D0786724

Wealth Building Strategies in Energy, Metals, and Other Markets

Wealth Building Strategies in Energy, Metals, and Other Markets

Chris Waltzek

WILEY

John Wiley & Sons, Inc.

Published by John Wiley & Sons, Inc., Hoboken, New Jersey.

Published simultaneously in Canada.

For general information on our other products and services or for technical support, please contact our Customer Care Department within the United States at (800) 762-2974, outside the United States at (317) 572-3993 or fax (317) 572-4002.

Wiley also publishes its books in a variety of electronic formats. Some content that appears in print may not be available in electronic books. For more information about Wiley products, visit our web site at www.wiley.com.

Library of Congress Cataloging-in-Publication Data:
Waltzek, Chris.
    Wealth building strategies in energy, metals, and other markets/Chris Waltzek.
    p. cm.
  Includes index.
    ISBN 978-0-470-63830-9 (hardback); ISBN 978-0-470-91265-2 (ebk); ISBN 978-0-470-91266-9 (ebk); ISBN 978-0-470-91267-6 (ebk)
  1. Investments. 2. Stock exchanges. 3. Strategic planning. 4. Precious metals.
  5. Power resources. I. Title.
  HG4523.W35 2010
    332.6–dc22   2010019079

Printed in the United States of America

10 9 8 7 6 5 4 3 2 1

To the thousands of wonderful Goldseek.com Radio listeners who have become friends and offered encouragement over the past four-plus years. To everyone who has fallen behind in their mortgage payments, entered foreclosure or bankruptcy as a result of the 2008 credit crisis.

Contents

Acknowledgments

I offer a special thank you to Jennifer and my parents Sandra, and Kenneth. To the sponsor of Goldseek.com Radio, Peter Spina, president of Goldseek.com. To the hundreds of guests who sacrificed their valuable time to entertain and inform GSR listeners over the past four-plus years. The great folks at the 203-year-old publisher, John Wiley & Sons, Debra Englander, Adrianna Johnson, Kelly O'Connor, and Claire Wesley. Also, to the numerous authors whose books, articles, and statistics provided inspiration. Lastly, thank you to my Lord and Savior, Jesus Christ.

A Musical Rainman

"Where words fail, music speaks."
—Hans Christian Anderson

"Music was my refuge. I could crawl into the space between the notes and curl my back to loneliness."
—Maya Angelou

Like so many young people, I was captivated by music of every sort at an early age. Between the tiny grooves of vinyl records I found a gateway to a new dimension. Although outdated in the digital world, the 33 revolutions per minute of the family record player were sufficient for me to develop substantial and enduring friendships with the great classical composers. Vivaldi, Handel, Chopin, and Bach became my mentors.

Meantime, on a routine visit with a physician, I was informed that I had a rare form of eidetic memory. Dr. Bruce helped me to understand that such nearly perfect musical recall was uncommon. While eidetic mnemonics imparted flawless audio memory, it also compelled the subject to relive verbal criticisms and harsh words with DVR-like recall, indefinitely.

Still, the malady did include interesting, albeit peculiar, side effects. Whenever life's challenges seemed intolerable, a repertoire of the world's greatest musicians magically whispered in my ears. The musical genius of E. Power Biggs and the London Symphony Orchestra with Sir Neville Marriner at the helm always provided a calming panacea for a weary mind.

Internal iPod

Eventually, I was exposed to every type of modern music, including the top 40 hits. The early passion for music morphed into a mental jukebox, allowing for instant access to every song that I'd ever heard. The ability was particularly useful while attending mundane lectures in windowless, dungeon-like classrooms. Confined within appalling, windowless walls, pinned like a bull en route to the slaughterhouse, I developed a blueprint for escape. Armed with only an internal iPod I would teleport to an outdoor concert event amid lush green fields and deep blue skies. All of a sudden, boredom became musical elation. If conditions were particularly unsettling, the course of treatment included a favorite Bach fugue and toccata masterpiece or a performance written for the king of England, *Water Music* by Handel.

As useful and entertaining as a powerful memory proved to be, it was destined to remain little more than a diversion. The ability offered little in the way of monetary rewards. I found the prospect of becoming a starving artist somewhat less than appealing. Millions of gifted artists will gladly attest to the fact, that without a source of income, all the talent in the world will not satiate a landlord's appetite for monthly rent payments.

The Rhythmical Economist

Just as the language of music is applied to a canvas-like score, one brush stroke at a time Wall Street carries on its discourse with investors via individual stock quotes. The striking visual and mathematical relationship between stock charts and musical arrangements first became apparent to me while away at school. Ergo, a degree in economics seemed the ideal transition from a potential life of penury into the more practical and promising field of investing.

My education in the challenging world of finance began at the library. Anxious to obtain the latest copy of the *Wall Street Journal*, before daily lectures, I'd dash from the student center with a freshly grilled Philly steak sandwich and side of French fries. Sitting comfortably in the library periodical reading room, I occasionally turned my attention away from the *Journal* to survey the remarkable campus. The view was filled with tall Georgia pines, majestic magnolia blossoms, and the pale blue southern skyline.

Meanwhile, the front page of the investing section provided the object of my obsession—a chart of the Dow Jones Industrial Average. Like the intense yet sublime melody of Vivaldi's *Four Seasons*, the Dow Jones prices seemed to adhere to a divine governing rhythm. Suddenly, a beguiling question struck me. Just as the human mind is capable of anticipating the next few notes of a musical performance—was it possible to profit from the basic melodies hidden within market prices? Answering the perplexing question became a personal quest.

Super Dome of Finance

The decision crystallized within me to pursue a degree in economics and finance. No longer was my career path to be dominated by music. While enjoying Christmas break, my resolve was further emboldened by a visit to the Chicago Mercantile Exchange. A close family friend and former member of the exchange invited my family on a tour of the vast trading floor. While strolling around the huge complex, I found the energy level and the roar of the adrenaline-filled traders to be intoxicating.

Afterwards, a new question entered my mind. Should a starving college student pursue a summer internship as a runner on the exchange floor? Unfortunately, the campus was nearly 700 miles away from the super dome–sized temple of finance.

Moreover, most if not all the brokerage positions required unpaid internships, endless cold calling, and boiler room–like conditions. Undeterred, I eventually secured a position as an industry analyst at the nation's largest law firm. Compared with the jobs I'd held while working my way through school, I found, for the most part, that lawyers enjoyed far more reasonable working hours.

My new office home from 9 to 5 P.M. towered 500 feet above the sprawling metropolis. The executive suite was lined with huge windows, which framed a breathtaking scene of the city skyline. Local news helicopters whirled through the city, sometimes several stories below eye level.

Meantime, I settled into a surprisingly comfortable leather office chair behind an impressive executive desk and began analyzing economic conditions for the firm's partners. I'd been hired with the understanding that I should expect large blocks of time, sometimes days, without steady projects. The work was challenging, albeit sporadic. Waiting for new projects to descend the imposing office hierarchy left considerable time for my market investigations. I found that my passion for the markets hadn't disappeared, but merely lain dormant.

Nonetheless, 500 feet below my office the shelves of a nearby bookstore held copies of the latest investing periodicals. During lunch hour I'd pass through the air-conditioned sky tunnels, which connected the marble tower to a shopping venue.

Similar to my daily visits to the university library reading room, my search now focused upon the latest issue of *Stocks & Commodities* magazine. I devoured each article with as much fervor as lunch— sometimes losing track of time in the process. As a typical neophyte, my quest for the holy grail of investing began with the field of technical analysis, that is, repeating rhythmic price patterns. Terms such as *stochastic, relative strength index, trend lines, Fibonacci* and *parabolic stop,* and *reverse systems* entered my vocabulary.

By 1998 the Internet stock market boom was front-page news. Trading opportunities seemed so boundless that I decided to pursue independent investing as a full-time career. My house was the first in the neighborhood to "jack-in" to the newly available broadband Internet technology. With blazingly fast cable modem wind in my computer's sails, I attempted to seize the unique trading opportunities offered by instantaneous market quotes.

Accordingly, lightning-fast Internet access and free real-time index charts did culminate with a significant breakthrough. I discovered that the underlying futures contract always changed direction before the NASDAQ at important market tops and bottoms. Although the brief glimpse into the future dissipated eventually, a million-dollar seat on the NYSE wasn't required to recognize the potential arbitrage opportunities. Armed with the latest technological marvels and a zealous lust for success, I found that providence favored the prepared mind. Trading losses eventually yielded to profits, albeit humble.

Moreover, as with so many endeavors in life, just when the riddle of the markets seemed to be solved, a fundamental shift occurred and everything changed. On March 9, 2000, the NASDAQ index climbed above 5,000 for the first time in history. Pundits proclaimed that the market ascent would continue, perpetually.

The Dow Jones Industrial Average gained more than 1,300 percent during the great bull market of 1982–2000. James K. Glassman and Kevin A. Hassett's book, *DOW 36,000*, forever captured the extraordinary hyperbole of the period. Many book titles were to follow, such as *DOW 40,000* by David Elias. But the crown and scepter of one-upmanship remains justly and firmly in the possession of Charles W. Kadlec. The title of his work, *DOW 100,000*, was the piece de resistance. Yet the additional 1,000 percent in gains required for Kadlec's *Dow 100,000* penultimate forecast to come to pass, never materialized. Kadlec's prediction was a contrarian wake-up call to liquidate stocks and diversify into Treasuries and commodities.

Dot.com—Dot.bomb

In the late 1990s, many executives desperately sought to secure their claim in the Internet Gold Rush. For a very brief moment in time, adding a simple web page and dot.com to the corporate logo worked wonders for share prices. But before long the Internet stock flash in the pan came to an abrupt halt. By the end of 2000, the market selloff seemed as harrowing to the legion of inexperienced investors as the tribulations of Job.

In Chapter 1, verse 21 of the Book of Job, the troubled protagonist says, "Naked came I out of my mother's womb, and naked shall I return thither: the Lord gave, and the Lord hath taken away." In similar fashion, just as the market had granted sizable profits during the late 1990s bull market, now that the stock market peak had passed, a scourge of losses promptly followed. As suddenly as the IPO phase of the bull market had arrived, it evaporated. Gone were the profitable days of investing in dot.com stocks. Just as Job was engulfed by his misfortunes, bullish investors suddenly faced a formidable bear market.

Correspondingly, by September 11, 2001, investing capital was dwindling as rapidly as market prices. In order to retain what little remained of an initial grubstake, a self-imposed trading hiatus was necessary. During the break, I began an exhaustive search for a solution to the bear market dilemma. The renewed quest for an investing holy grail included Metastock, a computer-based trading system platform.

During business hours, I designed and tested mechanical trading systems. In the evenings, my reading list included books covering the mathematical underpinnings of rules-based investing, such as system expectancy, risk-reward ratio, win-loss and Sharp ratio, and so on.

Accordingly, the due diligence process led to an epiphany. No matter what time frame I examined, whether it was tick by tick, five, 15 or 60 minutes, daily, weekly, or quarterly, one commonality always held true. Eventually, a lengthy/profitable trend emerged. Finally, the breakthrough arrived and persistence yielded dividends. An adaptive and robust trend-based system was to be my portfolio's savior. The faithful Job-like neophyte investor had escaped the clutches of financial capital punishment by carefully scrutinizing the markets.

The leap of understanding shares similarities with Euclid's five postulates. In his magnum opus, *Elements*, the Greek mathematician and founder of modern geometry provided mathematical proofs that, even 2,300 years later, form the support of every conceivable engineering wonder. In like manner, the realization that regardless of the time frame observed, all markets eventually establish a profitable trend was a career-changing insight. Suddenly price prediction seemed a wasteful, even futile, endeavor.

Moreover, as the seductive sea siren of Greek mythology and wailing banshee from Gaelic folklore lured seafarers toward the reef, so the promise of prediction draws the unsuspecting market mariner to his ultimate demise. Calm market conditions more often than not conceal a tempest of price complexity. As soon as an over-optimized system is exposed to actual data, it invariably crashes into the unyielding reef below, covering the sea floor with the contents of the portfolio treasure chest. The solution is simple. Investors must leave forecasting to the weatherman and instead concentrate on wealth building strategies that entail a portfolio rich in energy and precious metals investments.

The focus of Part I of this text is wealth building strategies in stocks and commodities. Relevant historical anecdotes add greater substance to the material and better illustrate the challenges facing the modern investor. For instance, stock market bubbles and panics are neither new nor rare occurrences. Extreme price volatility is actually the norm. From the South Sea Bubble all the way to the more recent 1929, 1987, and 2000 market implosions, former manias provide an excellent vantage point from which to investigate the recent 2008 credit crisis.

Nevertheless, there's far more to financial success than merely solid investments in stocks and commodities. At the end of the trading session, every investor must find someplace to call home. Yet the challenges facing homeowners today are overwhelming. During the past three years, securing a reasonably priced house has become a far more complex proposition. Currently more than 11 million families own homes worth less than their mortgages. Part II investigates the housing crash and provides an easy-to-follow roadmap to real estate bargains. Armed with three simple rules of thumb, readers will never again fall prey to high-pressure sales tactics. Instead, they'll know how to avoid the lemons and secure their dream home. Once the housing market fully stabilizes, most likely in 2012–2013, the reader will be prepared to purchase a safe and affordable house at a reasonable price.

Furthermore, until recently, domestic bank runs/banking holidays were rare occurrences. That all changed in 2008 when hundreds of IndyMac bank accounts were frozen and seized by the FDIC. With numerous banks expected to file for bankruptcy, would you know what to do if your lender suddenly closed its doors? Part III guides investors through the land mine–laden banking sector with practical procedures to protect the accumulated profits earned from the methods outlined in Part I and Part II.

In addition, over the course of five years in the field of business talk radio, I've answered thousands of thought-provoking questions. One universal theme remains constant throughout the stacks of letters and phone calls: Millions of real people are desperately seeking simple answers to tough financial questions. Thus, each chapter includes a Q&A section with inquiries from actual Goldseek.com radio listeners. Plus chapters wrap up with a Key Point summary of the most significant topics. So insert your ear buds and enjoy your favorite iPod tunes. You are embarking upon a unique and entertaining financial enterprise!

PART I

SUCCESSFUL INVESTING

CHAPTER 1

Winning Formula

THE INVESTING HOLY GRAIL

"October: This is one of the peculiarly dangerous months to speculate in stocks. The others are July, January, September, April, November, May, March, June, December, August, and February."

—Mark Twain

Welcome to the exciting world of personal finance. Written within the pages of this book are the keys to unlocking incalculable riches. The first step to financial success is a unique understanding of price behavior. This chapter begins a thorough investigation into trend investing, arguably the most profound breakthrough in finance since the first exchange opened for trade over 400 years ago. By examining market manias and the people who traded them, the reader will gain priceless insights into market dynamics including how and why securities enter protracted trends.

The Market Trend Enigma

For hundreds of years, the secrets to investing success were hidden away from the masses. Even the prodigious mind of Sir Isaac Newton was perplexed by market dynamics. When asked about the South Sea Bubble, the greatest scientist of the last millennia replied, "I can calculate the movement of the stars, but not the madness of men." His investing woes were further chronicled and corroborated by comments from his niece, "(Uncle Isaac) lost twenty thousand pounds (millions of dollars). Of this, however, he never much liked to hear." (See Figure 1.1.) Judging by the nearly vertical crash that followed the speculative mania, it's easy to understand why Newton was so mystified by market mechanics (see Figure 1.2).

Yet by the twentieth century the investing riddle was solved. The astonishing market operations of two great traders, Jesse Livermore and Richard Dennis, contained the blueprints for a trend investing revolution. Rumors persist to this day that Livermore, the boy plunger as he liked to be called, reaped $100 million in profits by correctly gauging the 1929 market crash and the subsequent downtrend that followed. (See Figure 1.3.)

In similar fashion, the Prince of the Commodities Pit, Richard Dennis, reportedly transformed a meager $400 of borrowed funds into $200 million by adhering to market trends. What Livermore and Dennis had independently discovered was a financial El Dorado that had eluded even Isaac Newton. The intrepid pair ignited an investing gold rush of riches beyond the dreams of avarice, available to everyone armed with the proper skill set.

So just what exactly is the enigmatic market trend? A trend is merely an unusually long price advance or decline that results from a powerful new cycle in a higher time frame. For instance, a powerful new upswing in the weekly stock price oftentimes results with a lengthy uptrend within daily prices. Examples of extraordinary trends that remained unbroken for decades include the U.S. stock market and the residential real estate market. Both trended higher for decades. (See Figures 1.4 and 1.5.)

Trends do not always follow a northerly pathway; at times prices decline for extended periods. For example, from 1980 to 2000 lower prices (a downtrend), dominated the gold market. The yellow metal subsequently reversed course in 2001, beginning a decade-long advance (uptrend). (See Figure 1.6.)

Simply Unpredictable

Thousands of investors have subsequently followed in the footsteps of Livermore and Dennis, embracing the trend investing methodology. Yet despite the fact that trend investing is profoundly profitable, it runs contrary to currently accepted industry and academic

Figure 1.1   South Sea Bubble

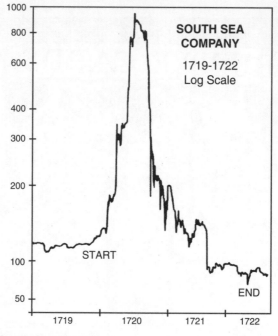

Figure 1.2   South Sea Crash

dogmas. Amid overwhelming supportive evidence, most main-stream pundits continue to promote the buy and hold technique as the closest that any investor can come to receiving a free lunch.

Still others insist that timing the market is possible. However, forecasting masks an insidious intellectual Gordian knot, which I refer to as the problem of prediction. Prices are governed by human emotions and are far more variable than predicted by standard models. Even Sir Isaac Newton failed to grasp the complexity of market dynamics. If the most prodigious mind of the past millennia suffered through the devastating South Sea Bubble implosion, how can the typical investor expect to produce better results? At first blush, the problem appears to be insurmountable.

However, to the trend investor, unpredictable markets are far from unsettling. The chaos actually presents unparalleled profit opportunities. Inevitable black swan events often lead to errors in groupthink, clouding the true market conditions. Statisticians and economists refer to these significant deviations from norm as 5-sigma events. While most of academia and Wall Street cling

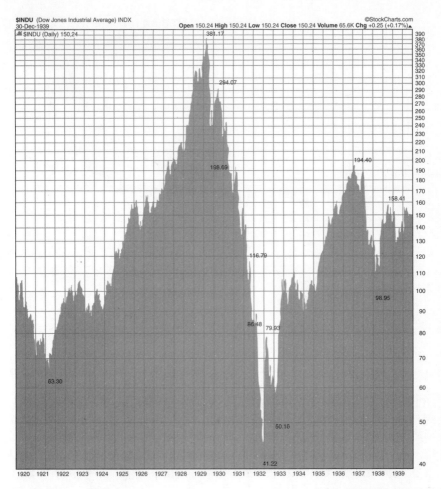

$INDU (Dow Jones Industrial Average) INDX   ©StockCharts.com
30-Dec-1939   Open 150.24 High 150.24 Low 150.24 Close 150.24 Volume 65.6K Chg +0.25 (+0.17%)▲

Figure 1.3 1929 Crash

tenaciously to Gaussian distribution models (the highest curve in
Figure 1.7), the cognoscenti view the bell curve representation of
the financial world as outdated—drastically underestimating the
likelihood of violent market reactions at either tail/extreme. Conversely, the Pareto distribution (the lowest curve in Figure 1.7) appropriately compensates for human emotions, presenting a more
adequate emulation of market behavior.

Although the outdated Gaussian market model remains highly
vulnerable to rogue market events, such as the crashes of 1987,
2001, and 2008, the Pareto model or fat tail distribution presents a

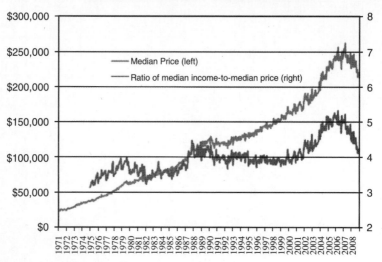

New Home Prices and Median Income

— Median Price (left)
······ Ratio of median income-to-median price (right)

Figure 1.4 Housing Bubble
Source: Census Bureau.

compelling alternative viewpoint. The Pareto interpretation accepts price variance as the norm rather than a once in a lifetime event. Thus precautions are essential to investing success. Pareto investing better prepares its adherents by underscoring the absolute necessity of adequate safeguards and contingency plans. Given these precepts, trend investing is greatly preferred to the buy and hold methodology and is the ideal means for extracting market profits and avoiding bear market losses.

Moreover, Nassim Taleb and the brilliant professor of mathematics, Benoit Mandelbrot, changed the way in which intelligent investors view the markets. Taleb and Mandelbrot agree that the Gaussian bell curve with its nearly static view of market behavior provides an inadequate emulation of market prices.

While the Wall Street crowd and much of academia remain bogged down in hyperbole, the discerning intellectual duo extol the virtues of the Pareto market model. Although Taleb is by no means a professed trend devotee, his books, *The Black Swan* and *Fooled by Randomness,* as well as his hedge fund results reveal a preference for market themes. The fact should come as little surprise, since practically all protracted market movements begin with black swan events.

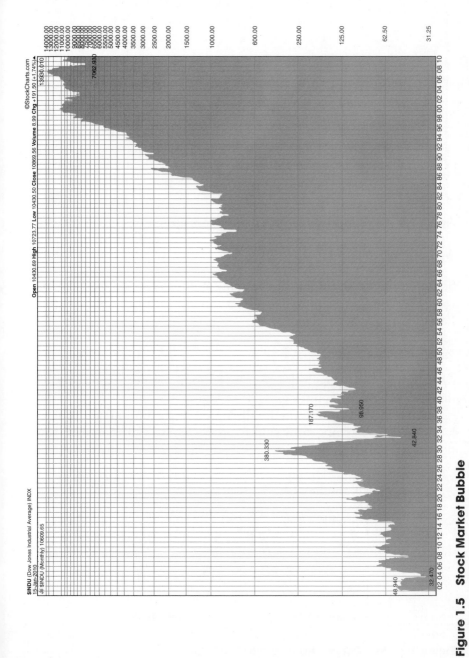

Figure 1.5   Stock Market Bubble

Source: StockCharts.com.

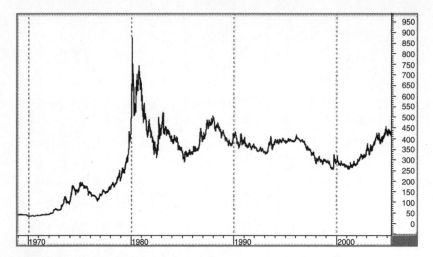

Figure 1.6   Gold Market: 20-Year Downtrend/Uptrend

Pareto-Waltzek Hypothesis

Standing on the shoulders of the great philosopher and mathematician, Vilfredo Pareto, as well as Taleb and Mandelbrot, I present the Pareto-Waltzek (PW) Hypothesis.

Pareto-Waltzek Rule #1

Although prices typically gyrate in a random manner, eventually all markets enter protracted trends. (See Figure 1.8.)

When market conditions are disrupted by a profound and singular event, prices temporarily shift from the typical Gaussian distribution into a Pareto distribution, resulting in a new primary trend. As

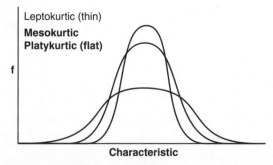

Figure 1.7   Bell Curve—Pareto, "Fat Tail" Curve

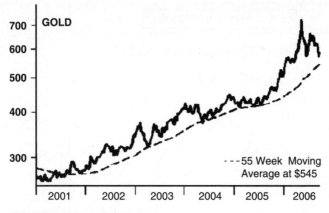

Figure 1.8   Market Trend (Uptrend)

long as the new factors persist, so does the trend. From the vantage point of statistical probability/game theory, the PW Hypothesis implies that a rogue event slightly improves the odds of experiencing a series of price advances or declines away from the 50 percent probability of a coin toss. For instance, if the probability of a winning day increases to 55 percent, the seemingly innocuous change creates the framework for the next profitable trend. Put simply, by increasing the odds of experiencing a winning session by only 5 percent beyond a coin toss, a major uptrend emerges. The graph in Figure 1.9

Figure 1.9   Random Number Generator (Uptrend)

Figure 1.10   Random Number Generator (Downtrend)

appears to represent market prices but is actually the result of a simple random number generator with graphical output. To my knowledge, this was one of the first attempts to illustrate, in graphical form, just how a fractional shift in perception can launch a new market trend.

Similarly, by reducing the likelihood of a favorable close by 5 percent, a primary downtrend unfolds, as seen in Figure 1.10.

Another critical component to deciphering the market trend riddle is a process I refer to as delayed participant response (DPR). Since investors react to new sea change events at a varied pace, the time delay between purchases or DPR creates an environment of gradual price adjustment.

At first seasoned professionals seize the new opportunity. The ensuing fresh wave of buy orders launches the initial stage of a fresh trend. Next, the next group of traders responds to the abrupt price advance by accumulating a position in anticipation of further gains. The second salvo of purchases sends the market steadily higher. Until that point, the natural price progression follows the convictions of individual investors. However, as the general public reacts to the opportunity, the final blow-off stage unfolds and a crowd mentality overtakes individual sensibilities. Clearly, if every investor reacted at precisely the same moment and in the same fashion, neither trends nor markets could exist at all.

Pareto-Waltzek Rule #2

All primary market movements (trends) are the result of at least one fundamental event, the significance of which is rarely recognized at the time.

Ergo, if the Federal Open Market Committee (FOMC) reduces its benchmark lending rate by 75 basis points, the liquidity injection will likely result in an economic revival as well as a stock market rally. Similarly, when a CEO makes a strategic decision, it's reasonable to assume that company earnings will improve along with profits/ share price.

Nevertheless, few sea change events are recognized as such at the time. The circumstances that transform market conditions into a sanctuary for Taleb's black swans always appear to go unnoticed by the majority of investors. Most traders overlook the singular events that ultimately lead to prolonged market movements. This is partially due to the time delay between important events and the resulting new trend. Put simply, most investors ignore black swan or random disruptions and fail to benefit from the trends that follow them. Thus without divine intervention or the patience of Job, valuation and forecasting methods are insufficient to identify most new primary trends.

Clearly, random walkers and "buy and hopers" should beware: Gaussian investing methods lead to a random stumble at best and at worst, a random disaster. Whereas the PW approach fills the sizable void left by outdated Gaussian-based investing methodologies.

The Soros Counterattack

For decades on Wall Street and Main Street alike, investors lined up on only one side of the housing Maginot Line—the buy side. Indeed, as the 2006 real estate peak came to pass, the "Housing can't lose" mantra was so deeply entrenched that contingency plans were deemed unnecessary, even supercilious. But by 2007 thousands of home loan companies, hedge funds, banks, and individual investors found that their worst fears were unfolding before their eyes. Despite the 75-year real estate boom, home prices were crashing—a new downtrend had begun in earnest.

Nonetheless, a fortunate handful of investors stowed away investing capital in foxholes, well out of range of enemy fire. Smaller still was the group with the foresight to launch a short-selling assault. The most prominent of the latter faction was George Soros. Among the housing market assailants, George Soros bet the proverbial ranch that the end was nigh for mortgage debt. Amid the financial Armageddon, billions in housing-related losses were transformed into short-sale profits and deposited directly into Soros's brokerage account.

Decades of higher home prices led to a mirage of paper wealth. The vast illusion first captured the minds of individuals, drawing them ever closer to the inaccessible profit oasis. As the housing bubble progressed, a fata morgana warped the collective groupthink, luring millions of unsuspecting house chasers into the grand deception. Still, in the financial kingdom the first to unveil the illusion is king. Sir Soros correctly identified the pandemic of housing hysteria as the root cause of the mortgage backed security (MBS) bubble.

Correspondingly, in Soros's philosophical treatise on market behavior, *The Alchemy of Finance*, he credits his reflexivity theory for his unique insight into human investing behavior. Soros contends that most investors, like gamblers, suffer from the affliction of overconfidence. For example, the downfall of the 158-year-old investment bank icon, Lehman Brothers, can be directly attributed to executive hubris. Overconfidence blindfolded management to the enormous risks posed by MBSs. Yet the incredulous Soros correctly surmised the situation and created a strategy to profit from the untimely demise of toxic mortgage debt. In the process, Soros's bank statement leaped in value by a remarkable $1.7 billion. The operation was by far the 78-year-old market alchemist's most lucrative victory. He had essentially transmuted MBS debt into gold by trading with the market trend.

So how did Soros profit so handsomely while the Masters of the Financial Universe on Wall Street were obliterated? The reflexivity theory and the PW Hypothesis hold the key. At the most basic level, financial pendulums tend to hyperextend. During the housing bubble, unbridled optimism resulted in a price eruption of truly colossal proportions. As logic would dictate, the return swing was quite profound. Consequently, investor fear and greed lead to far greater price variance than predicted by standard models, especially considering the massive leverage employed at the time.

In the final analysis, Wall Street was unprepared for the housing/credit crisis due to the lack of understanding of basic market underpinnings, such as market trends. If models had adequately adopted the Soros reflexivity model and/or the PW Hypothesis, millions of investors could have been spared billions of dollars in losses. The next few chapters delve more deeply into the market trend phenomenon to better prepare the reader to garner profits from extended price movements as well as to avoid devastating 2008-like market crashes.

KEY POINT

Although prices typically gyrate in a random manner, eventually all markets enter protracted/profitable trends.

Q&A

Listener Question #1: From across the Atlantic Ocean in the UK, Malcome, a friend of GSR, says, "Thank you for the show. I always listen each week. I wonder whether you could discuss the following question. Why can't larger countries who are aware of the U.S. government's manipulation of the gold and silver paper markets and the physical/paper disconnect, such as China, India, Russia, and the Arab states, do more to bring this manipulation to an end? Why is it that the U.S. manipulators are so strong?"

Answer: Hello, Malcome. By accumulating large amounts of gold and silver, officials in China, India, and Russia are doing their best to shield their respective economies from the weak greenback. A vast sea of wealth is being transferred away from Western countries and redistributed to the BRIC nations.

Additionally, the U.S. COMEX is the largest global futures exchange. As long as derivatives gimmickry is allowed to persist, precious metals will be held hostage. However, signs of a disconnection between the highly manipulated paper contracts and the solid physical market are emerging. Traders are instead choosing the precious metals ETFs. Now that gold has closed above $1,000 per ounce, the paper gold schemes are virtually certain to fail. Clearly, owning physical gold is the ideal choice. Thanks for the question, Malcome.

Listener Question #2: An anonymous phone caller says, "Although the euro has a small gold backing, it cannot be exchanged for the yellow metal. As a result, the benefits of the gold backing are insignificant."

Answer: Hello, caller. The euro has a nonredeemable 15 percent gold backing. Moreover, the euro zone, UK, China, and Russia are all expanding their money bases (as found in the back of *The Economist* magazine) following the lead of the U.S. Fed and Treasury. As a result, I continue to promote precious metals, commodities, and energy investments as ideal alternatives to the dollar and the euro. Thank you for your insightful question.

Listener Question #3: Hiro says, "Hi, Chris, thanks for your great work. In last week's show, you recommended a book by author Barton Biggs. What is the title of the book?"

Answer: Hi, Hiro, it's good to hear from you. Barton Biggs's new book is titled *Wealth, War and Wisdom.* Biggs provides a well-rounded perspective of the financial markets while proving how market prices are far better estimates of value than individual forecasts. I found his work to be as entertaining as it was educational and recommend it highly. The witty Winston Churchill anecdotes alone make the tome well worth the price.

Listener Question #4: Keith says, "Thanks for educating me. I have a question. I have purchased gold but in the event of a financial collapse, who is going to buy it from me? How can it be traded? How will I use my precious metals to buy a loaf of bread?"

Answer: Hello, Keith. Many GSR listeners have expressed similar concerns. As a highly condensed form of wealth, gold is particularly valuable in this dangerous geopolitical climate. If the credit crisis and debt dilemmas persist, the FDIC will likely require a bailout. Holding your savings in a digital form is not a prudent decision under such conditions. Instead, why not choose a tangible asset, likely to continue appreciating in value? Gold coins are easily transported and are universally accepted as sound money. Unlike dodgy bank balances, currencies, and stocks, gold has never dropped in value to zero and never files for bankruptcy. The yellow metal is the best line of defense against economic disaster. Plus U.S. silver dimes and quarters are useful for simple daily transactions in difficult times. Thank you, Keith.

CHAPTER 2

Money Machine

BUILDING A TRADING SYSTEM

"Rule No. 1: Never lose money. Rule No. 2: Never forget rule No. 1."

—Warren Buffett

The previous chapter examined the investing success and failure of three key individuals, Sir Isaac Newton, Jesse Livermore, and Richard Dennis. Newton failed to discover the trend concept and lost his fortune to the South Sea Bubble, whereas Livermore and Dennis embraced market trend investing and reaped enormous profits. However, of the three, only Richard Dennis retained his fortune. This chapter supplies the missing ingredient that enabled Dennis to succeed where his two gifted predecessors failed: money management. In addition, three trend trading systems with solid money management parameters are examined to better prepare the reader for financial success.

Go Investing

The world's most ancient board game, Go, originated in China approximately four thousand years ago. According to many enthusiasts, Go exceeds the challenging game of chess in complexity. Whereas chess is played on a board with 8 × 8 spaces, the tournament Go board encompasses a much larger 19 × 19 lines of play. In fact, mathematicians claim that a typical Go match is comprised of approximately 10 to the 170th power possible moves, more than the total number of subatomic particles in the known universe. Despite the modern digital gaming revolution, Go remains a global phenomenon.

As a Go player's skill level improves, one descends from the 30Kyu beginner's level down to semiprofessional 1Kyu. Ultimately the Go player seeks to qualify for Dan status. The Dan designation begins with 1Dan and completes with 7Dan, comparable to earning a black belt in karate. Interestingly, just like the demanding investing profession, winning at Go requires profound discipline and strategic reasoning skills.

By the same token, the rite of passage from novice investor (30kyu) to professional investor (1Dan) requires balance between risk and reward. By enduring the emotional stresses and financial strains of at least one major bear market, bona fide professional investor status is acquired. Any investor to survive such a test of character will agree that limiting losses is the most crucial aspect of a winning investing plan.

The patience and expertise gained from playing Go is certain to benefit every investor. Interested readers are encouraged to search the Internet for the free Go game software: IGOwin.

Money Management

The striking visual distinction between the black and white Go stones parallels the interplay between two dissimilar, yet vitally important investing methods—trend analysis and money management. Regrettably, safeguarding capital through money management remains an unsavory topic for most market participants. This fact is undoubtedly due to a peculiar human trait. Although the survival skill set should focus on protecting accumulated resources, instead, evolution seems to have hardwired people with an innate lust for "greener pastures."

Since the aurora of civilization, careful observation and prediction of global cycles, such as equinoxes and solstices, improved planting and harvesting results. The natural predilection toward forecasting is undoubtedly a remnant survival tactic from early subsistence farming days. Nowhere is the behavior better evidenced than in the neophyte trader's relentless pursuit of unattainable market tops and bottoms.

Meanwhile, great luminaries— including Copernicus, Galileo, Kepler, Brahe, and Newton—were required to unlock the elliptical nature of the planet's orbits. Their precise mathematical models allowed NASA to send spacecraft millions of miles, even beyond the limits of the solar system. While such models apply well to predicting the orbits of celestial objects, equations have surprising limitations when applied to market cycles. Unlike repetitive astronomical patterns, which often persist for millions of years, market rhythms are far too volatile to draw long-term conclusions. Black swan events quickly shift investors' perceptions, and suddenly the Earth is once again viewed as the center of the universe. The human decision process is clearly impeded by the agrarian mind-set. The successful investor must strive to overcome these limitations and instead evolve into an enlightened trend-following investor.

Straight-A-Itis

A peculiar malady plagues many investors of the more successful type. High achievers are accustomed to earning exceptional scores in school as well as excelling in the career path of choice. While a solid "B" grade point average is acceptable for many, to the more ambitious, the score equates with failure. This personality trait presents peculiar difficulties for trend investors. With a typical win/loss ratio of 40 percent, clearly the trend method earns an unbearable "F" average. Yet in the equally demanding field of major league baseball, a .400 batting average or 40 percent ratio would instantly lead to Baseball Hall of Fame status. Similarly, trend adherents with a track record of only 40 percent winning trades regularly produce spectacular fortunes.

Nevertheless, the professional investor acknowledges the limitations of forecasting, forgoing the fruitless quest for market tops and bottoms. Instead, within the market virtuoso's toolbox are two distinct, yet equally indispensable devices: protective sell stops and position sizing. Neglecting either fail-safe is akin to traversing a tightrope without a safety net, while adhering to both methods leads to remarkable profit synergies.

Furthermore, successful money management does not require sophisticated computer algorithms. In a nutshell, individual losses are simply limited to no more than 1–2 percent of total portfolio value. The logic behind the concept is elementary. Trend-based systems rarely produce a winning expectancy of better than 50 percent, so a string of losses presents a significant risk. Yet by limiting each trade to a 2 percent loss, a string of 10 consecutive losses puts only 20 percent of total capital at risk. Although a 20 percent loss is undesirable, a full recovery from the drawdown requires only a 25 percent gain.

Equation 2.1 calculates the scenario of maximum damage inflicted by a 10-trade losing streak and 2 percent risk per trade.

Equation 2.1 Money Management with 2% Risk/Trade

MM = [% risk of total portfolio] per # of trades
MM = [(% risk) (total portfolio $)] × (# trades)
MM = [(2%) × ($100,000)] × (−10)
MM = [$2,000] × (−10)
MM = (−$20,000)
MM = −$20,000 a 20% loss of total capital

(Assumptions: $100,000 portfolio; 2% risk per trade, including slippage and commissions; 10 consecutive losses.)

Although a 20 percent decline in capital may seem extreme, the situation becomes dire as the risk per trade parameter increases.

As you can see in Equation 2.2, with a 5 percent loss cutoff per trade, the portfolio is reduced by 50 percent. Recovery from such a blow requires a 100 percent return on remaining capital.

Equation 2.2 Money Management with 5% Risk/Trade

MM = [% risk of total portfolio] per # of trades
MM = [(% risk) (total portfolio $)] × (# trades)
MM = [(5%) × ($100,000)] × (−10)
MM = [$5,000] × (−10)
MM = (−$50,000)
MM = −$50,000 Loss − 50% Capital loss

(Assumptions: $100,000 portfolio; 5% risk per trade, including slippage and commissions; 10 consecutive losses.)

Equation 2.3 demonstrates the capital gain required to simply break even following a 50 percent loss:

Equation 2.3 Recovering from a 50% Loss

R% = LC/RC
R% = LC: ($100,000 × 50% = $50,000)/RC: $50,000
R% = LC: $50,000/RC: $50,000
R% = $50,000/$50,000
$50,000/$50,000 = 1 = 100%

Recovery percentage (R%) = Lost Capital (LC)/Remaining Capital (RC)

As you can see in Equation 2.3, recovery from a 50 percent loss in trading capital requires a 100 percent profit.

Consequently any risk per trade above the 2 percent parameter leads to unmanageable drawdowns. For instance, a string of 10 losses of even 3 percent results in a devastating equity drawdown (see Equation 2.4).

Equation 2.4 Recovering from a 30% Loss

$$R\% = LC/RC$$
$$R\% = LC: (\$100,000 \times 30\% = \$30,000)/RC: \$70,000$$
$$R\% = LC: \$30,000/RC: \$70,000$$
$$R\% = \$30,000/\$70,000$$
$$\$30,000/\$70,000 = 43\%$$

Recovery percentage (R%) = Lost Capital (LC)/Remaining Capital (RC)

As you can see in Equation 2.4, recovery requires a 43 percent profit.

Although most industry texts place marginal value on the unglamorous money management issue, the preceding equations prove that capital preservation is a critical component of investing success. In fact, this belief is shared by the Oracle of Omaha. Warren Buffett has publicly stated that the number one rule of investing is to never lose money. Clearly proper money management must be a primary focus of every aspiring investor.

Correspondingly, the allure of excessive profits can lead to investor impatience. Instead of waiting for the "best pitch," a "swing at any pitch" mentality develops due to simple boredom or as a knee-jerk reaction to unexpected losses. In a desperate attempt to recoup lost capital, novice investors forego rigorous money management discipline, choosing instead to swing at any trade across the plate. Oftentimes, investors overcome the temptation by paper trading for several months.

Determining Market Trend

With a firm grasp of the money management concept, the second necessary component to successful investing is trend identification.

There are at least as many ways to determine price trends as there are markets to trade. Since the market bias is entirely subjective, for the purposes of this investigation the following technical indicators are used: a 50 period moving average (50 ma) and the 200 moving average (200 ma).

As seen in Figure 2.1, a first-degree trend rating is triggered when the 50 ma crosses above the 200 ma.

Why use such an arbitrary gauge? In my experience the top money managers monitor both averages closely. Professional group-think inevitably leads to a self-reinforcing loop, providing an excellent proxy for market bias. Furthermore, the professional's tools improve the odds of identifying major market themes. (For those unfamiliar with moving averages, please navigate your Web browsers to stockcharts.com and type in a ticker symbol, such as DIA. The chart will automatically load both moving averages.)

Once the shorter 50 ma in the weekly chart moves decidedly above the longer 200 ma, a first-degree trend emerges (as seen in Figure 2.1).

First-Degree Trend:

1st Deg = (50 week ma > 200 week ma)

1st Deg = (50 ma > 200 ma)

Figure 2.1   First-Degree Trend

Source: StockCharts.com.

Next, a second-degree trend signal is said to occur when the price hovers above the 200 ma during an established market movement (see Figure 2.2).

Second-Degree Trend:

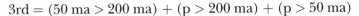

$2nd = (50 \text{ week ma} > 200 \text{ week ma}) + (\text{price} > 200 \text{ week ma})$

$2nd = (50 \text{ ma} > 200 \text{ ma}) + (p > 200 \text{ ma})$

Finally, as price hangs persistently above both moving averages without closing below either, the most desirable third-degree trend rating exists (see Figure 2.3).

Third-Degree Trend:

$3rd = (50 \text{ week ma} > 200 \text{ week ma}) + (\text{price} > 200 \text{ week ma}) + (\text{price} > 50 \text{ week ma})$

$3rd = (50 \text{ ma} > 200 \text{ ma}) + (p > 200 \text{ ma}) + (p > 50 \text{ ma})$

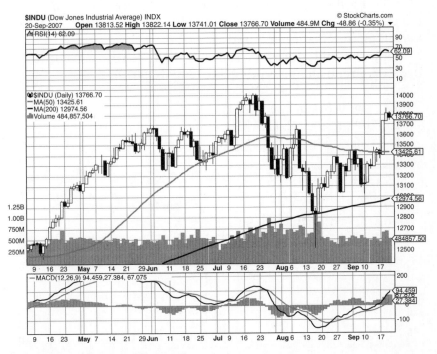

Figure 2.2 **Third-Degree Trend**

Source: StockCharts.com.

Figure 2.3   Gold Third-Degree Trend

Source: StockCharts.com.

Recent examples of powerful bull markets are revealed in the weekly charts of the short-term U.S. Treasury bond ETF ticker: SHY, as well as the gold and silver ETFs, tickers: GLD, SLV. Using the trend equations from the preceding section as a guide, only two primary markets currently qualify for bull market status (see Figures 2.3 and 2.4).

Only the underlined securities in the following list earn third-degree uptrend characteristics (as of August 2010):

1. Total U.S. stocks ETF: VTI
2. Foreign stocks ETF: VT
3. Dollar bullish ETF: UUP

Figure 2.4   SHY Third-Degree Trend

Source: StockCharts.com.

4. Foreign currency ETF: FXB
5. Corporate bond ETF: LQD
6. **Treasury bond ETFs: SHY**, TLT
7. **Gold ETF: GLD**
8. Real estate ETFs: IYR, ICF, VNQ
9. Crude oil ETF: USO

Judging by the fact that only two major indexes fall within the uptrend parameters, the credit crisis of 2008 clearly took quite a toll on the global financial system. Formerly impervious markets such as real estate and stocks were dethroned, leaving gold and short-term government bonds to successfully defend the title.

The GSR Goldilocks Trading System (GGTS™)

This section examines three trend-following systems with money management parameters. Only one of the three qualifies as a profitable trading system. In GGTS system #1, the nine-year uptrend in the gold market provides an ideal trading vehicle. Yet there is more to successful investing than merely trend adherence. As you can see in Equation 2.5, the risk factor per trade is a critical component.

Equation 2.5 GGTS System #1

Profits = Money Management × Trend

$P = MM \times T$

$P = MM[((\text{ideal \% risk}) - ((\text{actual \% risk}) \times (\text{\# of trades}))) >= 0]$
$$\times (50\,\text{ma} > 200\,\text{ma})$$

$P = [((20\%) - (3\% \times 10)) >= 0] \times (50\,\text{ma} > 200\,\text{ma})$

$P = [(20\% - 30\%) >= 0] \times [(50\,\text{ma} > 200\,\text{ma}) = 1]$

$P = ((-10\%) >= 0) = 0) \times 1$

$P = 0 \times 1$

$P = 0$

(Assumptions—T = gold = (50 ma > 200 ma); MM = 3% risk per trade)

As you can see in Equation 2.5, profits are equal to zero; the system is unprofitable.

Clearly, the favorable gold trend was insufficient to offset the risks associated with 10 losing trades and a 3 percent risk per trade parameter. The result is a 30 percent drawdown, requiring a 43 percent gain for full recovery. The system is deemed unprofitable.

With GGTS system #2, the investor reduces risk per trade to the prescribed 2 percent tolerance level. However, the index of choice is not currently experiencing a long-term uptrend.

Equation 2.6 GGTS System #2

Profits = Money Management × Trend

$P = MM \times T$

$P = MM[((\text{ideal \% risk}) - ((\text{actual \% risk}) \times (\# \text{ of trades}))) >= 0]$
$$\times (50 \text{ ma} < 200 \text{ ma})$$
$P = [((20\%) - (2\% \times 10)) >= 0] \times (50 \text{ ma} < 200 \text{ ma})$
$P = [(20\% - 20\%) >= 0] \times [(50 \text{ ma} < 200 \text{ ma}) = 0]$
$P = ((0) >= 0) = 1) \times 0$
$P = 1 \times 0$
$P = 0$

(Assumptions—market: stock market; 2% risk per trade) (MM = 2% risk per trade; T = 50 ma < 200 ma)

As you can see in Equation 2.6, profits equal zero; the system is unprofitable.

Even though the trader reduced risk per trade to an acceptable level, the 50 ma is lower than the 200 ma. Without a favorable market trend, the score is zero; the system is unnecessarily risky and unprofitable.

Moving on to GGTS system #3, which is shown in Equation 2.7, the investor wisely limits risk per trade to no more than 2 percent of the total portfolio value and chooses a market within an uptrend.

Equation 2.7 GGTS System #3 (Profitable)

Profits = Money Management × Trend

$P = MM \times T$

$P = MM[((\text{ideal \% risk}) - ((\text{actual \% risk}) \times (\# \text{ of trades}))) >= 0]$
$$\times (50 \text{ ma} > 200 \text{ ma})$$
$P = [((20\%) - (2\% \times 10)) >= 0] \times (50 \text{ ma} > 200 \text{ ma})$
$P = [(20\% - 20\%) >= 0] \times [(50 \text{ ma} > 200 \text{ ma}) = 1]$
$P = ((0) >= 0) = 1) \times 1$
$P = 1 \times 1$
$P = 1$

(Assumptions—market: gold; 2% risk per trade)
(MM = 2% risk per trade; T = 50 ma > 200 ma)

As you can see in Equation 2.7, profits are greater than zero—the system is acceptable.

In System #3, the investor limits risk to an appropriate 20 percent and the 50 ma is greater than the 200 ma. The favorable market trend and risk parameters lead to a positive score of 1. Ergo, by minimizing losses and adhering to the prevailing market theme, conditions are just right for profits. System #3 earns the GSR Goldilocks award.

In each weekly edition of the *GSR Spotlight Picks* newsletter, the current Goldilocks trading system results are displayed, including a list of bullish markets with low correlation. The free report includes the GSR Spotlight Stock Picks and Diversified Trend & Money Management Fund.™

Enhanced System Entries

System profitability can often be improved by tinkering with trade entries. Following a new trend signal, an investor can opt to purchase only a half position. If the first position remains profitable for a prescribed period of time, then the final half is accumulated. Conversely, if the trend falters and/or the first position is not profitable, the final trade is delayed. By slowly wading into the perilous waters, the investor gradually acquires the full position and exposes the portfolio to far less risk. The procedure minimizes losses in the event that the new trend fails and reduces the anxieties related with larger trade sizes.

Moreover, allocating no more than one-third of the available cash to any particular market/sector withholds adequate reserves for trends as they develop. The technique further reduces losses and the psychological impact of the drawdowns associated with unexpected market plunges.

House Money Method

In the next entry technique, the position size is limited to one-quarter of the available funds. For example, if an account is capable of purchasing a maximum of 4,000 shares of a particular security, such as the Dow Jones Industrials ETF, ticker symbol DIA, only 1,000 shares are accumulated. Once the account reaches a sufficient profit goal, the number of shares is increased by 100 percent, to 2,000. Again, the investor waits for additional profits to accrue and then the position size is again doubled to the full 4,000 number. Building a position with a fraction of the available margin drastically reduces initial drawdowns and ensures that only profits, not capital, are at risk. Essentially, this allows investors to play with the house's money.

Enhanced System Exits

Just as an object in motion tends to remain in motion, higher prices usually lead to further gains. However, if a market suddenly shifts course, the trend is likely finished. Intelligently planned exits provide further profit-boosting advantages. The ideal contingency plan includes a break-even stop for each position. The break-even stop simply defends existing trade profits. Plus, should the stop execute, additional funds are available for new opportunities as they develop.

Moreover, just as the thud of commercial airline tires meeting the tarmac signals the end of a flight, the markets often provide signs that a trend is nearing its end and money management becomes increasingly important. Tactful placement of trailing stops just below the 50 ma and 200 ma cushions the portfolio against abrupt market corrections. Trailing stops are simply automated failsafes, which secure unrealized profits and guard against losses. Thus if price penetrates the 50 ma in the weekly chart, a first-degree sell signal is registered.

Furthermore, trailing stops can be used to protect profits by automatically scaling out of half of an initial position. If price subsequently descends below the 200 ma, a second-degree sell signal is triggered and half of the remaining position is stopped out. Inevitably the 50 ma will cross below the 200 ma. At that point, the trend is over and only short positions are considered.

Nothing Succeeds Like Success

The incredible profit potential of trend trading and sound money management would impress even Sir Isaac Newton. Had the great scientist uncovered the two concepts a few centuries earlier, his investing account would have emerged unscathed from the South Sea market crash. Similarly, back-testing results prove that the GSR Goldilocks Trading System™ profited handsomely during every major bull market in history, as well as sidestepped each bear market, including the infamous crashes of 1987, 1998, 2000–2002, and 2008.

Likewise, the trading system registered a sell signal at the onset of the 2007 real estate crash. By simply selling short the related exchange traded funds, IYR and RWR, investors and homeowners could have earned spectacular gains, instead of enduring substantial losses. Only a handful of financial professionals can claim similar results.

Ergo, readers are now armed with a simple yet profound investing methodology. The Goldilocks system automates the entire process and eliminates the need for market newsletter subscriptions, advisory services, or data feeds. Investors can go about their daily routine, no longer shackled to video screens during business hours. The ease and simplicity of trend following allows the neophyte and professional alike to harvest profits effortlessly, perhaps even rivaling the results of the Wall Street elite.

Trend Portfolio Insurance

According to a Yale lecture series hosted by Dr. Robert Shiller, only 11 percent of people polled believe it is wise to time the stock market. Paraphrasing a pioneer in game theory and gambler extraordinaire, Geolamo Cardono, in his opus, The *Liber de Ludo Aleae*, the greatest benefit of gambling comes from not participating at all. But for those who are so inclined, I include a free web site that offers spectacular trade results for nearly all U.S. Stocks: http://americanbulls.com/Default.asp. Conversely, most investors are best served by building a solid, well-diversified investment portfolio with a simple market trend component. This section provides a pragmatic/inexpensive method to protect every portfolio from 2008-like downtrends without the need for advanced trading techniques.

Take, for example, a portfolio comprised of five markets with low correlation, such as: stocks, bonds, real estate, precious metals, and energy. Each quarter, the investor reviews the long-term chart of all five ETFs. If an ETF should drop below the 200 period moving average, a downtrend may unfold jeopardizing one-fifth or 20 percent of the account. Due to the difficulties of timing the market, plus trading fees, capital gains taxes, and so on, instead of selling the ETF, the investor opts to purchase Long-Term Equity Anticipation Securities (LEAPS), to shield the portfolio from a potential downtrend. A small LEAPS put position will cost less than 2 percent of the total portfolio value, but will guard against a 20 percent loss should the ETF lose all or most of its value.

Therefore, in 2008 as the stock and real estate ETFs dropped through the 200 period moving averages with scant ceremony, if the investor sold the ETFs, he or she would likely have missed the astounding recovery rally that followed in 2009–2010. By purchasing a LEAP insurance plan instead, the options offset 100 percent of the ETF crash losses, allowing the investor to sleep well at night. By 2010, the stock and bond ETFs fully recovered, and the investor only paid a tiny insurance premium of 2 percent if the LEAP options expired worthless.

Numerous calamities might have been avoided using the LEAP/trend insurance method. Imagine if the millions of investors who lost their entire fortunes in Enron, Fannie Mae, Bear Stearns, Lehman Brothers, Worldcom, and Sirius XM had employed the trend insurance method. Thousands of mutual funds, hedge funds, and municipalities could have been spared horrendous losses. Clearly the LEAP/trend portfolio insurance plan is a practical solution for protecting profits for individual investors as well as professionals.

An Orderly Walk up Trend Street

At this point in the investigation, the inadequacies of the Efficient Market Hypothesis have been established. Traders are encouraged to embrace the trend investing model instead of tossing darts at a list of ticker symbols. The Pareto-Waltzek theory from Chapter 1 fully anticipates the success of trend investing and money management systems. In the final analysis, market-biased investing is the most successful and widely tested method available. Success is virtually ensured for those who adhere to the market trend and disciplined money management.

After completing Chapters 1 and 2, the reader now has a firm grasp of the keys to investing success. However, just as knowing how a car operates does not entitle one to a driver's license, the prospective trend follower requires further training before risking actual trading capital. The remaining chapters in Part 1 further hones the investor skill set and better prepares the reader for Richard Dennis–style profits.

KEY POINT

Successful investing involves trend and money management skills, which limits losses to no more than 1–2 percent of total portfolio value.

Q&A

Listener Question #1: Ed says: "Hi, Chris. I love the show and listen religiously. I have invested 30 percent of my portfolio in gold and silver bullion as well as mining stocks. One of my holdings is the gold company Northgate Minerals Corp. Northgate has a relatively low production cost. Some analysts seem to admire the company, yet the price of the stock rarely moves higher. Can you please shed some light on Northgate? Also, I'm considering a career in short-term currency trading with the aid of a professional on the Forex currency exchange. I'd like your thoughts on this as well."

Answer: Hello, Ed. Northgate Minerals Corporation engages in gold and copper mining and exploration in Canada and Australia. The company is headquartered in Vancouver, Canada. If you are compelled to hold a portfolio of gold stocks, please consider diversifying your portfolio with StreetTracks gold stocks ETF, ticker symbol: GDX. The closed end fund tracks a basket of gold stocks.

Regarding your trading ambitions, while I applaud your initiative, day trading is an occupation that requires considerable acumen and self-discipline. Unfortunately, studies show that few people succeed as day traders and more than 9 out of 10 lose their entire funds. The costs associated with professional trading are actually comparable with college tuition. With merely a 10 percent chance of graduating, a degree in trading is not for the economically minded.

However, the following tips are provided for those who are willing to accept the associated risks and sacrifices. Since day trading involves emotional extremes, novice investors can benefit from longer term trading. Instead of day trading, why not try weekly trading? Weekly traders ignore the day to day market noise. Since weekly traders only place orders on the weekend, they are free to work full time.

Also, before investing a single dollar, a significant period of paper trading is essential. Each trade must be recorded in a log, including predefined percentage risk and sell stops. After months of meticulous paper trading with money management and trend following as the core methodology, the novice investor may place actual trades in small 100-share increments. Conservative positions provide much needed real-world experience while limiting potential losses.

Furthermore, professional traders must fund their personal health care and dental insurance needs. This requires a minimum expense of $150 per month. Next, mark-to-market trading status is a must for traders. The IRS designation allows trading losses to offset capital gains. Earning the status requires patience and a track record of regular trading. Plus, the tax benefits of an IRA trading account can be highly beneficial. Ed, thank you for the question and please keep me updated.

Listener Question #2: A caller asks, "What percentage of one's portfolio should be invested in precious metals?"

Answer: Hello, caller. While gold was formerly referred to by the Wall Street crowd as a barbarous relic, in fact gold has gained value for nine consecutive years. In times of political, social, and economic uncertainty, gold is the ideal insurance policy and one without recurring premiums.

Most financial advisors agree that precious metals are the ideal investment safety net. While the traditional gold allocation is 10 percent to 15 percent of total portfolio value, the potential for a period of unprecedented inflation warrants a 20 percent-plus commitment to precious metals. As the position becomes profitable, gold exposure can be expanded to 50 percent or more, via dollar cost averaging.

However, due to the highly volatile nature of the precious metals markets and the fact that long-range investing goals are subjective, individual risk tolerances must be adequately gauged. Most investors are best served by the balanced portfolio approach. A model portfolio includes exposure to all major asset classes, for example, 20 percent stocks, 20 percent bonds,

20 percent PMs, 20 percent miscellaneous, and 20 percent in cash. Every 12 months, the portfolio is rebalanced by selling a portion of the winners and reinvesting in lagging sectors to preserve profits and to maintain portfolio equilibrium. Thank you, caller, for the thought-provoking question and please keep in touch.

CHAPTER 3

Gold Bonanza

PROFITING FROM THE GOLD BULL MARKET

"Gold has worked down from Alexander's time. . . . When something holds good for two thousand years I do not believe it can be so because of prejudice or mistaken theory."

—Bernard M. Baruch (1870–1965),
American Financier

For several decades stocks and bonds dominated the global financial arena. But in the wake of the devastating 2008 credit crisis, investors are questioning the safety of such intangible assets. A growing number are turning instead to the gold and silver safe haven. Precious metals investments are once again becoming synonymous with financial success. This section provides extensive historical, fundamental, and technical evidence supporting precious metals as the ideal investment class for years to come.

A Brief History of Markets

Investors have suffered through financial calamities for hundreds of years. The unwashed masses are most vulnerable during periods of economic upheaval. To their great peril, most ignore the warning signals. Whether the lack of investor preparedness is due to complacency or misinformation is unclear. But one fact remains certain—

the psychological interplay between greed and fear has always been and will always remain at the core of every market mania.

Considering the intense societal anguish that accompanies boom and bust economic cycles, one would expect the cognoscenti of this computer era to implement a universal economic barometer. The fact that economists have not identified and embraced such a mechanism speaks volumes. In fact, the recent housing crash and credit crisis reveals how exposed and susceptible investors remain to economic downturns.

In the classic economic tome, *Extraordinary Popular Delusions & the Madness of Crowds*, Charles Mackay examines the South Sea Bubble of 1720, one of the more memorable financial manias. The British government struck a deal with the South Sea Company. The firm gained a trade monopoly over the South Sea region, in exchange for absorbing a portion of the sizable national debt. The agreement set in motion a series of events, which culminated with a financial bubble of Mt. Everest-sized proportions. In merely one year, South Sea Company shares soared by 1,000 percent. (See Figure 3.1.)

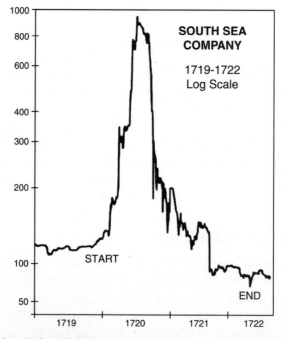

Figure 3.1   South Sea Bubble

Nevertheless, in the famous passage, "Men go mad in herds, while they only recover their senses slowly and one by one," Charles Mackay exposes the intricacies of crowd investing behavior. The sage investigator reaches the profound realization that during market manias investors collectively experience a peculiar form of groupthink. The manic conditions persist until the bubble inevitably bursts. Only then do a handful of sober individuals realize their folly. Most, however, refuse to acknowledge that the profit opportunity has forever passed and instead cling tenaciously to the false notion that the former glory days will someday return. Yet to date, a burst bubble has never been reinflated.

Accordingly, from the South Sea Mania of 1720 to the housing and credit implosion of 2008, little in the markets has changed. As it was hundreds of years hence, it remains today—only the most astute investor has the foresight to exchange soon to be worthless financial instruments for tangible assets, such as precious metals. The sheep-like herd of investors invariably overstays its welcome in paper assets only to be fleeced by the unforgiving market.

Moreover, financial history is replete with countless tales of inflation-ravaged currencies. For millennia, officials struggled to remedy economic distress by printing excessive levels of paper money. In fact, governments are actually bureaucratic herds, comprised of individuals who are equally susceptible to emotional extremes. This particular human failing explains why the temptation of easy money, that is, monetary expansion, is as seductive to policy makers today as it was to their predecessors.

Economic Early Warning System

More than two centuries hence, James Watt's steam engine ushered in the industrial revolution. From automobile airbags and antilock brakes to smoke detectors and home security systems, millions of people owe their lives and fortunes to the era of engineering marvels that followed. While many cities use early warning systems, such as community sirens, to warn of approaching tornadoes and related natural catastrophes, as for impending economic calamities, the masses are left to their own devices. Why haven't governments designed and implemented an economic early warning system? Widespread overconfidence in Keynesian and monetarist programs provides one likely explanation.

1970   1980

Figure 3.2   1980 Gold Bubble

Furthermore, for millions of Americans the gasoline shortage of the late 1970s conjures up memories of long lines at filling stations. Far fewer recall the simultaneous advance in precious metals. By the time that the masses recognized the inflation threat, gold was no longer at bargain prices. In 1980 the yellow metal climbed to a peak price of $850 an ounce and silver flew higher by twentyfold to $50 per ounce. (See Figure 3.2.) Clearly the predictive characteristics of precious metals make the asset class an ideal economic early warning siren.

Although the inflation of the 1970s was significant, it pales in comparison with that of the American Civil War. The Southern states experienced a devastating hyperinflation rate of 5,000 percent, which consumed family savings like a raging financial inferno. However, those who converted their Confederate bills into gold coins before the end of the war retained most of their wealth.

Nevertheless, as the twentieth century rolled forward several epidemics of inflation came to pass. Millions of people watched helplessly as their family savings evaporated in Europe. For example, the nation of Hungary struggled with hyperinflation rivaling even that of Weimar Germany. According to one source, Hungary experienced the most extreme monthly inflation rate ever: 41,900,000,000,000,000 percent.

War = Inflation

Following the tragic events of September 11, 2001, giant national military cogs were set in motion. The new war on terrorism, Operation Noble Eagle, was given a 10-year time horizon. Fortunately, no subsequent domestic terrorist attacks have materialized since that fateful September morning. However, freedom and wartime spending carry a hefty price tag.

Accordingly, no currency is impervious to government spending, not even the U.S. dollar. In fact, all protracted American wars concluded with periods of inflation and occasionally with hyperinflation. Close examination of every national conflict reveals a repeating pattern. War leads to deficit spending, currency devaluation, and inflation.

Early in American history wartime spending fomented three currency crises:

1. **The Continental.** Distributed during the American Revolution and best known for the stigma, "Not worth a Continental," the currency lost more than 96 percent of its prewar value—declining to less than 4 cents on the dollar. Due to overissuance and counterfeiting, trade came to a near standstill and the colonies entered a protracted recession.
2. **The Confederate Dollar.** By the end of the Civil War, the Confederate dollar was worth merely 2 cents per bill—representing a 98 percent loss of purchasing power. According to a Richmond, Virginia, newspaper article, the cost of a small family meal in 1860 was $6.55. Only three years later in 1863, the same meal skyrocketed by tenfold to $68.25, a 1,000 percent-plus price hike.
3. **The Greenback.** To avoid the 25–30 percent usury interest demanded by banks, Abraham Lincoln issued the first $150 million greenback tranche in 1862. By the end of the war a total of $450 million was in general circulation. The surplus ensured that even the victorious Northern states were straddled with an inflation burden of 80–100 percent. Yet despite

popular opinion to the contrary, the greenback was eventually redeemed.

In more recent times, episodes of domestic inflation have always accompanied war. Domestic prices advanced substantially during both World Wars. The War to End All Wars witnessed an inflation peak of nearly 20 percent, the highest adjusted annual rate of the century. By the end of the conflict, prices for most goods and services had doubled.

In similar fashion, vast deficit spending during World War II once again ended with higher prices. In the 1940s, domestic inflation peaked with an annual rate of nearly 15 percent. By 1945, the cost of living soared by twofold, following the precedent set in the First World War.

Furthermore, war spending during the Korean and Vietnam Wars generated higher domestic prices. Inflation topped 10 percent during the Korean War. Excessive military spending during the Vietnam War ended with the inflationary 1970s. By 1980 the 10,000-day war resulted in an inflation rate of 15 percent.

Clearly wartime deficit spending burdens society with a surplus of debt and inflation. As the money supply further shifts out of equilibrium, demand for the currency is diminished and basic necessities extend beyond the grasp of the typical American. A sea change in prices unfolds in everyday goods, such as groceries, energy, and basic materials. Eventually, the deluge culminates with a crescendo of scarcity in essential commodities as prices catapult to impossibly high levels, in turn jeopardizing the entire economic system.

Furthermore, with the war on terror underway, the dollar is once again vulnerable to devaluation. The economic cost of a 10-year war on terror necessitates careful scrutiny. For further reading on the damaging effects of inflation, the classic text, *Fiat Money Inflation in France*, by Andrew Dickson White is available for free download at the following website: http://www.gutenberg.org/etext/6949.

To Buy or Not to Buy Precious Metals

Nearly two-thirds of Americans admits to some degree of stock exposure, whether it is in retirement accounts or company reinvestment programs. In fact, nearly 200 million people own stocks domestically, nearly 10 times more than own a house. Of the inventory of 75 million American homes, only 25 million are owned outright with an additional 50 million mortgages outstanding.

Yet when queried regarding gold investments, the response is far less encouraging. Common replies include, "Why would I own gold and where would I store it? Is it safe? Does it pay interest? Isn't gold volatile and risky? Where do I buy gold? How do I know that it is genuine? Isn't coin collecting a hobby reserved for grandfathers?" Frankly, the amount of misinformation and provincial thinking surrounding precious metals investing is unnerving.

So how did gold's millennia-long reputation as the investment vehicle of choice become so tarnished? In one word: complacency. Following WW2, the nuclear age ushered in an unparalleled peace dividend to the Western world. The subsequent period of prosperity initiated a multidecade-long bull market stampede in stocks and real estate. The painful legacy of the Great Depression was eliminated from the memories of all but the most senior investors, economists, and market enthusiasts. Wall Street was impervious to bear raids and traders flaunted their Teflon jackets.

Nevertheless, as the stock, bond, and real estate markets enjoyed years of prosperity, precious metals lost its safe haven appeal. Without even the hint of a perfect storm on the horizon, gold and silver entered a protracted downturn in 1980–2000. Twenty years of abysmal returns sullied precious metals' reputation.

Furthermore, in the minds of most traders, gold and silver were permanently downgraded to that of base metals status. According to Warren Buffett, "It takes 20 years to build a reputation and five minutes to ruin it." By the same token, the two-decade-long bear market so marred the investment appeal of precious metals, even 10 years into the new bull market the stigma still haunts the sector. Ergo, generations of Americans are virtually oblivious to the benefits of gold ownership.

Return of the King

In 2001, against the backdrop of two decades of abysmal returns, gold made a remarkable resurgence. Precious metals and related stocks emerged as the investments du jour. While the yellow metal increased by nearly fourfold from 2001 to 2009, the coveted bellwether Dow Jones Industrials remained virtually unchanged.

Although the lucky stock picker occasionally laid claim to a rich deposit, most stock portfolios were filled to capacity with pyrite.

Nonetheless, the primary fundamental factor driving the gold bull market is first and foremost the ailing greenback. Most primary advances in precious metals have coincided with a weak domestic currency. Not surprisingly, since 2002 the dollar has remained within a primary downtrend. Only making matters worse, the Federal Reserve continues to peg its lending rate at 0–.25 percent. The resulting flood of liquidity has redirected a vast pool of global funds into precious metals and higher yielding alternatives such as the euro, yen, and Chinese yuan.

Consequently, despite the glowing red warning signs looming over the dollar, most professional money managers and pundits alike continue to promote stocks and bonds. Another equally unsatisfactory suggestion involves index diversification. Yet the advice is myopic, as it provides little to no protection from impending interest rate increases/declining purchasing power.

Moreover, according to Wall Street folklore, the market is a mechanism for extracting the largest sum of money from the greatest number of participants. Indeed, even under the most favorable of market conditions, investing is a challenging pursuit. But no matter how malevolent the market may seem, it is not a sentient being stalking investors on Wall Street and Main Street. Market prices are, instead, the culmination of highly diverse viewpoints and investing objectives.

Consequently, diversification via precious metals best compensates for the limitations of the typical portfolio. For instance, a $100,000 account consisting of only stocks and bonds recorded devastating results in 2008. The credit crisis was an equal opportunity destroyer of most corporate debt and equities. Worse still, when measured in terms of gold and silver, stocks and bonds have a hidden Achilles heel. The assets lost considerably more in terms of real money, that is, when adjusted for inflation.

Conversely, in less than one decade, a $25,000 investment in gold increased in value to more than $100,000. Thus a fractional investment in gold insulated the typical portfolio of stocks and bonds from not only a $50,000 loss but actually increased the overall principal by $50,000. Gold single-handedly protected the entire portfolio while yielding sizeable profits.

Despite protests from the Wall Street establishment, precious metals represent the perfect investment. Unlike fiat money, stocks, or bond certificates, precious metals are free and clear from liens and entanglements. On Goldseek.com Radio, I interviewed a very successful hedge fund manager who chose a risky stock instead of gold. Unable to liquidate the shares due to legal restrictions, the well-known financier became saddled to the rapidly depreciating asset. The purchase nearly destroyed his career.

Conversely, if the same hedge fund manager had instead invested in silver, over the same time frame, the account would have doubled in value. In point of fact, silver leaped from $8 to $16. Even if his timing was less than perfect, the uptrend virtually guaranteed an enviable equity curve.

Needless to say, any investment with great potential carries additional risk. A simple technique to offset market volatility is dollar cost averaging (DCA). By adding a fixed dollar amount each month or quarter, the investor secures a position before the next price advance. Accumulation during pullbacks lowers the average total cost. When markets display bullish trend characteristics, investors must ignore the prevailing wisdom and focus instead like a laser beam on consistent dollar cost averaging.

Further Support for Precious Metals

There exists a widespread misconception that money market funds, savings, and checking accounts are universally safe. This viewpoint is a non sequitur. Although such financial vehicles do protect funds from stock and bond market declines, the inflation threat remains intact.

Furthermore, stocks, bonds, currencies, and related paper assets are always hostage to the whims of corporate insiders and government monetary policies. Intangible assets can be created with the mere stroke of a pen and are vulnerable to 100 percent loss. Conversely, precious metals are scarce and never enter bankruptcy. In an era where diversification is so simple, protecting wealth via precious metals insurance is the only logical choice.

Indeed, astute investors understand that powerful economic themes such as inflation tend to persist for years, even decades. Thus intangible paper assets must be exchanged for tangible, inflation-proof investments. Since the supply of precious metals is fixed and cannot be overinflated, it remains the ideal solution to investment security and the only safe currency during market instability.

Silver or Gold?   Determining where the smart money is directing its capital is a wise investing tactic. In recent years, celebrated investors, such as Warren Buffett, Bill Gates, and George Soros, placed enormous bets on silver. Warren Buffett plowed $500 million into a 129-million-ounce investment in bullion. Bill Gates directed millions of dollars into the Pan American Silver Company, and George Soros acquired a substantial stake in Apex Silver Mines. Why did the distinguished financiers choose silver positions over gold? They undoubtedly concluded that silver was undervalued in comparison.

Moreover, during much of history, one ounce of gold could be exchanged for 16 ounces of silver, that is, a gold/silver ratio of 16:1. Yet by 2010, the gold to silver ratio stood at more than 60:1. Judging by traditional standards, silver is currently discounted by 400 percent relative to gold.

Furthermore, the discovery of the New World by Christopher Columbus coincided with the highest precious metals prices ever recorded. Statistics indicate that silver reached a historic zenith of $806 per ounce in 1477. Gold climbed to a penultimate peak of $2,400 in 1492 (see Figure 3.6).

Clearly, the American gold bonanza flooded the global marketplace with such a vast supply of gold and silver that the subsequent 500-year precious metals price depreciation that followed was inevitable. In fact, silver slid from $806 down to $4.00 in 2002—more than a 99 percent loss—representing the most protracted bear market in history. However, one person's loss is often another's gain, as illustrated by the amazing precious metals bull market of the past decade. From a contrarian perspective, silver now represents one of the greatest buying opportunities of all time.

The Dollar Dilemma   Government monetary authorities could learn much from the time-honored adage, "too much of anything is good for nothing." By choosing to ignore the lessons of the past, unsound monetary programs are now abundant. In the long run, the stimulus panacea invariably backfires, resulting in a currency crisis and the destruction of national sovereignty. In effect, the malevolent process essentially marginalizes the young, senior citizens, as well as the middle and working classes to that of medieval serf status.

Moreover, fiat money quandaries are hardly a modern affair. More than two hundred and fifty years ago, Voltaire expressed his disdain for paper money. The great writer and philosopher of the

French Enlightenment noted, "Paper money eventually returns to its intrinsic value—zero." At the heart of every inflationary episode lurks a depreciating currency.

Evidently, more than two centuries later, history is once again demonstrating its affinity for repetition. The great American experiment is following a similar monetary path as Voltaire's France. In 1921 only $55 existed for every man, woman, and child in the United States. Yet by 2009 the humble figure skyrocketed above $30,000 per capita! Clearly, a plaque with an inscription of Voltaire's warning should be placed on the desktop of every member of the Federal Reserve.

Thanks to Fed monetary gamesmanship the greenback has relinquished 99 percent of its purchasing power since the unconstitutional Federal Reserve seized control of the national money supply. Ergo, the rapid descent of U.S. dollar purchasing power should come as little surprise to anyone. Yet approximately 150 years have elapsed since the last inflationary crisis gripped the nation. As a result, most investors have been desensitized to the threat posed by increasing price levels, and practically the entire nation is oblivious to the inflation threat. Only a few investors are prepared to cope with the corrosive effects of rapidly increasing price levels.

Moreover, at all times and places, inflation is a clandestine form of wealth confiscation. The hidden tax lurks behind policies designed to stimulate economic growth and finance international conflicts. The outcome of such domestic programs is always excessive deficit spending. Government meddling is little more than a self-inflicted shotgun blast, further deteriorating the reserve currency status of the greenback.

In like fashion, profligate government spending negatively impacts the economic cycle. For instance, as interest rates leap skyward, bonds become less attractive. Coupon interest loses its appeal and underlying principal erodes in value. Private industry and the Treasury Department are then forced to pay higher interest rates to encourage bond purchases.

The Gold Standard: A Necessary Statute

The architects of the U.S. constitution voiced their concerns regarding unrestrained money growth. The Founding Fathers had first-hand knowledge of the deleterious effects of fiat paper money and worried that the fledgling republic could enter a crisis similar to the current dilemma. In a letter dated January 9, 1787, George Washington warned, ''Paper money has had the effect in your state that it will ever have, to ruin commerce, oppress the honest, and open the door to every species of fraud and injustice.'' At the onset of the Revolutionary War in 1776, one continental dollar purchased one ounce of gold. Yet by 1781, one gold coin was worth 200 Continentals. Put simply, the Continental was worthless. What went wrong? Six years of excessive monetary expansion destroyed the Continental. To finance the Revolutionary War, Congress printed $200,000,000, nearly a quarter billion dollars—a staggering sum for the era.

The devaluation of the Continental fomented staggering inflation within the burgeoning nation. For instance, before the war a loaf of bread cost $1. Just a few years later, the same purchase required $200. However, those with the foresight to exchange Continentals for gold coins before the end of the conflict fared quite well. The price of gold subsequently increased by 150-fold or 15,000 percent. To better illustrate the dilemma, if the price of gold climbed by 150 times today, the price would reach a staggering $150,000 per ounce.

Meantime, the Continental Congress enacted standards to ensure that a bimetallic standard would remain a permanent feature of American money. The national founders set the dollar upon an unshakable framework of gold and silver. On June 21, 1788, the newly ratified United States Constitution declared that all American money must be supported by gold and silver, as presented in Article One, Section Ten: ''No state shall emit bills of credit, make anything but gold and silver coin as tender in payment of debts, coin money.''

From 1792 onward, the Mint Act secured a dollar peg of 371.25 grains of silver or 24.75 grains of gold. Ironically, the current dollar system is the very antithesis of the mandate. Two hundred years after the gold standard was set in place, the dollar is now supported by little more than debt and tax revenues. Without the backing of gold or silver, the counterfeit fiat money has essentially thrust the nation into perpetual indebtedness.

Meanwhile, one year after the American states ratified the Constitution, the Founding Fathers observed the French Revolution and the devastating episode of hyperinflation of 1789 that accompanied it. Yet unlike the newly printed American dollar, the French

currency was not backed by a gold or silver standard. The bureaucratic foible and government largess resulted in a series of water-
shed events: currency devaluation, runaway inflation, and the
French Revolution.

Nonetheless, more than a decade after the onset of the financial
hardship, in 1801 Napoleon Bonaparte linked the national currency
to the gold standard. The bold move single-handedly ensured a
sound currency, revived economic confidence, and halted runaway
inflation. Many scholars agree that the resulting economic revival
was a direct result of Napoleon's decision to reestablish a precious
metals standard.

Likewise, in the 1930s, the U.S. dollar was supported by a mountain of gold in the N.Y. Fed/Fort Knox vaults. This fact alone
was sufficient to ensure a 24-karat reputation. However, in 1971
President Richard Nixon abandoned the Bretton Woods Agreement, removing the dollar from the gold standard. Put simply,
dollar holders were no longer proffered gold in exchange for greenbacks. The invisible bulwark that had secured global supremacy for
decades was forfeited via a mere pen stroke. The next section examines the mysterious black gold standard that replaced the yellow
metal as the dollar's primary support.

The Black Gold Standard

After the dollar was decoupled from the gold standard in 1971, the
reserve currency required an alternative life support system. From
1971 to 2000, global oil demand provided the perfect panacea,
known as the Petrodollar phenomenon. OPEC nations primarily accepted dollars in exchange for oil exports. As a result, the dollar became the lifeblood of the modern economy. Since 1945, only
nations with sizable dollar reserves were virtually guaranteed a constant supply of oil imports.

Accordingly, the fate of the entire industrialized world became
intimately coupled with the petrodollar. In order to insure a steady
flow of petroleum, for decades dollar stockpiles were maintained
outside the domestic shores. The resulting demand ignited a cycle
of unparalleled dollar expansion and global co-dependency. The
U.S. dollar was not only the biggest currency on the block, it
enjoyed a virtual monopoly. The lopsided trade arrangement effectively subdued inflation. However, according to Gresham's law, the
scenario could not be sustained indefinitely.

Gresham's Law

Sir Thomas Gresham (1519–1579) was an English financier and London native during the Tudor dynasty. Gresham is credited as the founder of the Royal Exchange and his financial counsel was highly sought after by King Henry VIII. Gresham's law bears his name due to his discovery regarding monetary affairs. Gresham argued that more valuable money, such as precious metals, is accumulated and removed from circulation while less valuable currencies are used for everyday transactions. To fully restore confidence in the troubled British paper notes, Gresham insisted that Britain must return to a gold standard.

Likewise, millions of Americans have unknowingly been affected by Gresham's law. In the mid-1960s the U.S. Mint reduced the silver content in coin production from 90 percent to 40 percent and then ultimately to 0 percent. Even so, for decades silver dimes or quarters could be found in pocket change. Yet the purchasing power of the dollar has now eroded to the point that most silver coins have been removed from circulation.

While both silver and nonsilver coins share the same face value, the silver content of the earlier 90 percent variety sets them apart from their younger copper-nickel siblings. Thus countless U.S. silver coins are held by shrewd collectors while comparatively worthless copper-nickel coins are used for regular purchases and payments. Gresham would be impressed with the nearly perfect example of his law. In the next section, a more serious example of Gresham's law is examined.

Gresham's Euro

At midnight on January 1, 1999, the nations of the newly founded eurozone collectively recognized the euro as the official currency. The dream of a unified European currency had been realized. Non-euro notes and coins remained legal tender and the exchange rates were fixed against participating nations until January 1, 2002. The most striking characteristic of the new currency was its irredeemable 15 percent gold backing.

The token precious metals support marked a sea change in global currency dynamics and the beginning of the end of global dollar dominance. Although it is true that the euro has gold backing within eurozone bank vaults, the notes cannot be exchanged for bullion. Still, the die is cast—the euro has indeed crossed the

Rubicon. Gresham's law predicts that the entire geo-economic structure will be forever inverted as global governments divert capital away from dollars in favor of the euro rival.

Although the 15 percent nonredeemable gold backing seems insignificant at first blush, in the kingdom of fiat currencies the one with marginal gold support rules. Just as U.S. silver coins are retained for their precious metals content, euros are now stockpiled. Many crude oil exporting nations accept euros in exchange for exports—a further threat to dollar hegemony.

Not Worth a Greenback

Interestingly, the perilous dollar market slide was perfectly correlated with the introduction of the euro. In fact, the relationship between the euro's birthday in February 2002 and the end of dollar supremacy is irrefutable. The awe-inspiring size and scope of the dollar conundrum is likely to lead to the greatest currency crisis in recorded history. (See Figure 3.3.)

When I first published my thoughts on this subject in 2003, I showed that ceteris paribus, all things being equal, during periods of warfare and uncertainty, trust in fiat money wanes and government policies rarely revive confidence. I argued in favor of a balanced budget policy at the federal, state, and local levels. Unfortunately, officials failed to heed the warning signs. Since that time the nation has entered the most protracted recession since the Great Depression. Many cities, counties, and even states are now facing imminent bankruptcy.

Furthermore, in the aforementioned article I alluded to the fact that the United States, Great Britain, Europe, and the global community must stop central bank gold sales and instead accumulate large reserves. At the time, gold was valued at merely $300 per ounce. Had officials acted appropriately, the damage would have been minimal. However, five years later the cost to secure the same gold reserves has increased by nearly 400 percent.

Clearly, officials sold hundreds of tons of gold reserves at vastly discounted prices precisely when strategic stockpiles should have been accumulated. Much of the bullion was absorbed by the governments of China, India, and Russia. Although Western officials failed to prepare, it is not too late for individual investors to take the appropriate actions.

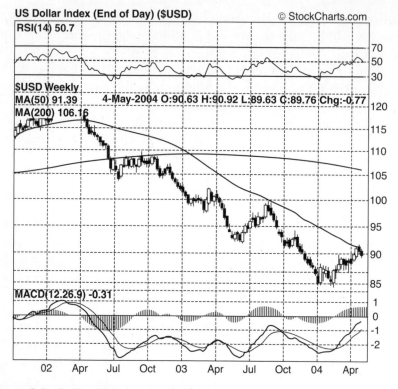

Figure 3.3   Dollar Downtrend Begins

The Investment Solution

Statistics show that as many as two out of three Americans own stocks. The domestic love affair with equities is partially responsible for the fact that comparatively few have opted to buy precious metals. On several occasions in the twentieth century, stock prices remained stagnant for years, even decades. At times, stocks make subpar investments. For example, in 1901–1921, 1929–1952, and 1965–1982, stock prices were subdued. In similar fashion, at the dawn of the new millennium the Dow Jones Industrial Average reached a peak price of 11,750. Nine years later, the index is still trading near 10,000.

Nevertheless, because precious metals never decline to zero in value, gold is widely regarded for its unique wealth preservation characteristics. Although the gold bull market has persisted for nearly 10 years, trends often last much longer than expected. The solid fundamental and technical underpinnings overwhelmingly increase the odds of success.

Even so, the dramatic shift from paper assets back into tangible commodities is a difficult transition for many investors. As the late Will Rogers said, "I am not as concerned about the return on my money as I am about the return of my money." Accordingly, for those interested in protecting wealth, nothing outshines precious metals. When governments fail to take the appropriate precautions necessary to secure basic living standards, individuals must make preparations. Gold and silver are the best remedy for what ails the dollar. Accumulating precious metals must become a top priority for every family.

Technically Speaking

Seemingly random market chaos provides clues to future price movements. Technical analysis attempts to profit from such clues. The power of technical prognostication is crystallized in the collapse of energy giant, Enron. Declining Enron share prices sounded the alarm well in advance of the bankruptcy announcement. For years the Wall Street blue chip Enron and its management were above reproach. Yet unbeknownst to legions of experts, Enron and its accounting firm Arthur Andersen clandestinely cooked the books. By the time that the full extent of the corporate malfeasance was revealed, millions had lost millions. The majority of shareholders were exposed to enormous risks, including the total loss of each and every dollar invested.

Since governments and corporations alike can cook the books, the effectiveness of fundamental research is dubious. In the final analysis it was technical research and not fundamental that proved to be invaluable. Subsequently, much of the wealth was transferred from the brokerage accounts of fundamental investors and deposited into those of market trend adherents.

Fundamentally Flawed

On the opposite side of the analysis spectrum, fundamental analysts claim that statistical metrics are the best determinant of true investment value. The fundamentally inclined present the compelling argument that prices reflect independent events, vastly limiting the predictive power of technical patterns. Markets are comprised of investors who occasionally misjudge "true" valuations. Thus, investors must only sell when prices are overvalued and accumulate when prices are deemed to be undervalued.

Returning to the Enron disaster parallel, fraudulent company statistics clouded the view of most fundamental analysts. In essence, fundamental investors were essentially flying while blindfolded. Although the value-oriented methodology is intellectually appealing, without a technical vantage point the technique is inadequate.

Conversely, the technical school insists that assets often remain overvalued or undervalued far longer than prescribed by fundamental analysis. Ergo, price alone is the best estimate of true value at any given time. This explains why most fundamental traders remained on the sidelines during the hugely profitable Internet stock boom of the 1990s, while technical investors ignored the warnings of nervous fundamental investors and instead participated in the bull market. More importantly, technical investors sidestepped the 2000 stock market crash.

Ultimately, I agree with the conclusion drawn by both Barton Biggs and James Surowiecki in their seminal works, *Wealth, War & Wisdom* and *The Wisdom of Crowds*, respectively. Market price is the ultimate determinant of value and the best mechanism available to shield investors from losses. When technical market trends are included, I propose that price is the only valuation method capable of preventing major losses in every market crisis of the past, present, and future. Put simply, price reflects the global knowledge base of relevant data, including fundamental metrics and even rumors.

Forecasting with Fibonacci

Born in the Italian city of Pisa in 1175, Leonardo Fibonacci forever changed the way that people view the world. Although his name translates loosely as "block head," he was far from simple minded. In his magnum opus, *Liber Abaci*, the great mathematician presented an ingenious numerical sequence. The Fibonacci formula is a recurrent law that describes countless global enigmas. The profound mathematical concept is based on the golden mean, originally discovered by the ancient proto-civilizations in Egypt and Greece.

Examples of the Fibonacci sequence are abundant throughout the natural world, including the sublime architecture of curved sea shells, the vortex configuration of sunflower seeds, the luminous arms of spiral galaxies, and even the length of human fingers, hands, and arm segments. Although the mathematical basis of the Fibonacci method is simple, the concept is quite profound. By adding two consecutive numbers in the series, the next Fibonacci number is derived:

$$1\ 1\ 2\ 3\ 5\ 8\ 13\ 21\ 33\ 54$$
$$(1+1) = 2\ 3\ 5\ 8\ 13\ 21\ 33\ 54$$
$$1\ 1(2+3) = 5\ 8\ 13\ 21\ 33\ 54$$
$$1\ 1\ 2\ 3(5+8) = 13\ 21\ 33\ 54$$

The Fibonacci phenomenon is not only woven within the fabric of the universe, but it appears in a startling array of human systems, such as market prices. When applied appropriately to technical analysis, it provides a marginally reliable form of price forecasting.

For instance, following a primary market movement, a Fibonacci retracement is common. The typical reaction involves a 38–50 percent retracement. However, prices sometimes overshoot the first two Fibonacci levels, stopping instead near the 62 percent level before resuming the initial direction. Therefore, the average of the two extremes, 50 percent, is the most practical guide. By extrapolating the midpoint of the prior move, a retracement target provides price projections and potential investing opportunities. In Figure 3.4, the 50 percent Fibonacci level offers an excellent target. Price rebounded sharply from that point.

An example of Fibonacci numbers in action is the 1980 silver bull market price peak. Following the $50 climax, a brutal 20-year bear market in silver commenced. In 2002 a penultimate bottom of $4 per ounce was reached. The 50 percent retracement or midpoint of $4 and $50 is $27. This provides a reasonable Fibonacci target for silver. Interestingly, silver did in fact breach $21 in 2008. Should prices exceed the $27 level a 100 percent retracement will likely catapult the price back to the former $50 price peak. (See Figure 3.5.)

Yet as grandiose as a $50 silver price forecast may seem, the long-term Fibonacci metric suggests it may be a conservative estimate. As mentioned earlier in the chapter, the price of silver reached a crescendo of $806 per ounce in 1477. The highest inflation-adjusted figure ever recorded was followed by the discovery of the New World and its seemingly inexhaustible supply of silver. The silver surfeit ultimately squelched demand which resulted in a 500+ year bear market. Silver crashed like Icarus from $806 to $4 an ounce (See Figure 3.6.)

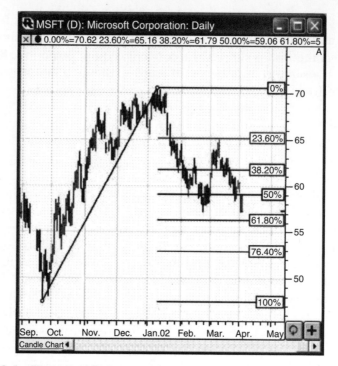

Figure 3.4   Fibonacci Retracement

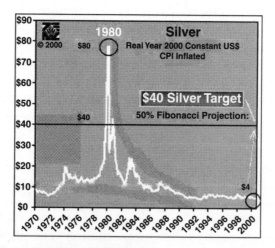

Figure 3.5   Potential Silver Bonanza

Source: Zeal LLC: www.zealllc.com.

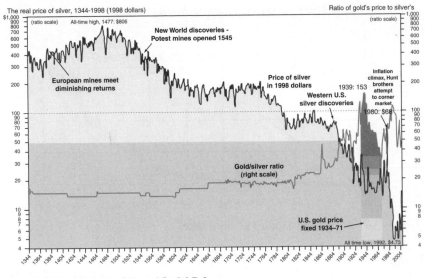

Figure 3.6   Historic Silver/Gold Price

Source: The Gold Information Network http://goldinfo.net/silver600.html.

However, over the course of five centuries the price of silver has yet to undergo a 50 percent retracement of the $806 price level. Using Fibonacci analysis as a guide, a price of $400 fulfills the 50 percent retracement requirement. While an astounding 100-fold increase from $4 to $400 seems implausible, the 1990s dot.com mania produced hundreds of stocks with equally astounding price increases. Will history repeat with another dot.com-like advance in the precious metals markets? Only time will tell. Yet, unlike the hundreds of now worthless Internet stock lottery tickets, silver is a far more secure investment that never enters into bankruptcy. After all, a stock certificate of a bankrupt company is worth less than a similarly sized sheet of paper. But if investment demand for precious metal disappears, jewelry and industrial demand will remain as strong price supports.

Accordingly, the astounding ascent of Microsoft's share price represents another example of a 100-fold advance. On a split-adjusted basis, Bill Gates' company climbed from 60 cents in 1990 to nearly $60 by the year 2000 (see Figure 3.7).

Although a similar 10,000 percent moon shot in silver seems improbable, recent market bubbles and Fibonacci statistics suggest that it may be imminent. Remaining skeptics are encouraged to consider the wisdom of author Jerome Smith who wrote, "Within

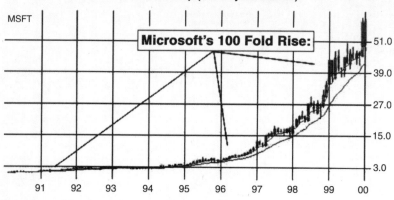

Figure 3.7 Microsoft Stock 100-Fold Rise

Source: www.iqchart.com.

our lifetime, silver may very well become more valuable than gold, as it was in ancient Egypt.''

Seasonally Speaking

As autumn approaches, the Indian wedding festival becomes an important component of precious metals projections. Indian parents present brides and grooms with gold and silver wedding gifts. Christmas and related holidays further increase jewelry demand.

However, to better substantiate the true value of the precious metals seasonal pattern, concrete data are necessary. According to standard econometric analysis 30 observations is the minimum number required to establish a statistically significant sample set. Since each year provides one data point, the past 30 years of XAU gold stock index prices supply ample data.

Although the seasonal hypothesis yielded encouraging test results, I was initially concerned that the observation period was skewed by the 20-year bear market in precious metals. The question remained as to whether the cycle had retained its predictive powers in the current bull market. Further examination of the XAU showed that all four primary bull market advances since 2001 occurred in the fall and concluded before the following summer—fully supporting my seasonal thesis. After crunching the numbers, I was pleased to find that the seasonal pattern concept was supported by the empirical data. Approximately 80 percent of the time, PM's related investments fared better in the fall and winter seasons and less well during the spring and summer months.

In like manner, silver underwent four primary bull market stampedes from 2002 to 2009. The most reflective of all metals ascended from $4 to $9 in its initial advance. In the next rally, silver climbed from $8 to $15. In the third movement, silver soared from $11 to over $21 in 2007–2008. Finally, in 2009, silver doubled in value. As if by divine decree, all four market movements occurred within the fall and winter seasons after completing an approximate 18-month trading range.

Then why not sell all precious metals in the first quarter and wait until the winter holiday season to repurchase gold? Unfortunately, the market is far too uncertain to justify such an approach. The cyclical pattern is useful as an indicator to increase precious metals exposure when the sap is running down the trees and reducing exposure when the mercury is climbing the thermometer.

Conclusions and Opportunities

As the sole issuer of the world reserve currency, the United States Treasury and The Federal Reserve exerted unprecedented influence over the global economy for more than half a century. Insatiable demand for petrodollars offset the inflationary effects of excessive monetary expansion, in turn virtually ensuring global dollar domination.

However, in early 2002 the reserve monopoly was challenged by the introduction of the euro note as well as reckless domestic monetary and fiscal policies. Due to the threat of further lost purchasing power, investors are advised to take appropriate action to preserve remaining wealth. The ideal hedge against capital erosion during such inflationary periods is an investment in gold and silver assets.

There exists considerable technical and fundamental evidence in support of precious metals ownership. One compelling metric indicates that gold is currently priced at a 50 percent discount below its inflation-adjusted 1980s peak price. Fibonacci projections suggest that a parabolic advance in the price of silver may be inevitable.

Given the current economic and market conditions, only precious metals offer the necessary wealth preservation and risk to reward characteristics. A passage from William Shakespeare's timeless classic, *Julius Caesar*, best captures the incredible opportunity,

"There is a tide in the affairs of men—which, taken at the flood, leads on to fortune." Similarly, the end of dollar hegemony is the sea change event that will secure precious metals' role as an essential investment lifeboat for years to come.

KEY POINT

Precious metals are the ideal insurance plan for every portfolio. Of the two metals, silver represents the greatest opportunity for extraordinary profits.

Q&A

Listener Question #1. An anonymous caller would like to know the best method for taking delivery of silver futures contracts.

Answer. Hello, caller. Opinions vary widely regarding futures delivery. In general, such contracts are used exclusively to speculate and/or hedge against market advances or declines.

There are costs associated with delivery. In most instances, shipping and insurance fees are substantial. Plus the exchanges only carry bulky 1,000-ounce silver bars, which require the added expense of assaying tests.

Alternatively, purchasing bullion through a dealer is the preferred method. Reputable gold dealers generally charge reasonable rates. Thanks to the Internet, buying metals is as easy as clicking a computer mouse button. Some online precious metals dealers allow debit card purchases. Orders can be easily insured and delivered to your home. Please visit www.bullionseek .com

Listener Question #2. Jeff writes, "Chris, after listening to your show for quite a while (and enjoying it, by the way), I know that you are quite bearish on real estate. However, I can't help but think of the similarities that real estate shares with precious metals. Mother Nature isn't making any more of either. Two—it takes time to develop both (mining with precious metals, and development of land into usable real estate). Three—you mentioned on your show how gold will never go to $0. Well, what about real estate? Buildings may depreciate, but it would seem to me to be very rare that underlying land would go to $0 in value. I'd be interested to hear any thoughts you have."

Answer. Hello, Jeff. You are correct that the supply of housing and precious metals is relatively fixed and neither asset is likely to fall to zero in value. These are two admirable characteristics for any asset class. However, there is at least one important distinction between the two. While the housing market recorded 75 years of consecutive higher prices, gold is recovering from a 20-year bear market. In other words, gold is inexpensive relative to housing. For example, there is an existing inventory overhang of more than 19 million unoccupied homes weighing heavily on the housing market. Conversely, gold remains a scarce precious metal.

Now that lenders have tightened lending practices, gone are the days of no money down, no-documentation loans. Easy credit is a relic of the past. Instead, the smart money is bracing for a double dip recession. Plus, millions of options ARM resets will lead to a new avalanche of foreclosures, which will in turn fall on the already glutted housing market. In general, home values will continue to depreciate and/or stagnate as gold shines brightly. Thank you for the question.

Listener Question #3. Dan asks if wealthy investors are responsible for the 2008 commodities bubble.

Answer. Hello, Dan. The primary factors driving the price of commodities to higher levels over the past few years is demand and supply imbalances as well as declining dollar purchasing power. As the greenback falls relative to global currencies, most goods and services increase by the same degree. Thanks to the Fed and competing central bank policies the global economy is awash in liquidity. The true culprits are clearly the central bankers and not wealthy investors. Thanks, Dan.

Listener Question #4. Louis writes: "I would like to express my deep gratitude to you for all that you do each week. As you mentioned on last week's broadcast, the Royal Bank of Scotland hit the panic button and issued a warning about an impending market crash. John Williams from Shadowstats.com also recently forecast a 90 percent decline in the value of U.S. stocks if the world succumbs to another great depression. I know that both of you have repeatedly advised investors to 'go long and stay long' in physical metals and their related shares. I have been a strong believer in this strategy as I have no time or the necessary skills to trade. Instead, I prefer to add to my positions on dips.''

"However, if the outlook is as bleak as the pundits predict, how do you see the performance of gold and silver mining shares in such an environment? I have invested heavily in some good-quality juniors but I am now wondering if it's better to sell into strength today, sit on the sidelines, and buy back in after the predicted crash.''

Answer. Hi, Louis. According to Ric Edelman's work, 98 percent of the time the buy and hold strategy beats market timing. However, when anxieties run high, rebalancing a portfolio oftentimes alleviates related anxieties. Thank you.

Listener Question #5. Howard from sunny Sarasota, Florida, writes, ''Thank you for discussing my comments last week concerning a general confusion regarding gold confiscation. I think it would be helpful to many gold supporters to hear your view on how to know when it is time to sell gold?''

'' . . . The general consensus seems to agree that it's best to wait until we see masses of people flocking to coin dealers. At that point the public will be fully involved and it will be time to put on our contrarian caps. But even then, what would I want to exchange for my valuable gold? We certainly would not want to sell out for a debased paper currency just because they are willing to give us more of it. Should we think along the lines of trading some of our gold for some other tangible? Your opinions are always important to me and I start every weekend with the goldseek .com radio broadcast and reading all your printed articles.''

Answer. Hi, Howard. If asked to pick the most significant benefit of owning precious metals, the wealth preservation characteristics would be high on the list. Put simply, precious metals represent a phenomenal financial insurance policy. Once the public becomes cognizant of the opportunity, it will then be time to distribute a portion of your gold and silver proceeds into paper assets selling at fire sale prices. But for the next few years precious metals will likely continue to outshine most competing assets.

Listener Question #6. Matthew writes, "Hello, Chris. I'm an avid listener of your radio show and I invest in many numismatic coins like the $20 Saint-Gaudens, $20 Liberty, and $1 Morgan and Peace silver dollars all with various mint state (MS) quality. I was under the impression that investing in this segment of the precious metals market was the most profitable means to take advantage of the gold and silver bull market. I was listening to your interview with Rich Dad, Robert Kiyosaki. He wasn't much of a fan of investing in numismatic coins. I like what you said about the potential return in numismatic coins when the market mania phase begins in earnest. I would like to hear any additional comments you may have on this issue."

Answer. Hello, Matthew. We suggest regularly on GSR that investors focus on the inflation-fighting and wealth preservation characteristics of precious metals. After a new investor secures a core bullion position, an investment in numismatics may be advisable, but only for speculative purposes. The decision hinges upon individual risk tolerances and financial goals.

Nevertheless, after establishing a core holding in bullion, an investment in the rare coin market may be considered. However, only coins with PCGS, MS-63, or higher grading are worthy candidates. PCGS coins are hermetically sealed and graded by professionals. Quality is guaranteed and standardized. When it comes to numismatics, caveat emptor, let the buyer beware. Conversely, when thinking of gold and silver bullion, caveat venditor, let the seller beware. Thanks, Matthew, for another great question.

Listener Question #7. Mr. Ho from Anaheim, California, is concerned about platinum prices.

Answer. Hello, Mr. Ho. The other white precious metal, platinum, earned its name from the Spanish term *platina*, which translates as "little silver." Platinum is far more scarce than silver or gold. In the eighteenth century, its rarity convinced King Louis XV to announce that platinum was the only metal fit for a king.

The platinum market struggled along with gold and silver in 2008. Platinum was also negatively impacted by the current recession. When the economy catches a cold, industrial commodities catch the flu, and platinum was no exception to the rule, thanks to reduced auto maker demand for platinum-rich catalytic converters.

However, once the global economic recovery begins in earnest, platinum-filled catalytic converters will experience resurgence in demand. Lastly, the typical fuel cell requires up to 2 ounces of platinum. So as fuel cell technology becomes more widespread, platinum demand will soar. Thanks for yet another thought provoking question, Mr. Ho.

Listener Question #8. From Toronto, Canada, Daryl says, "Chris, I've been listening to the show for about four months and really enjoy the insights shared by you and your guests. With the shortage of physical silver, I've started to accumulate 1,000-ounce silver bars. I've heard that in order to sell them later I'll have to reassay the bars. I was wondering if you could give me some advice on how best to store them and whether a new assay would be required. Thanks for your entertaining and educational shows."

Answer. Hello, Daryl. 1,000-ounce silver bars do require the additional cost of assaying in order to verify the silver content. At over 70 lbs. per bar, they are quite heavy. My personal preference is for 100-ounce and smaller silver bars. Thanks, Daryl, for the questions and best of luck with your investments.

CHAPTER 4

Inflation—Deflation
STRATEGIC WEALTH POSITIONING

"Government is the only institution that can take a valuable commodity like paper, and make it worthless by applying ink."

—Ludwig von Mises

As far back in history as ancient Rome, rising prices have threatened the wherewithal of entire nations. Even today, to satisfy extravagant policies such as funding expensive wars, currencies are regularly debased. The result is predictable; inflated prices put basic necessities outside the reach of the masses. Similarly, signs of domestic/global inflation abound. Will modern leaders make the same mistakes as their predecessors, culminating in a hyperinflationary disaster, or will a deflationary crash be the ultimate result? Chapter 4 delves more deeply into the inflation/deflation debate while providing ideal methods to protect against much higher prices.

The National Razor

In 1792 the French Revolution gave birth to a cruelly efficient form of capital punishment. The guillotine was a gruesome killing machine that rivaled even "Dr. Death," Jack Kevorkian's macabre creation. Barely one year old, by 1793 the fearsome device had decapitated more than a thousand aristocrats in the city of Paris alone.

By the close of the whole affair the guillotine had claimed a total of 15,000 regal and noble heads.

Sacre Bleu

According to legend, in response to pleas for bread from a starving crowd, Marie Antoinette exclaimed, "*Qu'ils mangent de la brioche*," translated as, "Let them eat cake." Whether the queen of France actually made the remark remains open to debate. Yet considering her public sobriquet, "Madame Deficit," the story may have merit.

Meanwhile, Marie Antoinette's husband King Louis's careless spending bankrupted the national treasury. Thanks in no small part to the royal couple's lavish lifestyle the nation of France found itself on the verge of insolvency. Anecdotally, King Louis's contributions reportedly turned the tide in favor of George Washington's campaign for American independence. Yet instead of making the necessary cutbacks, the king chose the monetary debasement escape route, which has devastated every nation before and since. The result was disastrous hyperinflation and ultimately the forfeit of King Louis's and Marie Antoinette's heads to the National Razor.

Monarchy—Democracy—Tyranny: Louis and Marie—Robespierre—Napoleon

Following the royal couple's untimely rendezvous with the guillotine, the oratory genius Maximilien Robespierre seized the national reins. Yet Robespierre's mob rule failed to undo the economic chaos that accompanied the revolution. Ironically, "The Reign of Terror" was governed by the Committee of Public Safety, which shares a disturbingly similar title with the current U.S. Department of Homeland Security. Restoring the economy required a second national "Terror," Napoleon Bonaparte.

Although Napoleon did indeed terrorize most of Europe, the people adored him. He quickly established the Bank of France and a gold standard. The economic maneuvers proved to be financial dynamite for the French economy. Of course, the extraordinary feat required the military conquest of much of Europe. Euphemistically speaking, the Emperor Napoleon borrowed most of the yellow metal from neighboring countries. Regardless of his methods, returning to the gold standard reversed decades of economic chaos.

For more on this fascinating chapter in economic history and the similarities with the current domestic situation, please enjoy a free copy of *Fiat Money Inflation in France* at the following website: www.radio.goldseek.com.

Let Them Eat McDonald's

According to reports, millions of Americans require assistance to simply put food on the dinner table. Emblematic of the severe housing downturn and recession, the alarming statistic also represents a new threshold in domestic poverty. The fact that more than 1 in 10 Americans are struggling to feed their families seems trivial from a statistical vantage point. Samuel Clemens captures the irony of the statistics with his warning, "Figures don't lie, but liars figure." An earth-shattering 41+ million people are on the verge of starvation—more than the entire Canadian populace of 33 million.

In similar fashion, the notion that the global bread basket and the land of milk and honey is now home to 41 million serfs on the verge of starvation is unconscionable. In the United States, food stamp usage has soared by more than 10 percent in only one year. It remains to be seen how long the sole remaining global superpower can bear the stigma of so many of its citizens living one food stamp card swipe away from starvation.

Moreover, as Wall Street bank executives dine on lavish bailout banquets, millions of Americans on Main Street rely on food stamps for frozen TV dinners. Although action is required to combat the epidemic of poverty, the moral hazard associated with reliance on government handouts is of equal concern. For instance, the Ireland potato famine, as well as the food shortages that accompanied the Second World War, is emblematic of such government failure. As shown in Figure 4.1, the Zimbabwe hyperinflation disaster and the ensuing food shortages is another recent example. In less than one year the Zimbabwe dollar lost virtually all of its value.

. . . Doomed to Regret It

According to Samuel Clemens history does not repeat, but it rhymes. The twentieth-century essayist George Santayana echoed Clemens's sentiments in his memorable statement, "Those who do not read history are doomed to repeat it." In like manner, the

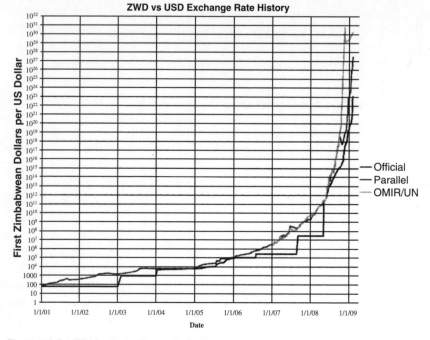

Figure 4.1   Zimbabwe Hyperinflation

current inflation pandemic closely resembles that which followed the French and American Revolutions.

Accordingly, as the Federal Open Market Committee (FOMC) officials spewed hawkish rhetoric to the media in 2007, bailout money coursed throughout the financial sector. So it's little surprise that domestic gasoline prices approached $4.00 in many metropolitan centers. The inflation specter effectively transformed the ritual weekly trip to the gas station into an outrageously expensive ordeal. According to urban legend, when Federal Reserve Chairman Ben Bernanke learned of his chauffeur's gasoline bill, he exclaimed, "Let him use regular unleaded gas!"

Nevertheless, I agree with many of my rogue economist colleagues that the national statistics have been intentionally massaged. For example, in order to present a best case scenario to the general public, officials removed two essential components from the core Consumer Price Index (CPI) figure: food and energy prices. As duly noted earlier in this chapter, for 41 million Americans, food and energy represent a significant portion of total monthly income. The sleight of hand eliminated approximately one-quarter of all consumer expenses from the core CPI number.

Officials claim that food and energy are too volatile to be included in the CPI figure. However, artificially low inflation essentially reduces government Social Security obligations by billions of dollars each year. Fudging the inflation figure also decreases government employee payrolls as well as interest on Treasury Inflation Protected Securities (TIPS). Falsifying inflation numbers foments a dangerous pattern of monetary debasement, which, according to history, inevitably will end with catastrophic inflation and socioeconomic turmoil.

Inflation Barometer—Gold

As discussed in Chapter 3, the most legitimate litmus test of excessive money growth has always been and will always remain the current gold price. In 2000–2001 the smart money correctly surmised that the 20-year gold market downtrend had reached a conclusion and stocks were overpriced. Since that point, gold has increased in value by almost 500 percent, shining brightly as an alternative to erroneous official inflation statistics. How high could the yellow metal climb? When adjusted for inflation, the 1980s peak price of $850 approaches $2,500. Will gold climb to $2,500? Only time will tell. But once the typical investor realizes that runaway inflation is rendering the greenback virtually worthless, a volcano of gold purchases will erupt. Figure 4.2, shows that the long-term trend in gold began in 2001.

The Buffet Proviso

In a page torn directly from the Keynesian school of economic thought, government officials are attempting to ameliorate the credit crisis via bailouts. Yet history has proven conclusively that such bureaucratic panaceas provide little more than temporary relief at best. Conversely, business leaders often construct far more pragmatic solutions to economic issues. For example, Warren Buffett shared his practical answer to the inflation dilemma. According to Buffett, when the CPI rises above an agreed-upon level, a new election must be held to identify a more inflation-conscientious Senate. His solution is particularly interesting considering that his father was a U.S. senator.

Although I applaud Warren Buffett's efforts in the struggle against government-sanctioned inflation, the questionable accuracy

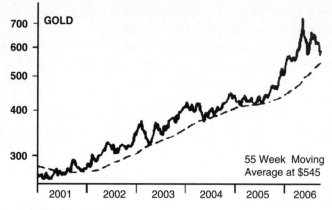

Figure 4.2   Inflation Barometer

of the CPI figure presents a significant hurdle to the plan's success. Again, due to the exclusion of critically important food and energy costs, the CPI remains a poor representation of domestic inflation. While the CPI performed well during the greatest housing/economic boom in history, amid the commodities bull market, currently the metric is virtually useless.

Clearly the CPI is an inadequate inflation measure, only useful for gauging covert government wealth confiscation. If one assumes a CPI reading of 5 percent, the true inflation rate is more likely to be 10 percent when energy and food are properly taken into account. In essence, a hidden 5 percent tax is levied on every taxpayer without his or her consent.

However, by removing the dubious CPI figure and instead relying upon an independent inflation measure, Warren Buffett's plan would work well. For instance, a standard regression of the monthly gold price data would provide a more accurate gauge of inflation and help the Buffet Proviso accomplish its intended objectives. Investors would be protected from covert wealth confiscation and government employees/beneficiaries would receive fair and adequate compensation.

Revenge of the Greenback

By the summer of 2008, the downtrodden dollar had endured a brutal six-year bear market. Relentless short selling had crushed the greenback to such an extent that practically every investor and analyst was bearish regarding its prospects. But rumors of its demise were premature. From a contrarian perspective, the greenback was deeply oversold. In simple market parlance, that which refuses to decline tends to rise. The dollar built an impressive base over a five-month period, which provided a launching pad for an inevitable rally. The dollar emerged from the multiyear bear market in an astounding relief rally, which continued unabated for three consecutive months. Yet just as abruptly as the dollar rally began, it once again plunged back to terra firma, forfeiting half of its gains.

Nonetheless, the question remained unanswered as to whether the dollar rally could sustain the upward momentum. Indeed, would inflation once again exert its gravitational influence and plunge the reserve currency headlong to terra firma? In the next section, a careful examination of the domestic money supply solves the dollar rally conundrum.

Will the True M3 Figure Please Stand Up?

By early 2008, it appeared as though the inflation/deflation debate had resulted in a decisive victory for the inflation camp. Gold and crude oil reached $1,000 per ounce and $147 per barrel respectively—the highest recorded prices in modern history. While the inflation crowd rejoiced with celebratory champagne (a glass of nonalcoholic for me), *The Telegraph* ran an article claiming that the money supply growth had dropped from 19 percent to nearly 2 percent. Penned in the summer of 2008, the UK newspaper noted, "The U.S. money supply has experienced the sharpest contraction in modern history, heightening the risk of a Wall Street crunch and a severe economic slowdown in coming months." Understandably, the report raised the eyebrows of numerous GSR listeners, many of whom filled my e-mail inbox with messages.

The stack of messages shared a singular theme. How could inflation persist amid crashing money supply conditions? Initially, the solution eluded me. But upon further examination of the data, it became increasingly clear that the inconsistency was due to a misunderstanding over the money supply rate of change.

In the 1990s as a graduate student, I spent countless hours crunching numbers on mainframe SAS program linear regression models in the mathematics building. Quite often we identified promising forecasts that seemed to predict future performance. Yet the ever skeptical Professor Karsten was fond of asking, "Do the results make sense?" More often than not, the statistical models were too closely fit to the data, which made predictions irrelevant. Likewise, the deflationists had made a similar miscalculation. Although the sharp drop in the M3 figure was significant, the argument for sustained deflation simply didn't make sense. The M3 data indicates that inflation had not come to an end but instead, had merely gone dormant.

Although the annual rate of money growth as reported by the Money Zero Maturity (MZM), a reliable measure of true money growth, dropped sharply from 17 percent to 10 percent by November 2008, the figure remained well above the 2 percent figure implied by the *Telegraph* article. In actuality, during the 2008 credit crisis the true annual inflation rate remained near 10 percent. Clearly, the deflationist argument that inflation had been conquered was at best premature and at worst, specious.

The Dismal Deflationists

By mid-2008, it was painfully obvious that trillions of dollars in mortgage backed securities (MBSs), collateralized debt obligations (CDOs), and structured investment vehicles (SIVs) had evaporated and a full-blown credit crisis was at hand. Since inflation is always the result of monetary expansion and **credit expansion**, the resulting credit crunch was certain to offset years of inflationary money growth. Further supporting the deflation thesis, the M3 data compiled by Lombard Street Research fell by almost $50 billion in July 2008, the biggest one-month decline since modern records were first kept in 1959. Plus, from February 2008, the U.S. MZM number crashed from 17 percent to 10 percent, where it remained until late 2009. The inflation culprit seemed to be contained, albeit temporarily.

After seven unbroken years of stubborn inflation, in 2008 the deflation camp finally declared victory. According to the much maligned group, plunging housing, equities, and commodities prices heralded the end of the inflation boom and the inception of global deflation. The deflated MZM money supply figure seemed to add further support to their thesis. Since money and credit are the lifeblood of the economy, as credit evaporated from the waterlogged system, the liquidity crisis subdued the inflation specter— absorbing much of the excess money sloshing around the globe.

However, the deflationist argument proved to be only partially correct. The markets did indeed fall sharply, aided and abetted by the combination punches of declining institutional credit, hedge fund redemptions, and margin calls. Yet despite the abrupt decline in the domestic money supply, the invisible fly in the deflation ointment was the stubbornly persistent nature of price inflation, particularly in regard to everyday goods and services.

Meanwhile, the credit crisis–induced dollar rally ignited a stagflationary recession, which temporarily stifled commodities gains and inflation. But against the backdrop of $12 trillion in government bailouts and stimulus plans, a hyperinflation bonfire was becoming inevitable.

Furthermore, it was the government bailout of Freddie Mac and Fannie Mae that turned the dollar currency to port. With half of all domestic mortgages written on Fannie Mae and Freddie Mac balance sheets, crashing home prices sent the two primary lenders of last resort into the market abyss. However, the tide reversed course the moment that the GSE government bailout was announced. The event became a primary force driving the dollar to surprising heights in 2008.

Likewise, by the summer of 2008, government bailouts ensured that $5 trillion of toxic GSE debt no longer weighed heavily on the greenback. Dollar bears were further thwarted by competing European and Asian central bank rate cuts. As foreign central bankers lowered their lending rates, a sea change in global money flows directed a currency tidal wave toward the greenback. The net effect temporarily removed the dollar from the endangered currencies list.

Moreover, dollar strength dealt consumers a temporary reprieve from inflation via lower gasoline prices. After a remarkable run from under $50 to $147 per barrel, crude oil collapsed to $35, representing a near $110 loss. The price at the pumps soon followed, falling from a lofty $4.00 per gallon to below $1.50.

In similar fashion, the benchmark Dow Jones Industrials index experienced a 50 percent decline. By February 2009, more than 7,000 points evaporated from the world's most closely watched stock bourse. The subsequent losses dealt a deadly blow to millions of 401k pensioners. Fed officials quickly marched to the rescue. By means of quantitative easing as well as nearly zero lending rates, the Fed effectively uploaded 13 trillion digital dollars into national arteries, securing the Fed chairman's title as Ben "Broadband" Bernanke.

Nevertheless, once inflation enters its more insidious stages, prices will resume a skyward trajectory. The highly incendiary mixture of easy money, liquid hydrogen, and zero lending rate, liquid oxygen will be the rocket fuel launching prices into the stratosphere. As prices for basic necessities enter a perpetually high orbit, depleted grocery store shelves will lead to intense social unrest. The government will follow the Keynesian precedent. Grocery prices will become regulated and grocery chains will be nationalized. Despite the potential for a Zimbabwe-style hyperinflationary crash, officials will continue to ignore the warning signs.

The China Connection

According to one media report, a primary driver behind the astounding dollar advance of 2008–2009 was intervention in the currency market by China's central bank. New commercial bank currency rules increased reserve requirements sharply, leading to dollar hoarding. China currently holds a massive stockpile of $1.8 trillion, the largest in the world.

However, China can hardly be blamed for accumulating dollar reserves. Holding China's central bank accountable for the dollar rally is tantamount to faulting investor purchases of the gold ETF for the entire bull market in precious metals. China's dollar policy was simply an ancillary factor and not the catalyst itself. The preponderance of evidence regarding China's supposed malevolent dollar manipulation demands a mistrial.

On the contrary, the liquidity crisis was the primary impetus behind the temporary dollar shortage in the United States and around the world. Plus, global central bankers were forced to mirror massive Fed interest rate cuts in order to halt the credit crisis tsunami from slamming into their shores. Lastly, unwinding of carry trade positions transformed the greenback and the yen into the currencies du jour.

Carry Trade

The stock market rally of 2003–2008 was further encouraged by a huge influx of foreign capital, resulting largely from the dollar carry trade. Institutional investors borrowed heavily from Japanese banks at nearly 0 percent interest and then directed the funds primarily into domestic MBSs, stocks, and bonds. A vast sea of liquidity flooded the domestic housing and stock markets in pursuit of a nearly risk-free return, that is to say, a free lunch.

But investors soon discovered that there's no such thing as a free lunch on Wall Street. The arbitrage play actually reincarnated the dollar currency phoenix, which subsequently climbed from the ashes as investors, bankers, and governments desperately sought to unwind dollar-denominated carry trade positions.

The Great Lakes Effect

By 2008 the profound inflationary effects of the dollar carry trade were reverberating throughout the domestic economy. The situation amounted to the Atlantic Ocean (carry trade–related global capital flows) emptying into the comparably tiny Great Lakes (U.S. stocks and real estate). Yet as the dollar rally unfolded, the Saint Lawrence Seaway reversed course, returning half of the Great Lakes contents back into the Atlantic Ocean, that is, U.S. stocks and real estate lost half their value. Now that domestic stocks and real estate have rebounded from the 2009 nadir, global money flows have temporarily returned to a natural equilibrium state. But many analysts are understandably concerned that the entire process could repeat itself, effectively undoing the 2009 stock and housing market gains.

Meanwhile, record demand from foreign banks added further momentum to the explosive dollar market advance. The housing/MBS collapse created a vast disparity between dollar supply and demand, setting into motion a ghoulish deleveraging process. High on the unwinding list was the now infamous CDS payoffs. CDS were originally marketed as insurance for the highest quality CDO tranches. But before long unusually high interest rate returns transformed the CDS into a must-have investment. Global and domestic investment banks and municipalities accumulated hundreds of billions of CDS. Yet the paper promises amounted to a bottomless pit filled with nearly worthless paper—requiring billions of dollars in settlements.

Banker, Can You Spare a Loan?

As MBS sold for pennies on the dollar and hedge fund margin calls reached a fevered pitch, the deleveraging process set off a chain reaction of selling, leaving practically no asset class untouched. In typical Keynesian manner, the Federal Reserve, Treasury Department, and global central banks responded to the credit crisis with emergency loans. By absorbing toxic MBS and related debts, the Fed essentially nationalized many of the major U.S. banks.

Although central bank meddling temporarily reset the timer on the global thermonuclear inflation device, it only postponed the ultimate day of reckoning. Eventually, quantitative easing and related government intervention will detonate the unstable inflation ordinance.

Moreover, insidious financial debt and leverage share striking similarities with fallen woodland timber. Without the natural cycle of forest fires, heavily wooded areas accumulate dangerous levels of kindling. Forest rangers regularly eliminate highly flammable debris via closely controlled burning programs. Carefully supervised forest fires stimulate new growth by releasing essential nutrients back into the soil as well as increasing available sunlight.

Likewise, the 2008 credit crisis ignited a decade of inflation kindling in the form of leverage, debt imbalances, and lending excesses that burned brightly into 2009. However, instead of allowing the natural process to undo decades of inflationary monetary policies, Fed officials ignored the instructions of the great economic forest ranger, Ludwig von Mises.

Accordingly, Wall Street bailouts amounted to an aerial water drop on a raging inferno. Although the action temporarily contained the blaze, eventually a flare-up will engulf the national landscape. Simply put, by expanding the existing money supply beyond all rational means, that is, fighting fire with fire, bailouts will eventually devalue the purchasing power of each dollar, in turn sending grocery bills, gasoline, and related necessities sky high.

Regrettably few Americans understand how inflation threatens their personal savings. Retirees on fixed incomes and the working classes are particularly vulnerable to the damaging effects. Most will be helpless as the price of inflated goods and services devours dwindling disposable income.

Bernanke vs. the Great Roubini

A member of the small tribe of economists who correctly predicted the housing smash and the ensuing great recession, Nouriel

Roubini gave the Federal Reserve chairman, Ben Bernanke, poor marks for his economic crisis management and blamed the carnage on his predecessor, Alan Greenspan. The economic philomath said that Greenspan deserves most of the credit for the dilemma due to his decision to lower interest rates too far and too low. He further added, "The regulators should investigate themselves for bailing out Fannie Mae and Freddie Mac." According to Roubini, "It is privatizing the gains and profits, and socializing the losses, as usual. This is socialism for Wall Street and the rich. . . . Ultimately, the American taxpayer is going to pay the bill." The price tag will be unimaginably large.

Clearly the Fed's hands are tied with the benchmark lending rate locked at virtually 0 percent since December 2008. If monetary authorities raise rates, the remnants of the housing market will crumble and unemployment will surpass Depression levels.

Nonetheless, with trillions of free dollars available to the banking sector, the excess liquidity is setting the stage for a nightmarish "Crack-Up Boom." As described by Ludwig von Mises, over the course of just a few weeks a currency collapse leaves only tangible goods and services with any value. Examples of the Crack-Up Boom include the U.S. Revolutionary War, the French Revolution, and post–WWI Germany. As impossible as it may seem, all the stars are aligned for a modern Crack-Up Boom economic disaster.

Inflation—Shortages and Riots

Reports of food shortages and riots were commonplace in 2008. In response, the United Nations secretary-general set up a task force to help alleviate the global crisis. The UN Food and Agriculture Organization (FAO) developed a billion-dollar plan to provide seeds for farmers in the poorest countries. Yet soaring fertilizer and energy production costs persuaded farmers to plant less, further exacerbating the shortage issue. Plus inflation encouraged farmers to retain crops longer in expectation of much higher prices. The net effect was soaring demand and decreased supply in global cereals, dairy produce, meat and sugar prices—the perfect recipe for famine.

Meanwhile, some analysts blamed the huge population of China for higher agricultural costs, especially for rice, and the resulting famine. Yet China actually exports more rice than it consumes. The true culprit pushing food products beyond the means of millions of people remains global money-printing machinations. The net effect will be worldwide global hyperinflation and subsequent starvation on a truly devastating scale.

Furthermore, supply disruptions wreck havoc on domestic communities. In the wake of the 2006 gasoline shortage following Hurricane Gustav, for weeks, filling stations in my scenic town in western North Carolina limited fuel transactions to $40 while others closed their pumps altogether. Long lines of cars wrapped around filling stations. The sight was eerily reminiscent of the oil crisis of the 1970s.

Moreover, with forecasts of $200 per barrel of crude oil considered conservative, the American consumer must brace for $15–$20 per gallon at the gas pumps, assuming that fuel is available at any price. While gasoline is a crucial consumer good, groceries are far more important. Yet without diesel fuel, the vast grocery distribution system will grind to a halt, emptying local store shelves in the process. In the new decade, rural areas, which require extra shipping costs, will be especially hard hit by grocery shortages.

Clearly, energy price inflation and rationing are but a prelude to food shortages and even starvation. Yet determining which culprit will ultimately lead to the tipping point is challenging. One likely candidate could be an unusually difficult hurricane season. Hurricane Ike single-handedly disabled much of the southern states' refining capacity. However, such acts of God are merely catalysts of the coming Crack-Up Boom. The true threat lies in underlying monetary inflation.

Surviving Inflation-Related Shortages

Following the 9/11 terrorist events, government officials advised Americans to make preparations for subsequent disasters. Stockpiling rolls of duct tape and clear plastic sheets was high on the list of suggestions. The concept was simple. By taping plastic sheets to windows, terrified homeowners could render harmless chemical and biological attacks, such as anthrax. However, cowering alone in a room while sealed up within air-tight plastic sheeting is highly dubious advice.

Moreover, following the fateful 9/11 tragedy, the administration and mainline media both insisted that increased shopping activity was a patriotic duty. The misinformation created a legion of loyal flag-waving citizens who believed the key to economic recovery was excessive spending and debt accumulation, that is, consumption. In fact, former Fed head Alan Greenspan advised Americans to refinance their mortgages from conservative fixed-rate loans into risky ARMs. Not since the days of John Law and the Mississippi Scheme has one man been so closely tied to a market bubble.

Greenspan also supported the use of risky CDSs and MBSs within the lending industry. With such short-sighted advice, it's little wonder that millions of families are barely treading water above the poverty line or facing foreclosure. The next section offers a few basic steps to prepare for the coming socioeconomic threats.

Fat-Free Farm

Food shortages and rationing are commonplace in times of rampant inflation. Yet a home-based safety net can be purchased for less than $5 per week, by simply adding a few canned items and/or a 5 lb. bag of rice to the grocery store shopping cart on each visit. Gradual accumulation minimizes effort while ensuring invaluable peace of mind. After a few months, the cupboard is filled to capacity with an emergency food supply.

Another valuable survival resource is the home vegetable garden. Gardens are often overlooked by career-minded professionals with lengthy workdays and commutes. Millions choose instead to spend valuable time in front of the television or at a fitness center. Why waste money on overpriced membership fees, workout clothing, gasoline, and car expenses when the home garden fitness center beckons? By reducing TV viewing time by only 30 minutes per day, the home garden fitness center provides similar results at a fraction of the cost.

Moreover, gardening strengthens family ties while paying dividends in the form of physical fitness, healthy air, vegetables, and sunshine. Crop surpluses can be bartered with neighbors. A home garden/alternative fitness center can significantly improve the odds of survival.

Survival Spud

Topping the list of ideal home garden crops is the basic potato. Easily prepared in a variety of dishes, pound for pound of yield, the potato requires 75 percent less garden space than does grain or rice. Since potato tubers grow underground, unlike tomatoes, corn, and so on, hungry neighbors are far less inclined to borrow a meal without express written permission.

According to one urban legend, a lady provided ample food for her large family via a novel potato cultivation method. With little more than a few used auto tires from the local junk yard, she set a plan into motion. First the industrious gardener placed a sprouted potato eye in the center of each tire and filled the tires to capacity with composted soil. Within a few weeks, potato stems emerged and hovered 12 inches above the tires. Next a second tire was placed atop the first and a fresh layer of soil was applied. The additional compost encouraged a new crop of edible tubers within the new tires. The entire process was repeated until each stack contained four tires.

As the growing season progressed, the tires were emptied of new potatoes, which provided ample meals without affecting plant growth or total output. Two large potatoes per meal provide approximately 50 grams of protein each day, fulfilling the minimum recommended daily allowance.

In 2008 Jennifer and I planted two potato gardens, one in spring and one in fall. Each patch produced a one-month supply of potatoes. A personal favorite recipe involves chopping two large potatoes into small cubes. The pieces are then placed in a large covered plastic bowl with a quarter-cup of olive oil. After being shaken thoroughly, the potato pieces are then placed on a cooking sheet in a preheated oven at 350 degrees for about 45 minutes, longer for a more crispy texture. Next a slight coating of sea salt is added and bon appétit. The method significantly reduces fat and calorie intake over the more popular fried potatoes, without sacrificing taste.

For the time-strapped chef a microwave, fork, and paper towel are all that's required. Each potato is poked several times with a fork. Next, the tuber is wrapped in a paper towel and then cooked in a microwave for 5–10 minutes. After allowing the potato to cool for 5 minutes, slice the center open and press both ends together. Voila, a perfect baked potato. Although it may seem like provincial thinking at first blush, the ease and simplicity of survival gardening ensures that any family, regardless of income level, can enjoy the numerous associated benefits and better prepare for the approaching inflation storm.

KEY POINT

Due to massive global government bailouts/monetary expansion, an inflation disaster is inevitable. The price of gold will likely reach $2,500 in the coming years. Gold represents the best safety net for every portfolio.

Q&A

Listener Question #1: Sharif writes, "Thank you, Chris, for your article regarding the *Telegraph*'s M3 mistake. I read it twice with great interest. When looking for further answers, I found that their statistics are based on three-month moving averages. How could the moving average collapse and not the year over year figure?"

Answer: Hello, Sharif. In a discussion with John Williams of Shadow stats.com, he agreed that the annual time frame is most relevant for viewing the M3 rate of change. Everything else is noise. So the three-month moving average is little more than a statistical anomaly. Thanks for another thought-provoking question, Sharif.

Listener Question #2: Nikolay from Bulgaria writes, "Thanks, Chris, for the good analysis on the M3 article."

Answer: Hello, Nikolay. GSR listeners filled my inbox with their concerns. It was pleasing to find a simple resolution to the puzzle. Thanks and keep in touch.

Energy Crisis

BLACK GOLD

" . . . the days of persistently cheap oil and natural gas are likely behind us."

—Ben Bernanke, Chairman of the U.S. Federal Reserve,
Economic Club of Chicago, June 15, 2006

The global ebb and flow of petroleum supply/demand has shifted markedly in recent years. Demand for crude oil is accelerating at a time when the world oil supply has passed its peak. Against the backdrop of "Peak Oil" and unprecedented global demand, the international energy chess match is rapidly approaching a checkmate scenario.

However, the credit crisis of 2008 sharply reduced demand and the price of energy providing a much needed time out. The temporary reprieve has presented a rare window of opportunity for the global community and individual investors alike. This chapter outlines the appropriate steps necessary to protect against the corrosive effects of higher energy prices while reaping sizeable profits with minimal risk exposure.

The Oil Crisis Strikes Back

The long-standing American love affair with cheap and abundant energy has created a society that is highly dependent upon foreign crude oil imports. Home to merely 5 percent of the global population, the United States consumes 25 percent of the total global oil output. Gas-guzzling SUVs and an endless assortment of plastic products devour petroleum like the super-massive black hole at the center of the Milky Way.

However, growing demand in China and India threatens to surpass even the domestic affinity for petroleum. As our trading partners emerge from third world status, the resulting increase in demand for cheap and abundant energy is alarming. With a combined population of more than two billion people, one-third of the entire global populace, "Chindia" is expanding like an uncontrolled nuclear reaction. Unfortunately, the current sea change in global crude oil dynamics is occurring precisely when supply has been capped by what scientists refer to as "Peak Oil."

Peak Oil—An Inconvenient Fact

In 2007–2008 Al Gore's documentary film, *An Inconvenient Truth* outlined the alleged effects of global warming. Moviegoers viewed emotionally charged images of the environmental impact of soaring fossil fuel pollution. With dramatic flair, Al Gore ascended in a scissor-lift elevator to emphasize the astounding increase in global greenhouse gas emissions (carbon dioxide) credited to the industrial revolution.

Meanwhile as *An Inconvenient Truth* reached the height of its popularity, an equally startling event came to pass. A second inconvenient truth occurred not at the movies, but within the financial theatre. Crude oil mounted a spectacular climb from under $50 to $147 per barrel. The nearly threefold price advance warrants the use of the same scissor-lift elevator used by Al Gore.

Figure 5.1 illustrates how the crude oil contract moved continually higher on a parabolic vector. As a result, the average price of a gallon of gasoline climbed to a new record, above $4.00.

Working to Afford the Commute

Before the Oil Crisis Part II began in 2003, the average retail price of a gallon of gasoline was less than $1.50. At such low prices, a $20 bill was ample to fill the fuel tank of a compact car with sufficient spare change remaining for refreshments and a small donation box contribution. If one assumes that the typical gas station attendant

$WTIC (Oil - Light Crude - Continuous Contract (EOD)) INDX
1-Jul-2008
©StockCharts.com
Open 140.60 High 143.67 Low 139.17 Close 140.97 Chg +0.76 (+0.54%) ▲

Figure 5.1   Crude Oil Bull Market

Source: StockCharts.com.

earned little more than $5.75 per hour in 2003, filling a 15-gallon gas tank for the weekly commute required about $22, approximately 4 hours of labor.

Yet by 2005 gasoline prices doubled to $3.00 per gallon. For the next three years, the domestic median price settled within the $2.00–$3.00 range. Not until 2008 did the price break free above $4.00 per gallon. Even with an increase in the minimum wage to $7.25, the same worker required a day of labor, 8 hours of work just to afford the commute.

Despite analysts' forecasts, crude oil didn't remain at such lofty levels for long. By the end of 2008, the price plunged in violent fashion back to the bull market starting line from five years earlier. Oil cratered from $147 to near $40. Similarly, the median price of gasoline fell from a high above $4.00 only to find a floor near $1.50. (See Figure 5.2.) Thus ended one of the most spectacular bull market runs in modern history.

Global Bread Basket—Oil Pipeline

Although difficult to fathom today, only a few decades earlier America was not merely the global bread basket but a leading petroleum supplier. However, suburban commuting and convenient plastic consumables put an end to domestic energy self-sufficiency. The nation now consumes over 25 barrels per capita each year, equating to over 1,000 gallons of crude oil for each American. When compared

Figure 5.2   Crude Oil Plunge

Source: StockCharts.com.

to Chindia's approximate five-barrel per person consumption level, the domestic number seems impossibly high. In fact, insatiable domestic demand for black gold now exceeds one-quarter of the entire global output. Similarly, if the state of Alaska devoured one-quarter of the U.S. gasoline supply, hypothetically speaking, legislation would likely be enacted to annex the region back to its former Russian owners, with scant ceremony.

Meanwhile, only a few decades ago streets in China were filled with bicycle commuters and few automobiles. But in 2010 a transportation revolution of abundant automobiles has relegated bicycles to less urban centers. Factors driving demand for gasoline include longer commutes, the vastly improved salary levels of the burgeoning middle class, plus government gasoline price subsidies. Petroleum demand in China will continue to expand, eventually rivaling even that of the United States.

The Oil Must Flow

In 1964, a U.S. naval destroyer engaged three North Vietnamese torpedo boats in the Gulf of Tonkin. Although the alleged attack was later determined to be a false positive report, the Gulf of Tonkin incident became the flash point widely credited with drawing President Johnson and the U.S. military into the Vietnam War.

Similarly, in 2008, U.S. naval ships guarding the Strait of Hormuz nearly fired upon five hostile Iranian boats. Analysts insist that such heightened geopolitical tensions could lead to a "Gulf of Tonkin"-like event between the United States and Iran. Every day 18 million barrels of oil pass through the small 34-mile stretch of water, approximately 30 percent of global daily crude output. The strategic significance of the Strait of Hormuz must not be underestimated, as the oil tanker route is the exclusive pathway for the combined oil supply of Iran, Iraq, Saudi Arabia, and Kuwait.

The potential for an oil supply disruption is ever present and would prove to be a catastrophic blow to the energy-hungry Western economy. The scenario is eerily similar to the line from the classic movie based on Frank Herbert's book, *Dune*, "He who controls the desert, controls the spice and he who controls the spice controls the universe. . . . The spice must flow." Rephrased in terms of the Energy Crisis Part 2, "He who controls the Strait of Hormuz, controls the entire Middle East oil supply. . . . The oil must flow."

Energy Crisis Solutions—The Smart Money Knows Best

In any military engagement, intelligence is a key and determining factor. Knowledge of the opposing commander plus the strengths and weaknesses of his or her forces is of incalculable value. Likewise, the smart money always seems to be privy to foreknowledge of primary market moves. In 2008, billionaire investor and philanthropist George Soros was no exception. Soros claimed that the "bubble" in crude oil prices was the result of energy index speculation as well as favorable supply and demand conditions. He pinned $40 of the $110 crude oil advance on speculators and another $40 on supply constraints.

In testimony before the Senate Committee on Commerce, Science, and Transportation, Soros stated, "The bubble is superimposed on an upward trend in oil prices that has a strong foundation in reality. . . . The rise in oil prices aggravates the prospects for a recession." In one of the best market calls of 2008, Soros insisted that the crude oil bubble would burst and investors should steer clear of crude oil investments. Like clockwork, the price plunged from well above $140 to $40. Oil investors who heeded Soros's advice were spared hefty losses.

In 2008 media pundits announced the end of the crude oil bull market. But according to billionaire and oil raconteur T. Boone Pickens, thanks in part to record global demand, the uptrend was far from over. Given the soaring demand and dwindling supply estimates, Pickens and many others will likely be proven correct in the coming years.

In the meantime, government officials have attempted to heap responsibility for price inflation squarely on the shoulders of energy market speculators. Bureaucrats cite the remarkable 200 percent price advance as prima facie evidence of market manipulation. However, purchasing an appreciating commodity is hardly a display of insatiable greed but merely a wise investment decision. For example, who would fault shoppers for clearing local grocery store shelves in anticipation of a tornado or a hurricane? Similarly, investors are merely protecting their purchasing power amid the global inflationary firestorm. As an essential commodity, gasoline displays strong price inelasticity, which portends a far more precarious outcome for the domestic economy.

Nevertheless, the fact remains that Americans consume over 25 barrels of crude oil per capita per year—more than a thousand gallons per person. Clearly, profit-minded speculators are not the root cause of the Oil Crisis Part 2. Instead, record domestic and global demand, unfettered money growth, and peak oil should be the targets of government investigations. Unfortunately for the nation as a whole, investors will likely become more frequently vilified by the mainline media. Eventually, public backlash will lead to draconian regulations. In response, investment capital will flee in search of alternative global energy markets.

Corn-enol

Inexpensive conversion kits allow diesel engines to utilize food-grade oil as a viable fuel source. Although the United States produces 70 percent of the global corn crop and half of its soybean crop, organic ethanol and used restaurant grease may not present practical energy solutions, due to volatile grain prices and related costs. For instance, corn prices rocketed from under $2.00 a bushel in 2006 to over $7.50 in 2008, making the energy source an expensive alternative.

While commodities prices have declined somewhat, ethanol remains a highly energy-intensive petroleum substitute. Production requires considerable fertilizer and heavy diesel machinery. High energy production costs make corn a questionable alternative to gasoline and diesel fuels.

Furthermore, ethanol fuel production ultimately leads to increases in corn prices, a critical component of the domestic food supply, precisely when most families are struggling to deal with high grocery expenses. Plus, crops are limited by natural events, such as the devastating 2008 Corn Belt flood, which sent the price of corn into the stratosphere.

Furthermore, alternative fuels such as wind and solar power remain only somewhat viable energy alternatives. While recent breakthroughs in solar cell technology are promising, the cost of production still exceeds output, requiring years to recoup large initial outlays. Solar panels will not become cost efficient for the typical consumer for another 10 years at least.

In addition, across the Atlantic Ocean giant windmills provide residents of the Netherlands with a surprisingly cost-effective solution to growing electricity needs. Yet wind power is only useful for fixed residential and commercial applications and virtually useless for transportation energy requirements.

Moreover, the commuting preference of the domestic consumer is broadening beyond energy-inefficient SUVs to include electric auto hybrids, such as the Prius. However, gasoline and diesel fuels still satisfy over 90 percent of total domestic transportation needs. Studies indicate that years will pass before the current inventory of gas-devouring SUVs is cleared from the roadways. The nation is still decades away from replacing petroleum as the primary transportation energy resource.

Missing the Bus

Trains, buses, and subways could remove considerable pressure from the petroleum-based system. However, America may have missed the bus with regard to mass transit. Thanks to record foreclosures and declining tax revenues in 2008–2009, many municipalities are grappling with bankruptcy. Tax protests are becoming trendy with hundreds of communities hosting mock tea parties. Most cities are burdened with budgets that simply cannot afford the massive initial outlays associated with infrastructure upgrades.

Furthermore, the dilemma is further exacerbated by the widespread perception that mass transit is a service reserved for less fortunate folks. In the foreseeable future, auto commuting will remain deeply engrained as a status symbol in the American psyche.

The Energy Investment Paradox

In the United States, investing has evolved from an activity once reserved for the wealthy elite into a national passion of the middle class. Due in large part to the modern love affair with stock-based mutual funds and IRAs, over half of Americans now own stocks. This is the highest ratio in history, especially when compared with the roaring twenties, when only 2.5–10 percent of Americans shared ownership in national corporations.

Over the course of the next few years, the average price of a domestic gallon of gasoline will exceed the former peak of $4.00 and climb to seemingly impossible heights. At that point, prices at the pump and blood pressures alike will reach critical levels. However, the fact that 200 million Americans have some degree of stock ownership plus the near certainty of soaring energy prices forms an intriguing economic paradox. The majority of Americans could invest in energy ETFs and sound energy companies to offset the economic hardships associated with soaring prices at the gas pump/heating costs. I refer to this proposal as the Waltzek Energy Investment Solution (WEIS.) The plan could potentially provide an inflation safety net for two out of every three Americans. Still, only a small fraction of the population will wake up to the opportunity in time to share in the benefits.

Free Is an Excellent Price

Identifying energy stock candidates is challenging for professionals and much more so for neophytes. Novice stock pickers are encouraged to avoid individual companies and focus exclusively upon energy ETFs. Experienced investors searching for oversized capital gains and dividends will enjoy a free subscription to the *GSR Spotlight Picks* newsletter. The weekly periodical regularly includes a list of high-yielding energy stocks. In 2010, the free newsletter surpassed the 175th edition landmark.

During the 2007–2008 bull market, the Spotlight Pick portfolio trounced the Dow Jones Industrials performance by over 17 percent. The list of winning picks includes Batex energy stock with its 64 percent gain. Next, Teloz's stock gained 50 percent, not including the 13 percent dividend. But it was Fording Coal (FDG) that stole the show. The stock recorded an earth-shattering 115 percent capital gain in only a few months' time. The potential for capital appreciation and high-dividend yields once again make energy companies highly attractive portfolio components.

However, individual stock results offer limited perspective. A far more reliable measure of gains is the weekly portfolio percentage change. During the first half of 2008, the typical GSR portfolio recorded a capital gain of 25 percent plus an additional 10 percent dividend yield. From the 2009 low to April 2010, the stocks continued to outperform the general market.

The Energy Manhattan Project

While government officials busily chase energy crisis red herrings, such as speculators, the impending energy dilemma rolls forward. At this late stage, the situation demands much more than finger pointing. In order to sidestep the coming economic emergency, I propose that an organized think tank of the top business and economic minds must be assembled to tackle the challenging energy issues, including the following talking points:

- **Improved mass transit: diesel trains/maglev trains:** Locomotive transport is several times more energy efficient than air travel. A mandatory ride on a modern European maglev railway would likely impress upon our leaders the significant breakthroughs in mass transit and the potential for domestic application. The massive infrastructure updates required by such projects would provide new jobs for the struggling economy.
- **Nuclear power plants:** According to one source, not a single domestic atomic reactor facility has been built since 1996. This is partially due to the emotional fallout of the Three Mile Island and Russia's Chernobyl accidents. However, empirical data suggest that the dangers of nuclear energy sources have been vastly exaggerated by an extremely vocal and well-financed environmental movement. France has set an exemplary example and debunked nuclear power paranoia by deriving 75 percent of electrical needs from the clean energy source.
- **Tax breaks and incentives:** Immediate government relief efforts are required to better manage the crisis. Tax breaks for metro residency will encourage mass transit and reduce gasoline-intensive suburban commuting. Plus tax relief for

employers that compensate employees for train commuting will further alleviate gasoline consumption.

- **Glass and aluminum container alternatives:** Due to the high petroleum demands of plastic manufacturing, glass and aluminum are preferable. Although plastic items are generally less expensive to produce—lightweight, the aluminum and glass manufacturing process uses mostly electrical sources, not petroleum. Plus paper products are a renewable resource. Conversely, plastic bag manufacturing utilizes crude oil, a nonrenewable source. Encouraging the use of paper bags over plastic in grocery and retail stores would be a step, albeit small, toward reducing national crude oil dependency.
- **Energy conservation:** Unlike the energy crisis of President Jimmy Carter's era, the current dilemma will plague the nation for decades. The country as a whole ignored his valiant efforts and warnings, skipping the ounce of prevention method. As a result, a ton of cure is now required. The energy shortage will subject millions of people to electrical outages. Ergo, school curricula must be shifted away from the over-hyped global warming agenda and instead to promoting the virtues of energy conservation.
- **Individual energy-related investments:** Crude oil and natural gas ETFs, stocks, and mutual funds present an opportunity to offset rising energy costs for up to 200 million stock-owning Americans. The resulting improvement in capital flows would greatly encourage oil exploration as well as research and development projects.

Up, Up, and Away . . .

According to a newspaper report, in 2008, a 48-year-old gas station owner completed a 200-mile aircraft journey without the use of a single drop of gasoline, diesel, or even electrical power. Instead Kent Couch crossed the Oregon desert into the neighboring state of Idaho on his lawn chair. His craft was rendered weightless by 150 giant helium-filled balloons.

Moreover, Kent covered a total distance of 235 miles in about nine hours. The chair weighed nearly 400 lbs., and a parachute added 200 lbs for a grand total of 600 lbs. Each of the 150 balloons provided 4 lbs. of lift, sufficient to send the craft and its occupant skyward. The contraption included a hand-held global positioning device with altimeter and a satellite phone. One GPS was reserved for the pilot and the other for the chair, in the event that he was forced to evacuate the craft. Food supplies included boiled eggs, jerky, and chocolate.

The event marked Couch's third balloon flight. In an earlier attempt in 2006, he was forced to make an emergency parachute jump after popping too many balloons. In 2007, he flew 193 miles to the sagebrush of northeastern Oregon, just short of his goal.

Originally, the intrepid adventurer was uncertain how he would land his aircraft. Traditionally balloonists descend by expelling warm air via an overhead release valve. As warm air rushes out of the balloon, it gradually loses lift.

However, Kent Couch chose a slightly less conventional landing method. He modeled the procedure after a headline story from over two decades earlier. In 1982, a TV show highlighted Larry Walter's seminal lawn chair flight over Los Angeles. The aviation feat led to folklore status and a stiff $1,500 fine for violating air traffic regulations.

With Mr. Walter's heroic flight in mind, Kent decided to emulate the performance by shooting one balloon at a time with a hand-held BB gun. Each exploding balloon reduced lift, slowly returning the lawn chair and its pilot back to terra firma. Kent commented, "I'd go to 30,000 feet if I didn't shoot a balloon down periodically." The mission was completed with the use of a Red Ryder BB gun and a dart pistol equipped with steel darts. He also carried a pole with a hook for pulling in balloons.

As one might suspect, the lawn chair landing created quite a spectacle in the small Idaho farming town where it came to rest. Similar to an unidentified flying object on a starry night, Kent was greeted by cheers and fanfare from dozens of locals. The fearless aviator received an offering of cool water to quench his thirst. As a token of appreciation, he shared several helium-filled balloons with local children. Luckily, none of the town's youth embarked upon a skyward adventure of their own.

Although the townspeople were thrilled by Couch's arrival, his wife Susan was more reserved, noting, "There's never been a dull moment since [she'd] married him."

In tribute/commemoration of Kent's groundbreaking energy-saving mode of transportation, I was proud to announce on

Goldseek Radio my plan for a similar flight. However, the maiden voyage was cut short by rumors that locals had hatched a plan to improvise an alternative landing method for my craft. It wasn't the quick descent that troubled me, but the sudden stop at the end.

Kent Couch deserves a hat tip for ingenuity and courage. Without the use of a single drop of fuel, he traveled over 200 miles on what must have been a remarkable voyage. Although highly unconventional, such creative thinking will lead to future breakthroughs in energy conservation.

KEY POINT

Due to peak oil/soaring global demand, the age of cheap gasoline has passed. To better prepare for the Energy Crisis Part 2, every portfolio should include exposure to energy investments.

Q&A

Listener Question #1: Nick from Russia says, "Hi, Chris. What do you think about Petrobras stock? Why is it so low; any ideas?"

Answer: Hi, Nick. Although the oil company Petrobras (PBR) has solid fundamentals including yearly and quarterly earnings; I've included several appealing alternatives in the *Spotlight Picks* weekly report. Plus the energy stock ETFs offer diversification at a reasonable expense. Energy stock ETFs also provide dividends, which act as a safety net against ill-timed purchases. Thank you, Nick and best of luck.

Listener Question #2: Anthony writes from Los Angeles, California, "Hi, Chris. I'm a big fan of the show and listen every week. One thing I would love to hear you discuss is this correlation that is often cited between the exhaustible commodity crude oil and gold. In a world where companies are finding ways to replace oil with alternative sources of fuel, why should honest money (gold) be correlated to the price of a barrel of oil? There are electric vehicles and compressed air vehicles that are either starting to sell now or will in the future—not to mention bio-fuels. Even Sweden intends to be completely oil independent by 2020. . . . I would love to get your thoughts on this."

Answer: Hello, Anthony. The ratio is useful to better determine when gold is inexpensive relative to oil. In my view, large institutions, hedge funds, and money managers benefit far more from the gold/oil ratio than you or I. Regarding alternative fuel sources, currently there are no economically viable solutions to the dilemma nor are there likely to be for at least 5–10 years. By that point, the Energy Crisis Part 2 will be fully underway. Thanks for the question, Anthony.

Listener Question #3: Tom from Arizona calls with a question regarding the sale of the US Sugar everglades real estate tract.

Answer: Hi, Tom. US Sugar announced a $1.7-billion, 300-square-mile sale of its everglades land to the state of Florida. Following the transaction, the largest national sugar company will be granted the right to farm the land for six years. I'm sure you'd agree that it is a "sweet deal."

Due to government overregulation and the efforts of hostile environmental folks, wastewater treatment costs are the most likely source of company distress. The militant activists that hounded the company will view the land sale as a major victory. However, I concur with your thoughts that the transaction represents the loss of a renewable source of ethanol. Clearly, by allowing the swamp to reclaim a cheap and abundant green energy source, the efforts have backfired.

Listener Question #4: Peter writes, "Dear Chris: You have mentioned many oil stocks with high dividends on the show and I am impressed with their quality. For someone who has less money and is interested in an oil stock fund, is there a fund of multiple oil companies that also pays a high dividend? I'd like to avoid company-specific risks if I can."

Answer: Hello, Peter. Yes, there is at least one ETF that offers oil company exposure and a solid dividend—iShares Dow Jones US Energy (ticker: IYE). For more impressive yields, direct oil company exposure is required. By limiting losses to no more than 2 percent of portfolio value, you'll be certain that all of your eggs are not held in a single basket. Thank you, Peter.

Sun Tzu—The Art of Profits

ANCIENT WISDOM FOR MODERN INVESTORS

"To subdue the enemy without fighting is the supreme (Art of War)."

—Sun Tzu

Similar to the sting of an adversary's weapon, one false step in the investing field leads to cataclysmic results. Without calculated forethought, discipline, and planning, trading capital disappears without a trace. Anyone who spends enough time in the highly volatile financial world eventually comes to the realization that the market is indeed an unforgiving battlefield. But there is hope for the burgeoning investor. In China more than two thousand years ago, Sun Tzu penned an ancient war tome of enormous strategic significance. This chapter applies Master Tzu's wisdom to the field of investing in simple terms to vastly enhance trading discipline and performance.

The Pacific Ring of Fire ascends from the southern tip of South America, follows along the U.S. west coast and extends to the Bering Strait. From there the most active global seismic belt begins a lengthy journey southward along the Asian Pacific coast finishing near Australia. The seismic zone is prone to fearsome earthquakes and tsunamis. In fact, the Pacific belt is home to 90 percent of all earthquakes and 75 percent of volcanoes.

Paradoxically, the destructive Ring of Fire is a critically important global life support system. Geologists and biologists concur that continental drift is essential to maintaining life on the earth. The yin and yang–like perpetual creation and destruction of great land masses acts as a global recycling mechanism, exposing the biosphere to the building blocks of life, such as iron and calcium. Without such a life support system, essential minerals would remain inaccessible.

However, the life-giving qualities of the great seismic belt are sometimes eclipsed by its destructive force. Unfortunately for the people of China, the ring of fire runs along the eastern coastline. In 2008 a devastating 7.8 magnitude earthquake shook the national foundations, culminating with a mind-numbing death toll of 40,000.

Nonetheless, the national tragedy was punctuated by an amazing tale of survival. Hidden beneath tons of rubble for a harrowing 196 hours, a 60-year-old woman defied the odds. The heroic survivor withstood eight days in the hostile environment, escaping with only minor scrapes and bruises. For most people, living under such extreme conditions for only eight hours would be intolerable.

Moreover, the amazing tale of fortitude shares a striking resemblance with China's national heritage. As the world's oldest civilization, it has withstood millennia of warfare, plagues, and natural catastrophes, only to emerge as a thriving and vibrant culture. En passant the ancient society has accumulated an impressive array of contributions to society, which could easily fill a museum, particularly within the discipline of warfare. For instance, gunpowder and the Great Wall are two well-known Chinese innovations that greatly enhanced national defenses.

The Pen Is Mightier Than Gunpowder

Against the backdrop of numerous noteworthy technological and military advancements, China is home to the world's oldest and most widely respected military masterpiece. Approximately 2,500 years ago, a Chinese general named Sun Tzu compiled a list of military tactics in a book titled *The Art of War*. The original book title is believed to be *Sun Tzu*, which translates into Master Sun. Scholars believe the master strategist lived from 544 B.C. to 496 B.C.

According to historical accounts, King Wu asked Sun Tzu if his military principles were universally applicable. The general insisted that any army could successfully implement his methods. Sun Tzu was so confident, that he agreed to transform 360 court women into soldiers in a single session.

Sun Tzu first instructed the group of 360 concubines to divide into two companies consisting of 180 each. Next, the king's two most adored companions were placed in charge of each company. Initially, the undisciplined group of ladies giggled and laughed as the stranger barked out commands. But the unruly behavior didn't persist for long. In response to the outbursts, Sun Tzu severely punished the leader of each group, despite the intense protests of the king. The women were shocked by the abrupt turn of events. If King Wu's two favorite concubines could receive such treatment, what might befall the rest? From that moment forward, the rag-tag harem of 358 remaining soldiers ceased to giggle with scant ceremony and performed the military maneuvers with flawless accuracy.

Sun Tzu understood that the truest measure of a great military general is revealed by the discipline and devotion of his troops. While his harsh training methods are completely unacceptable by modern standards, the tactics did provide the desired results. The display so impressed the king that Sun Tzu quickly ascended the military ranks to the position of field marshal.

Meanwhile, Sun Tzu's first military conquest was the capital city of Ying in the state of Ch'u. His troops crushed the powerful adversary in 506 B.C. Next, the great commander turned his military ambitions upon the two northern states, Ch'i and Chin. Sun Tzu successfully subdued both provinces, an act that some authorities link to the modern national identity, Chin-a.

Across the Pond

The Art of War was far too significant a document to remain forever confined within the exclusionary walls of China. Eventually the oldest and most significant military treatise found its way across the Sea of Japan. According to sources the war manuscript so impressed the Japanese that it became an important component of bushido, that is, national chivalry and the samurai code of honor.

Moreover, *The Art of War* has even become intertwined within Western popular culture. Widely regarded as the most influential Japanese film, Akira Akurasawa's *Seven Samurai* is teeming with lessons from *The Art of War*. The plot revolves around the heroic defense of an impoverished Japanese farming village against 40 ronin, renegade warlords. The terrorized villagers employ a wise, Sun Tzu–like samurai to resist the ferocious marauders. The battle-hardened leader and his handpicked motley crew of only seven warriors liberate the farming village by defeating a force five times in size. The military strategies employed as well as the character of the samurai would surely impress Sun Tzu. The morality play remains a perennial favorite of movie enthusiasts due to the timeless message of honor, duty, self sacrifice, and military strategy.

Sun Tzu Investing

The career of the professional investor compares remarkably well with that of a veteran military commander. Just as life-threatening conflicts are commonplace for the seasoned battlefield leader, investors experience the gut-wrenching carnage of bear markets.

On the contrary, the novice investor is overly obsessed with profits and dangerously oblivious to risks. He acts in a rash, awkward manner, ignoring the subtle intricacies of investing warfare. Akin to a deadly eighteenth-century pistol duel, every new trade thrusts the unprepared participant into the direct pathway of a financial slug fired by an equally determined and merciless adversary.

Nevertheless, with a nearly endless variety of markets and investment vehicles from which to choose, hope truly springs eternal. So how can investors avoid becoming cannon fodder for Wall Street warlords? Sun Tzu's *The Art of War* contains immense wisdom for the novice and professional investor alike. In this section, several of the great general's most salient stratagems are applied to real-world investing scenarios, beginning with the following:

> Sun Tzu, "He will win who knows when to fight and when not to fight. He will win who knows how to handle both superior and inferior forces. He will win who, prepared himself, waits to take the enemy unprepared."

The first sentence, *"He will win who knows when to fight and when not to fight,"* closely parallels knowing when or when not to invest. Since the financial markets are available throughout the business week, tens of thousands of stocks, mutual funds, options, futures, and commodities present a seemingly endless array of opportunities. As a result, identifying the ideal moment to strike is a daunting task. Unfortunately, most rely on the opinions of other investors. However, long-term success requires that each trader must individually determine when to buy or sell.

Nevertheless, without first carefully gauging market conditions or relying too heavily on the advice of experts, the unprepared investor unwittingly chooses to engage a superior foe in financial combat without the proper weapons and armor. Similar to David's great fortune while battling Goliath, the investor might experience beginner's luck, but the odds overwhelmingly favor defeat. The prepared investor must build a system that signals the precise time to initiate market maneuvers as well as determines the appropriate contingency plan to defend against the inevitable counterattack.

Professionals employ a vast array of techniques to improve market entries and exits. When markets are trending, dollar cost averaging is a particularly effective and simple position-building tactic. By adding a predetermined dollar amount on a regular basis a solid core position is established with minimal exposure to the emotional swings associated with greed and fear.

Continuing with Sun Tzu's instruction, *"He will win who knows how to handle both superior and inferior forces."* Likewise, at the onset of a new market trend, the trader faces superior forces. Yet after the entire core position is accumulated and profitable, he ascends the ranks to the level of supreme commander. A perfect example of successful dollar cost averaging is revealed by the untold millions of investors who profited handsomely during the 1980s and 1990s stock market advance. Put simply, dollar cost averaging is an automated system, which helps everyday investors to maximize profits during major market movements.

Additionally, a technique for position building that has gained favor over the years is the 50 percent retracement method. The technique searches for discounts during market reactions. Instead of fleeing the battlefield and retreating, the strategic investor stands firm and gains even more ground. The wise commander would clearly approve of the tactic, *"He will win who, prepared himself, waits to take the enemy unprepared."* In like manner, the supreme investor benefits from his trading adversaries' fear during market reactions.

Sun Tzu, "If you know the enemy and know yourself, you need not fear the result of a hundred battles. If you know yourself but not the enemy, for every victory gained you will also suffer a defeat. If you know neither the enemy nor yourself, you will succumb in every battle."

The next pearl of wisdom parallels a peculiar investment paradox. The world of high finance conjures up images of wealthy tycoons as well as the destitution associated with the Great Depression. How is it that Wall Street creates such incredible opportunities and simultaneously so much despair? As with warfare, the market is both enemy and ally. To the victor go the investing spoils and to the defeated go the losses.

Consequently, just as Sun Tzu insists that the successful warrior must understand his foe, he'd undoubtedly agree that a solid grasp of the underlying market dynamics is a necessity for investing success. For instance, what is the current market bias: uptrend, downtrend, or choppy? With typical genius and brevity Sun Tzu reduces the complex world of warfare and investing down to the most basic components. In Occam's razor–like fashion the point is so relevant to trading success that it could have just as easily been written by the investing legends, Jim Rogers or Jesse Livermore.

The second crucial aspect of Sun Tzu's challenge, understanding oneself, is equally important. Identifying and embracing inner strengths and weaknesses is essential to success in any of life's pursuits but particularly germane to investing. Readers are encouraged to answer the following questionnaire:

- Do you readily submit to expert opinions or rely instead upon your own judgment?
- Do you have the intestinal fortitude to hold a position through a market downturn?
- Would watching profits evaporate shake your resolve?
- Are you a speculative gambler who throws caution to the wind or are you determined to become a sophisticated investor who carefully scrutinizes probabilities and market trends and employs sound money management?

The student investor is encouraged to practice or paper trade until he or she can answer all these questions in the affirmative.

Performing an objective evaluation on a semiannual basis is also beneficial. In order to best surmise the market trend and to implement a successful money management strategy, the intelligent investor must continually monitor and improve character flaws while enhancing personal strengths.

> Sun Tzu, "The victorious strategist only seeks battle after the victory has been won, whereas he who is destined to defeat first fights and afterwards looks for victory."

The next extraordinary saying is perhaps best translated with the following statement: Do not make an investment until conditions overwhelmingly favor victory. Few investors expect to be greeted with losses when entering a buy or sell order. However, one of the two participants involved in the transaction is destined to fail. By accurately identifying the prevailing market trend, investors vastly increase the odds of winning market skirmishes.

Furthermore, Sun Tzu reveres the ability to anticipate events. Foreknowledge grants the wise commander a strategic advantage over his adversaries. In similar fashion, the sharpest financial minds insist that the commodities downturn of 2008 was a temporary setback within the context of a major bull market uptrend. I concur and expect gold to climb above $2,000 by 2012. Soaring monetary growth and resulting inflation overwhelmingly support the case for much higher yellow metal prices. Ergo, victory should resonate within the core psyche of every gold investor.

However, the concept of predetermination does not fit well with the traditional Western view of the world. Most folks still cling tenaciously to a highly linear perspective of reality. Yet Sun Tzu transcends the archaic mind-set by acknowledging the fluidity and flexibility of time as well as warfare. From his vantage point, every investor who bets against the prevailing trend forfeited his money before the order was even placed.

Nonetheless, if Sun Tzu were alive today, he would harshly reprimand any subordinate who scoffed at the profit potential of gold and silver investments. The general would focus like a crossbow bolt's cold steel tip on the fact that fundamental and technical analysis ensures that victory for the legion of gold investors is merely a matter of time and discipline.

> Sun Tzu, "Fighting with a large army under your command is no different from fighting with a small one: it is merely a question of instituting signs and signals."

Similarly, long-term trend investing works remarkably well with either 100 or 100,000 shares. However, smaller accounts do suffer in comparison due to the regressive nature of trade commissions and slippage expenses. If one assumes a total of $20 in round-trip commissions and slippage per trade, 100 share orders result in a minimum of $2,000 in expenses. So a $20,000 account requires a 10 percent profit to simply break even. Yet a $100,000 account only requires a 2 percent gain to cross the break-even threshold. Clearly, larger accounts benefit from economies of scale.

> Sun Tzu, "Whoever is first in the field and awaits the coming of the enemy, will be fresh for the fight; whoever is second in the field and has to hasten to battle will arrive exhausted." "Move not unless you see an advantage; use not your troops unless there is something to be gained; fight not unless the position is critical. If it is to your advantage, make a forward move; if not, stay where you are."

In the first statement, "Whoever is first in the field . . . ," Sun Tzu presents another priceless gem from a treasure trove of wisdom. This concept best applies to resisting the all too human tendency of chasing prices. The characteristic is most likely a remnant survival tactic from the bygone days of tribal hunting. The animal instinct to chase game as it bolts away from the ravenous hunting party still haunts the modern human psyche. Professionals wage a personal battle against this archaic habit.

Instead, Sun Tzu's teachings advocate waiting patiently and confidently as market adversaries squander valuable resources in the pursuit of frothy market prices. Once the rival tribe/beast has exhausted itself, the patient hunter may pounce. In like manner, since prices tend to meander in a sideways fashion, the supreme investor observes the natural rhythm to better identify opportunities. By adhering to this method, the trend follower avoids chasing prices as they roll over the edge of a cliff.

> Sun Tzu, "Move not unless you see an advantage."

In one brief sentence, the ancient general details how inaction is oftentimes a profitable investing decision. For instance, in 2006–2007 gold bulls and bears were equally matched within a narrow range from $600 to $700. An entire year passed before choppy prices yielded. From that point onward, the gold market stampede was unstoppable, and the market quickly advanced to $800 and then on to a new all-time record price of $900. Sun Tzu would be pleased with those who ignored the price gyrations. By avoiding whip-saws, the warrior-investor builds a profitable position only when a distinct advantage develops.

Sun Tzu, "So in war, the way is to avoid what is strong and to strike at what is weak."

Occasionally, prices are chaotic, like the somewhat manic yet inspirational melody of Chopin's *Minute Waltz*. At other times, the markets enter clearly defined trends and are comparatively subdued and sublime, as with Pachelbel's *Canon*. Building a position when market prices are in harmony allows traders to vastly increase the odds of success. With the support of empirical data at his side, the supreme commander cooperates with the bulls during an uptrend, essentially joining forces with the strong and trampling underfoot that which is weak.

Sun Tzu: "An army may march great distances without distress, if it marches through country where the enemy is not. You can be sure of success in your attacks if you only attack places which are undefended. You can ensure the safety of your defense if you only hold positions that cannot be attacked."

Next, the ancient commander warns investors to guard against placing boundaries that are too restrictive around the market. Picture the neophyte investor with both eyes fixated on dual LCD computer screens, one sweaty palm grasping the computer mouse tightly and the other hand nervously tapping the keyboard. Unsure of the new trading system, the investor is tempted to place overly conservative stops. The mistake essentially allows fear of failure and loss to override discipline. Without providing a wide enough berth, the beguiled investor will watch helplessly as volatile and fast market conditions relieve him of his position.

However, by placing stops well away from the prevailing market trading range, the investor applies the proper degree of respect for random, unexpected price swings. He is rewarded with a position that remains well beyond the reach of his adversaries and impervious to attack.

> Sun Tzu, "Military tactics are like unto water; for water in its natural course runs away from high places and hastens downwards. . . . Water shapes its course according to the nature of the ground over which it flows; the soldier works out his victory in relation to the foe he faces. Therefore, just as water retains no constant shape, so in warfare there are no constant conditions. He, who can modify his tactics in relation to his opponent and thereby succeed in winning, may be called a heaven-born captain."

Ignoring Sun Tzu's next insight is undoubtedly hazardous to portfolio wealth. Since market prices do not always follow the normal bell curve distribution, as John Meriwether and his team at LTCM discovered to their great dismay, the victorious investor must design a robust system that readily adapts to every imaginable market condition. Sun Tzu's water parallel perfectly illustrates how an investor must move with the flow; just as water gracefully courses past every imaginable object in its path.

At any given moment, prices fall into only one of two primary categories, trending or non-trending. Since markets tend to remain range bound for as much as 70 percent of the time, trend followers must develop methods for avoiding whipsaw market activity. The trend follower learns to conform to the market topography, effectively gliding past the obstacles and hindrances presented by choppy market conditions. In fact, after years of crafting trading systems, I have developed a simple method for avoiding up to 80 percent of market whipsaw conditions. Simply wait for the new potential trend to retrace and then place a buy/sell stop just above the peak price. This method has provided just as favorable results in real time as it has in back-testing.

Moreover, the trading system of the heaven-born captain adapts to every imaginable condition. Once the volatile market behavior passes, calmer waters provide the stability to strike like a lightning bolt at the onset of a new trend. Likewise, after more than one hundred years, trend-based systems remain the most flexible and adaptive to market conditions.

> Sun Tzu, "Do not interfere with an army that is returning home. When you surround an army, leave an outlet free. Do not press a desperate foe too hard."

Sun Tzu's next instruction is strikingly similar to the old market adage, "Never catch a falling knife." When a market exhibits runaway conditions, many trapped investors desperately seek to unload positions. The event compares with Sun Tzu's, "Death Ground," where the foe has nothing to lose and transforms into a formidable opponent.

In like fashion, it is a common neophyte mistake to search for bargains under declining market conditions. However, Sun Tzu makes it abundantly clear that successful warfare involves attacking that which is weak and avoiding what is strong. Instead, selling or shorting a falling market is the ideal response. Afterwards, the financial warrior waits patiently for the ideal moment to make a purchase. By ignoring falling daggers and allowing prices to build a base from which to rebound, investors avoid a dangerous conflict with a homeward-bound enemy.

> Sun Tzu, "Throw your soldiers into positions whence there is no escape, and they will prefer death to flight. If they will face death, there is nothing they may not achieve."

The ancient strategist's next suggestion is quite apropos to the world of investing. As with all creatures of the animal kingdom, warriors are also susceptible to the fight or flight instinct. Thus when cornered and faced with imminent destruction, there's no other choice than to fight without compunction. This advice compares to a trader's inability to accept seemingly incorrect or ambiguous trading system signals. It is only human nature to question everything, but in the world of mechanical trading, this tendency is counterproductive. The investor must accept every trade provided by the system, essentially embracing the fight instinct and rejecting the flight impulse.

One method to aid investor perseverance is paper trading or practice trading. Paper trading involves following system signals without putting actual capital at risk. The approach helps to strengthen the resolve of investors during unfavorable market conditions.

While paper trading is an essential component of every investor's education, armchair trading with imaginary dollars is merely a prelude to the psychologically demanding financial battlefield. In other words, play fighting with wooden swords is only marginally beneficial. Actual combat is considerably more challenging. Not until real funds are at stake, does one truly experience the full range of emotions, that is, the tug of war between greed and fear. Only after completing several months of practice trades is the fledgling trend follower prepared to lead the troops into battle via the Internet and the click of a computer mouse button.

Moreover, there is simply no substitute for trading experience. Similar to a skydiver or paratrooper, one must first jump from an airplane at 10,000 feet with little more than a flimsy helmet and a large nylon sack. Until the leap of faith has been taken, one cannot truly appreciate the myriad of intense emotions associated with skydiving.

Likewise, investing requires exceptional training and discipline. Once trading discipline is fully embraced and the fear of losing money has been conquered, the investor can focus upon the inevitable emergence of a profitable trend. At that point the neophyte becomes a professional who has attained self-actualization, and no mortal enemy or market condition can separate him or her from trading capital/profits.

> Sun Tzu, "To capture the enemy's entire army is better than to destroy it; to take intact a regiment, a company, or a squad is better than to destroy them. For to win one hundred victories in one hundred battles is not the supreme of excellence. To subdue the enemy without fighting is the supreme excellence."

In the statement above, the Asian general's wisdom reaches its ultimate crescendo. Although a dominant military commander may harass and harangue the enemy with an endless series of victories, it is the final battle that determines the victor. In like manner, the brilliant tactics of Napoleon led to an undefeated track record, with the one exception of his final conflict at Waterloo. The defeat ended his bid to reclaim his former role as emperor of France.

Accordingly, although the elation and emotional appeal of numerous winning trades can be alluring, the trend follower must avoid such pitfalls. In lieu of a high winning rate, trend followers seek the spectacular profits that accompany protracted market movements.

The brilliant commander crystallizes the supreme Art of War with arguably the most significant statement of the entire treatise. The ultimate goal of a victorious commander is to win the conflict without ever engaging the enemy. Unfortunately, the fine art of diplomacy seems to have been relegated to the past. In the modern arena, the ever ravenous war machine seems to adhere to the dogma of shoot first and ask questions later.

However, the first Persian Gulf War provides one recent example where Sun Tzu's principles were successfully applied. In blitzkrieg-like fashion, the Allies invaded and subdued the enemy in merely four days. Stormin' Norman Schwarzkopf was extremely well versed in military history and undoubtedly studied *The Art of War*. The use of a vast, Sun Tzu–like intelligence network combined with superior technology provided a striking military victory.

Furthermore, overzealous investors often rush to battle in search of exceptional profits. But oversized returns require excessive risks and related account drawdowns. Recovery from such steep declines in equity can be difficult if not impossible. Yet by limiting losses to no more than 2 percent of the total portfolio value, investors guard against imminent failure and ensure victory. At that point, an investor can rest assured that his or her position is well defended against enemy assaults.

Sayonara

Like a modern casino with its myriad of captivating lights, sounds, slot machines, live music, and shows, the financial markets offer a seemingly endless array of choices. To avoid against being fleeced like the typical casino patron, both the neophyte and professional alike will benefit from Sun Tzu's ancient warfare wisdom.

Although the markets are far too complex for mere mortal investors to unravel on a regular basis, garnering exceptional profits is possible. By heeding the long-term trend and limiting losses with protective sell stops, the modern Sun Tzu–trained captain preserves troops, that is, capital, for future victories, thus achieving the highly coveted title of heaven-born investor.

KEY POINT

Once an individual investor identifies and conquers personal weaknesses via paper trading, substantial investing profits will follow.

Q&A

Listener Question #1: Emily says, "I congratulate you on your fine work and listen every week. I have been reading that gold is entering a bear market. I am heavily invested in both gold and silver on margin at much higher prices and would like to know what you think."

Answer: Hello, Emily. The situation that you have outlined is troublesome. Whenever I have an unprofitable position, I sell half and then set protective stops on the remaining half. Therefore, if the price should continue to decline, losses are minimized. But if the market rebounds instead, the remaining half of the original position will offset most, if not all of the losses. By selling half of a losing position, one can reload at lower prices and relieve much of the psychological stress of holding a loss. Thank you for your kind words. Please keep me updated.

Listener Question #2: Randy writes from Atlanta, Georgia, "Hello, Chris. What exactly are the advantages of stock dividends for long-term investors? On the ex-dividend date, most dividend-paying stocks drop in price to compensate for the payout. So, it appears that the investor is left with no more value—possibly less value due to taxes on the distribution. What am I missing? What's the big deal about dividends?"

Answer: Hello, Randy. Studies show that stocks with solid and consistent dividends tend to outperform the market as a whole. Although it is true that shares sometimes experience a strong downdraft after the ex-dividend date, more often than not, prices recover. Therefore, companies with a regular history of dividend payouts are worthy of close examination.

Furthermore, dividend payments help compensate for ill-timed stock purchases. For example, in a weak stock market a 7 percent dividend will effectively offset a 7 percent decline in the underlying share price. Thus, in volatile market conditions investors with dividend-paying stocks are less inclined to engage in panic-related selling. Thank you for the thought-provoking question, Randy.

PART II

THE HOUSING BUBBLE

7

The Real Estate Mania

THE END OF A 75-YEAR ERA

"A house divided against itself cannot stand."

—Abraham Lincoln

In the wake of WWII, the United States emerged virtually unscathed as the lone global superpower. One key peace dividend was the 75-year domestic housing boom. Relaxed lending standards and artificially low Fed rates further pushed domestic home prices skyward. Generations of mortgage holders became convinced that annual price increases were as certain as death and April 15th.

However, the 2007 subprime implosion and the 2008 credit crisis that followed brought about an abrupt halt to the housing euphoria. The median U.S. house price tumbled by more than 32 percent. This first chapter of Part 2 begins the investigation into the housing market bubble/crash with a review of the dot.com mania. Understanding the similarities between the stock/housing bubbles is crucial to avoiding future crashes as well as participating in the next market trend opportunity.

The Great Crash of 2000

From 1997–2000 a tulip mania swept across the nation. Investors clamored to fill their portfolios with dot.com stocks. The feeding

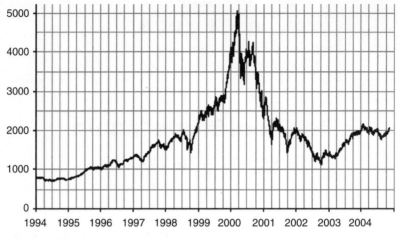

Figure 7.1   The NASDAQ Bubble-Crash

frenzy for anything and everything Internet-related was underway. Executives caught Internet fever and promptly added .com to company logos. Following the announcement of the new corporate Web page, share prices more often than not skyrocketed.

Nonetheless, my uncle, a former president of SouthTrust Bank, is fond of saying, "Trees don't grow to the sky." Well, perhaps not, but by the year 2000 the NASDAQ stock index certainly dwarfed even the most ancient giant sequoia in Northern California. In fact, the technology-laden index climbed to 5,000, representing a price increase of severalfold, as viewed in Figure 7.1.

Yet by 2002, three years of brutal selling on the NASDAQ exchange ended with an 80 percent crash. In many respects, the Internet stock bubble was eerily similar in depth to the Great Crash of 1929. But this time the Working Group on Financial Markets, that is, the Plunge Protection Team, came to the market's rescue. Plus, the Fed slashed rates to the lowest level in years. In response, bargain hunters snapped up discounted shares, which resulted in the remarkable 2003–2007 rebound.

Meanwhile, stocks weren't the only asset class to benefit from the Fed liquidity party. The decision to cut rates to the lowest level in 40 years proved to be financial nitroglycerin for the housing market. The rally was further aided and abetted by lax lending standards, which culminated with the blow-off phase of the greatest bubble in human history. In fact, estimates indicate that the housing bubble was nearly six times larger in scope than the Internet bubble.

In the wake of the dot.com bust, the Fed slashed its benchmark lending rate to 1 percent in order to hold the economic house of cards together. With such low rates, who could resist a mortgage? After all, in 2002 the housing bubble was still inflating at a rapid clip. With the support of low rates, lax lending standards, and endless demand for MBSs and CDOs, lenders were desperate to extend ARMs to anyone gullible enough to sign on the dotted line.

Do Home Prices Always Go Up?

For 75 consecutive years the median national home price increased in value. Not since the Great Depression had the American housing sector endured a single losing year. (See Figure 7.2.) As far back in history as the original Amsterdam stock exchange of 1602, nothing has ever approached the American housing bubble. In fact, I challenge the reader to identify a market with an unbroken annual

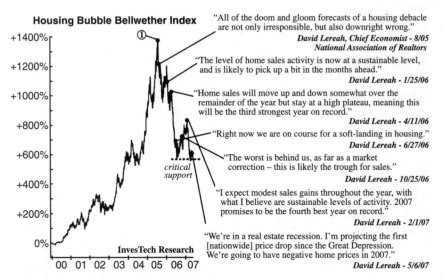

Figure 7.2   75-Year Housing Bubble

Source: Robert J. Shiller, Irrational Exuberance, 2nd ed., 2006. With permission from www .doctorhousingbubble.com.

winning streak spanning three-quarters of a century. Not even the amazing American bull stock market of the past 100 years can compare.

Moreover, by the early 2000s, the housing bubble reached a new threshold and began to take on a life of its own. In less than a decade, house prices doubled across the nation. Las Vegas, California, and Florida experienced unprecedented price advances of 200–300 percent and higher. The market was even immune to recessions. Economic downturns proffered bargain prices, which only emboldened home hunters all the more.

Yet to the economic cognoscenti, such as Yale economist Robert Shiller, creator of the graph in Figure 7.2, it was abundantly clear that the situation was unsustainable. Housing was ripe for a correction.

In 1999 the hit TV movie, *Pirates of Silicon Valley,* based on the book *Fire in the Valley: The Making of the Personal Computer,* by Paul Freiberger and Michael Swaine, told the remarkable tale of Bill Gates, Paul Allen, Steve Ballmer, Steve Jobs, and Steve Wozniak's race to dominate the computer industry. Gates' character, played by Anthony Michael Hall, made the memorable statement, "Success is a menace. . . . It fools smart people into thinking they can't lose." The well-crafted statement perfectly encapsulates the faulty mind-set that led to the housing disaster. Seventy-five years of success had convinced tens of millions of people that housing was a sure bet. The phrases "Home prices only go up" and "If you don't buy now, you won't be able to afford a house later" became national mantras. Sadly, such frivolous slogans will continue to haunt millions of mortgage holders for generations to come.

Lender Implosion

The first cracks in the housing market foundation emerged in late 2006. In only 12 months, more than one hundred major lenders shut their doors. By 2007 the number of defunct mortgage lenders soared to 250. At the peak of the crisis, on average one lender per day closed its doors while thousands of small local firms vanished overnight. Even the mainline media began to proclaim that something was rotten in the state of housing. News outlets were beginning to accept the housing crash thesis.

The vastly reduced pool of mortgage lenders presented significant challenges in securing a mortgage. Borrowers found it increasingly difficult to exchange their toxic adjustable rate mortgages (ARMs) for more prudent fixed-rate loans, even with the lowest lending rates in recent memory.

Meantime, by 2008 the traditionally favorable spring season brought little relief to the ailing housing industry. A closely watched gauge of domestic prices, the S&P/Case-Shiller Home-Price Index, posted its biggest drop on record. The Case-Shiller index of the top 20 U.S. metropolitan areas had crossed the event horizon. Escaping the massive subprime singularity was impossible. House prices plunged 12.7 percent from the year earlier. More notably, the metric declined every month since January 2007. While tame compared to today's headlines, at the time the news was shocking.

Moreover, Yale University professor and chief economist at MacroMarkets LLC Robert Shiller was one of the few analysts to accurately predict the dot.com crash as well as the housing bust. Shiller's 10-city composite index fell 13.6 percent by February 2008—the worst showing in its 21-year history. In fact, 19 out of 20 of the component cities experienced declines with only the resilient Charlotte, NC registering a meager 1.5 percent increase.

Therefore it's small wonder that the often controversial and usually correct Congressman Ron Paul blamed much of the housing mess on unscrupulous lending practices and artificially low Fed lending rates. Before a congressional panel Dr. Paul said:

> . . . many in Washington fail to realize it was government intervention that brought on the current economic malaise in the first place. Artificially low Fed interest rates created the loose, easy credit that ignited a voracious appetite in the banks for borrowers. People made these lending and buying decisions based on market conditions that were wildly manipulated by government. But part of sound financial management should be recognizing untenable or falsified economic conditions and adjusting risk accordingly. Many banks failed to do that and are now looking to taxpayers to pick up the pieces. This is wrong-headed and unfair, but Congress is attempting to do it anyway.

Dr. Paul further outlined the major flaws with the housing bills:

> . . . they attempt to hide the very problem that the Fed
> created with more government shenanigans that the only
> solution is for our elected leaders to let go of the reins and let
> the market adjust naturally. Although it will be very painful
> at first, it will dissipate the excesses as well as discourage the
> massive moral hazard that's developing with the seemingly
> never ending bailout packages.

Dr. Paul clearly identified the problems with government-sponsored housing bailouts. Providing aid to careless mortgage holders actually punishes those without mortgages including renters and the frugal.

Fed Wheel of Misfortune

After holding rates steady at 5.25 percent for over one year, Fed governors tore a page out of their regulation playbook. Officials slashed the benchmark lending rate in hopes of reinflating the housing bubble. Yet despite a surprise 75 basis points cut, the unprecedented action wasn't enough to revive the ailing housing sector. Additional cuts plunged rates down to 3 percent. Still, the economic albatross continued its death spiral. After only a few months, the blink of an eye in economic terms, rates fell to 2 percent and then down to 1 percent. The Fed's desperate bid to support the teetering economy was too little, too late. The Fed was no longer pushing on a string; it was leaning on a wet noodle.

What officials had failed to realize was that the burst housing bubble could not be reinflated. The Fed rate blitz merely postponed the day of reckoning. The best that could be expected was a temporary halt to the housing deluge. Fed Chairman Ben Bernanke and former Treasury Secretary Hank Paulson must have spent many long, sleepless nights mulling over the dilemma. The housing downturn was only in its early stages, yet it was clearly destined to surpass all but the most dire forecast. The crash threatened the very underpinnings of the entire global economy.

In the next few chapters, we'll delve more deeply into the housing crash and its implications for aspiring homeowners as well as the nation as a whole.

KEY POINT

The 75-year housing bubble has burst. The recovery will require several years. Caveat emptor.

Q&A

Listener Comment: Veronica writes, "A heartfelt thank you—I've been listening to your radio program from the UK now for over a year and always find it informative and amusing with those silly but wonderful spot effects you use to cheer us with the weekly news!

"I'm a single mother who struggled out of debt for the first time in 2006. I inherited a modest property in 2006, sold it, and bought 20 percent gold and 80 percent silver with the funds, entirely because of your program. At the time I was told I was crazy to sell the property and buy precious metals, but look at me now!

"I'd like to thank you, along with my young son, so very much for your humor and your wonderful banter with Bob Chapman. You are both remarkable people and are truly unsung heroes to us listeners. After struggling out of debt, at last my son and I are able to raise our heads and look forward to a brighter future. Thank you. Veronica."

Answer: Hello, Veronica. Your success story is inspirational. Your shining example is likely to motivate others to take the appropriate actions to escape mortgage debt bondage. Congratulations and please keep us updated with regard to your progress.

Listener Question: Amit writes from the UK, "Although I am no expert in stock investing, I am learning bit by bit. I am a UK resident and currently work as an adviser and problem solver for a property development family. I have been tasked with forecasting the economy over the next two years. I am finding this nigh impossible, but have uncovered some startling truths. It seems that the best advice I can give the family is to sell all property and buy silver. Am I being too pessimistic or is that good advice? Please help!"

Answer: Hello, Amit. Considering the turbulent economic conditions and volatile financial markets, many folks share your concerns. A glance at a chart of the UK housing bubble reveals a frightening picture. The angle of ascent far eclipses even that of the U.S. real estate bubble. It's clear that the subsequent decline will be unpleasant. All sources now indicate that the UK housing market, especially London, is even more overpriced than even Southern California or Florida.

But there is a silver lining to this story. Just as fads tend to originate on the U.S. West Coast and migrate to the East Coast, awareness of the looming real estate crisis is only now emerging in the UK. While median home prices are off nearly 15 percent in the United States, across the pond prices are only now declining—down approximately 3 percent from the peak. So a window of opportunity remains open for UK mortgage holders to prepare for the impending housing crash.

With regard to your silver purchase comments, I continue to view silver bullion as a bargain. As for emigrating to another part of the world, if folks follow the steps outlined on GSR each week, hopefully such drastic measures won't be necessary. Thank you for the great questions, Amit.

House of Cards

THE HOUSING BUST

"Almost any man worthy of his salt would fight to defend his home,
but no one ever heard of a man going to war for his boarding house."

—Mark Twain

As 2006 came to a close, so did the decade's long real estate boom. In just a few months, years of speculative housing froth was washed away. By April 2010, millions of homes were in some stage of foreclosure. Due in part to the widespread use of toxic mortgages 12 million stunned homeowners owe more than their property is worth. Before the storm fully passes, the number is expected to surpass 25 million, representing half of all mortgages outstanding. Millions will walk away from overpriced properties in pursuit of more affordable housing.

This chapter uncovers how the shift away from traditional lending practices and the widespread dissemination of exotic mortgages drove real estate prices beyond all reasonable valuations. The section also examines the faulty belief system that ultimately convinced millions of borrowers/lenders that house prices "always go up."

Worst Housing Crash in History

In late 2006 the real estate bubble reached its zenith. The sublime concerto of escalating prices came to a deafening halt. By early 2007, with the median home price off only 2–3 percent, I warned GSR listeners of an impending housing bust. For over six months I referred to the inevitable real estate crash as the most significant event of the decade. A handful of listeners heeded my warning, sold their overpriced real estate, and purchased gold.

Conversely, the mainstream talking heads were nearly unanimous in the opinion that the 2–3 percent pullback in residential house prices presented an excellent buying opportunity. After all, for 75 years every housing slump had provided bargains for aspiring home-debtors. The American dream of owning a home seemed to be a sure-fire wealth-building stratagem. Since prices always recovered and then ascended to new heights, why not accept a risky ARM with little or no down payment?

However, by 2008 the cliché "it's different this time" was disturbingly appropriate. The "buying opportunity" morphed into a 20 percent crash. In just over one year, the median home price fell through the ceiling. Suddenly, millions of home debtors learned why, in high-stakes financial poker, going "all in" has dangerous implications. Moody's chief economist, Mark Zandi, commented on the dire situation, "We could argue this is the worst housing downturn ever. . . . Negative equity and unemployment are the driving factors. Things are getting worse, not better." Things were indeed getting worse, much worse. At the time Zandi made the comments, prices were only halfway to their ultimate destination.

By the time that the mainstream media finally recognized the true nature of the housing dilemma, the process was reaching critical mass. Millions of borrowers continued to fall into the home-debtor-ship trap. The *Washington Post* announced that conditions could rival the 1929 housing crash. Experts eventually drew the same conclusion that I had two years earlier. A 25–50 percent drop in the typical median home value was inevitable.

Easy Money

For as long as buyers and sellers have used exchanges to trade financial instruments, every subsequent market bubble was the direct result of abundant/accessible credit. The global real estate bubble is a textbook example of such excessive leverage.

Under the more strict lending practices of decades past, most borrowers avoided precarious debt levels. Traditional 20 percent down payments and fixed-rate loans ensured reasonable monthly payments. But the 1996–2006 real estate boom years created insatiable demand for mortgages/MBSs. In response, regulators reformed formerly stringent lending standards. As a result, millions have lost their homes to default and even more will face foreclosure in 2010–2013.

Nonetheless, the sea of abundant credit that developed during the bubble era created a self-fulfilling cyclone of higher prices. Home prices ballooned to unsustainable levels in the 10-year-long real estate mania phase. The typical house price skyrocketed several times above average income. Ergo, millions required the leverage of jumbo loans, $417,000 or more, to purchase a modest house.

In his Doric speech at Syracuse, Archimedes told the Greek cognoscenti, "Give me a place to stand and with a lever I will move the whole world." While Archimedes may have had the intellectual wherewithal to singlehandedly shift the earth into a new orbit, the size and scope of the derivatives leverage threatening the global economic foundations would have likely confounded even his prodigious mind.

Moreover, as credit flowed like cheap champagne at a New Year's Eve bash, a glib attitude permeated the entire real estate sector. Industry shills proclaimed that a new era in housing had arrived. Why should anyone who really wants a new home go without one? After all, it is different this time. Anyone capable of signing his or her name was offered a home loan. Traditional mortgage determination factors, such as three times gross annual household income, were relaxed. Borrowers were extended loans of up to nine times their annual gross income, 300 percent beyond the established safety guidelines.

The real estate binge resulted in decades of price advances and the widespread misuse of toxic mortgages. A hangover was inevitable. Thanks to crashing prices, record unemployment, and related social dislocations, analysts now expect the median residential house to decline an additional 10–15 percent, resulting in a 50 percent fire sale from the 2006 peak. The seismic shock waves will traverse the national borders from sea to shining sea, in turn sending tsunamis across both the Pacific and Atlantic oceans.

Subprime, Alt-A, Ninja, and Options Only Villains

The housing implosion began with trouble in subprime mortgages. The term itself, sub-prime or less than a prime mortgage, was the first warning sign. Subprime loans required lower credit scores, smaller or nonexistent down payments, and dodgy income track records. Before 2007 the term "subprime" rarely entered everyday conversation. Indeed, "subprime" was more likely to conjure images of low-quality steak at a greasy spoon restaurant. But the housing smash brought the shady mortgage to the forefront. Suddenly the second-class loan, which proffered homes to people less likely to return the borrowed funds, was headline news and the subject of endless blogosphere discussions. In Figure 8.1, one can see the massive number of subprime ARM resets, which ran from 2006 until the end of 2008. The two-year, $1 trillion subprime fiasco is represented by the first large group at the far left.

Furthermore, despite insistence to the contrary, real estate industry insiders roped the unsuspecting herd into impossibly high debt traps known as liar's loans, aka Alt-A. Liar's loans earned the ominous title due to the shady practice of allowing borrowers to exaggerate income levels in order to secure financing.

Suddenly the 20-year-old pizza delivery man could call a new McMansion home. The builder sold a house, the realtor made a

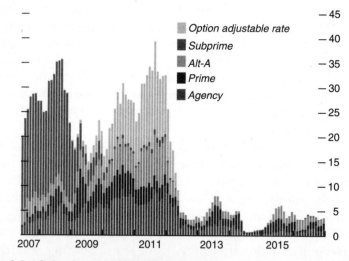

Figure 8.1   Subprime/ARM Reset Disaster

commission, the bank created a new loan and the investment banker packaged and sold the dodgy mortgage in a basket of thousands of top-notch debt instruments on Wall Street. The municipality that purchased the MBSs earned a high interest rate. The economy created new jobs and the president's approval rating went up. Everyone benefited, for the time being.

Those lucky enough to escape the Alt-A ambush succumbed to ninja loans (no documentation, no down payment). While Alt-A's earned the liar's loan designation, ninjas took the deception to a new level. Ninjas lured millions of aspiring homeowners with practically no qualifications whatsoever into expensive loans far beyond their ability to repay. Once the ninja mortgages reset, monthly payments quickly increased by 50–100 percent or more. Reasonable $750 monthly mortgage payments transformed into $1,500 nooses around the necks of many borrowers.

However, of the toxic debt arrangements, by far the most destructive type is the options-only ARM, also known as the pick-a-payment loan. Most borrowers picked the option that led to negative amortization, that is, the principal actually climbs after each monthly payment. Options ARM resets are expected to approach $1 trillion, comparable in size to the subprime disaster. Monthly payments will surge by 60–80–100+ percent, sending millions into foreclosure. The threat will not pass until 2011–2013, as seen in Figure 8.2.

After reporting of the imminent options ARM collapse since 2007 on Goldseek Radio, *The Economist* magazine finally picked up the story in 2008. An article outlined how soaring delinquencies in options-only recasts would pour a fresh supply of foreclosures atop the existing mountain of unsold homes. The options ARM is investigated in far greater detail in the next few chapters.

Flip-Floppers

Easy credit/lax lending standards encouraged a seemingly boundless number of new mortgage lenders to open their doors. With a lender on every corner, conditions were ripe for the notorious "Flipper" investor. Flippers purchased properties with the sole intention of making a quick sale/profit. Flippers were singularly interested in capital gains and had no intentions to use a foreclosed property as a personal residence. The investor quickly "flipped"

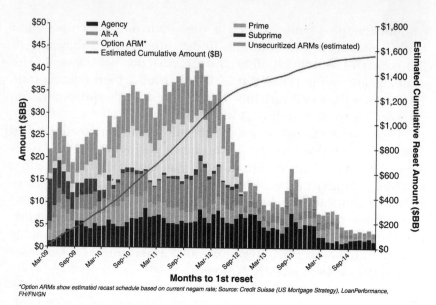

Figure 8.2   Option ARM Resets

Source: Credit Suisse.

(sold) the property and moved on to the next foreclosure opportunity.

When the housing bubble reached the 2006 apex, many flippers had accumulated large portfolios of houses. But as real estate values plummeted throughout 2007–2008, the get rich quick scheme transformed flippers into a new breed of speculator I refer to as floppers. Panicky floppers were forced to sell houses at whatever price the market offered.

Turning Japanese

The great Japanese housing boom of the 1980s was also fueled by easy credit as well as government disincentives to sell. Sellers were penalized so harshly, it made little sense to do anything other than accumulate and hold real estate. A "buy only" mentality, similar to that which permeated the American culture for decades, emerged in Japan. Likewise, a self-fulfilling prophecy of higher prices was inevitable, as was the bubble/crash that followed. According to one source, at the time of the bubble peak the Imperial Palace in Tokyo surpassed the value of the entire state of California.

Yet all such Ponzi schemes eventually fail. The entire fiasco disintegrated, ending with an epic real estate sell-off. Many boom areas eventually recorded 80 percent losses in real estate value. Japan continues to struggle with the economic aftershocks of the 20-year housing crash even today.

Much can be gleaned from the epic Japanese struggle with deflating real estate prices. Although the U.S. mortgage holder has fewer disincentives to sell, both nations made extensive use of leverage. U.S. banks funneled an enormous 10 percent of American savings into subprime CDOs. Godzilla-sized MBS and CDO monstrosities levered the national system to the breaking point. One hundred dollars invested in a CDO provided $10,000 dollars in subprime loans, truly remarkable leverage indeed.

However, CDOs were packaged under the assumption that no more than 1–2 percent of the underlying subprime loans would enter default. But far more than 1–2 percent of subprime loans eventually imploded. The actual rate approached 20 percent. Merely a 5 percent loss on subprime loans was sufficient to sink the entire CDO security, in turn affecting an untold number of individuals and firms. Retirees should be particularly concerned since pension funds purchased nearly 20 percent of the dangerous CDO tranches.

California Dreaming

In 2009 the Golden State registered a magnitude 9.0 mega-quake on the foreclosure Richter scale. Every business day, 1,300 new foreclosures were added to the growing rubble pile, a total of $100 billion over the course of two years. Statewide, more than 100,000 default notices were sent out by authorities, an increase of 150 percent. According to the California Association of Realtors, the median home price peaked at $597,640 in April 2007. Yet by 2009, the typical house price dropped to $350,760, an astounding loss for the typical California mortgage holder of 41.3 percent or $246,880.

Thanks in particular to the prevalence of highly exotic mortgages, few states embraced mortgage debt like California. Since the state is home to approximately half of all of the toxic option ARMs, conditions will likely deteriorate from already dire levels. Many borrowers are married to impossibly expensive mortgages of five to seven times the typical family annual income far above the traditional two to three times figure. Many Californians remain highly vulnerable to precipitous real estate price declines. According to ForeclosureRadar.com, the state default rate tripled in only one year. Most California homes entering the foreclosure stage were originally purchased between July 2005 and August 2006. With more than 1,000 houses added to foreclosure auctions every day, the $4 billion California relief plan to encourage local foreclosed home purchases was insufficient to compensate for the mountain of defaults and impending aftershocks.

Meantime the Santa Ana winds continued to spread the foreclosure flames across the majestic California landscape. Home sales plunged to the lowest figure in 15 years. The region recorded the worst summer sales number since 1993. According to DataQuick, San Diego foreclosures climbed 550 percent. The report indicated the largest number of defaults on record. The city by the bay witnessed a 1,600 percent increase in foreclosures. Considering that many analysts view California as a national early warning indicator, the housing fallout was destined to spread throughout the nation.

Trail of Foreclosure Tears

In a modern Trail of Tears–like reenactment, millions of American families are facing foreclosure. To fully illustrate the harsh reality, in some states the repossession process begins after merely 30 days. In Alabama, for instance, only one month after receiving a delinquency notice a home can be lost to foreclosure. Statutes in New Hampshire, Mississippi, and several other states require approximately 60 days, while in California residents have 120 days before default takes effect.

However, in 2009 many Chicago residents facing foreclosure no longer feared finding their belongings strewn along the street curb. A local sheriff instructed his deputies to halt the eviction of tenants in foreclosure. Sheriff Dart cited the increase in the unreasonable practice of evicting tenants without any notice whatsoever.

Similarly, millions around the country have chosen to "squat," stop making mortgage and rental payments. Although the Robin Hood–like practice of, "stealing from the rich to give to the poor" makes appealing movie plots, the method reaps havoc in capitalist societies. If local authorities fail to enforce mortgage obligations, a tidal wave of delinquencies could overwhelm the system.

Her Name Is REO

With nearly 20 million vacant homes in the United States, bank repossessions are now commonplace. Repossessed foreclosures, also known as REOs, are flooding the rosters of many banks. Every home returned to a lender creates enormous financial strain on the institutions. On average $50,000 is required to refurbish and sell a foreclosed property. In addition to repairs, every day that a repossessed property remains on the bank balance sheet represents a loss in terms of carrying/opportunity costs. The dilemma is only magnified by the deflated market conditions.

Additionally, the difference between the time the default notice arrives and when the occupant actually vacates the premises is of particular concern. Over 6–12 months is usually required before a defaulted home returns to a lender. Ergo, foreclosure numbers often underestimate the problem. Plus the blogosphere is filled with numerous tales of squatters who stopped making mortgage payments years ago, but remained in the home nonetheless. Clearly the system will continue to be taxed by a flood of millions of new foreclosures in the coming years.

Chapter Foreclosure

Charles Mackay crystallized the desperate plight of the typical mortgage holder in his magnum opus, *Extraordinary Popular Delusions and the Madness of Crowds*, "Men go mad in crowds and return to their senses, slowly and one by one." Similarly, the sudden and violent transition from housing boom to bust came as a surprise to millions of Americans. While hundreds of mortgage lenders have closed their doors, borrowers are only now returning to their senses.

As difficult as the housing crisis has proven to be thus far, the end game promises to be far more frustrating. The stark reality facing the nation is that the typical house price will not reach a final nadir until 2012–2013. After that, prices will likely remain flat for the rest of the decade. The first two chapters of the real estate section prepared the reader with a brief overview of the dilemma. The remaining chapters cover the topic in far greater detail. The discussion concludes with easy-to-use home purchase tips, including how to calculate the fair price for any house.

KEY POINT

Due to the mountain of toxic Alt-A and option ARM mortgages expected to reset in 2011–2012, the number of underwater homeowners is expected to double to 25 million. The resulting flood of inventory will further glut the already crowded market and suppress prices for years to come.

Q&A

Listener Question: John says, "Chris, I have closely observed the real estate markets of various cities I travel to, like Orlando, Los Angeles, San Diego, and Washington, D.C. These cities, referred to as the 'hot cities,' also enjoyed incredible price increases during the real estate boom, in stark contrast to the cities of the southeast, such as Raleigh and Charlotte, North Carolina, where few people complain of the 'real estate crash.'

"Real estate is not dropping like a rock here in North Carolina; housing prices are holding up well. Most residents claim that real estate in North Carolina will remain strong. Do you think that the real estate crash will miss these southern cities or is the North Carolina crisis simply delayed?"

Answer: Hello, John. You probably are aware that my home is in North Carolina. I agree with you that real estate prices have held up far better in this state than in many others.

However, this is a tale of two housing markets. Until recently, the North Carolina banking sector withstood the housing crisis, but as listeners know all too well, the sector eventually succumbed to the credit crisis. Therefore, as industry-related layoffs increase, I expect the subsequent rise in home foreclosures to glut the market and home prices to fall in line with the national average. Thanks for the question, John.

CHAPTER 9

Mortgage Contagion

THE HOUSING CRISIS SPREADS

*"What we call real estate—the solid ground to build a house on—
is the broad foundation on which nearly all the guilt of this world
rests."*

—Nathaniel Hawthorne

The stability of the real estate bubble created an atmosphere of exuberance within the lending industry. New and exciting mortgage instruments promised riches beyond the dreams of avarice to banks/lenders willing to accept no down payments from risky borrowers. But now that the residential housing market is in decline, owners without any "skin in the game" have little reason to remain shackled to toxic mortgages. Plus with millions already in mortgage default amid the worst housing crash since the Great Depression, the stigma associated with foreclosure is now far less intense. Thus, more than five million underwater mortgage holders are expected to walk away by 2012. The resulting inventory flood will be further exacerbated by exotic ARMs. The net effect will further push domestic house prices lower by another 10–15 percent by the end of 2012. Afterwards, prices will remain stagnant for years to come, punctuated with numerous false rallies along the way.

Chapter 9 makes a thorough examination of the modern debt/ leverage instruments that fomented the housing bubble. In the next few sections you'll follow the money footprints like a financial investigator to determine just who benefited/lost most from the real estate mania. Lastly, you'll see how usurious lending rates and the foreclosures that followed have decimated the American Dream. For many people, the new American Dream is renting a home.

Not So Prime Time Mortgages

As mentioned in earlier chapters, the year 2000 dot.com bomb significantly shook investor confidence in equities. Millions of scorned investors searched for a safe haven to park remaining funds. As formerly high-flying stocks continued to fall from the sky, many investors turned to the residential housing sector. A vast sea of wealth was diverted away from the stock market and funneled directly into the housing sector.

In response to the stock market rout, Alan "Bubbles" Greenspan dropped interest rates to 1 percent, the lowest level in half a century. By lowering rates so abruptly, the Federal Reserve actually aided and abetted the housing bubble. Inexpensive borrowing and lax lending standards was the perfect recipe for a five-year bull run in real estate. The only missing ingredient was ubiquitous access to easy credit. Nature abhors a vacuum; the void was quickly filled by exotic debt instruments.

ARM Candy

In the early 2000s it seemed as though everyone was profiting from the real estate bonanza. Bookstores and library shelves were filled to capacity with get rich with housing guides. The king of real estate Donald Trump's books disappeared from inventory as quickly as they arrived. But with home prices climbing so fast, 50–100 percent annually in the hottest regions, the American Dream was outside the reach of many Americans. How could the typical family keep up with the Joneses?

For legions of borrowers, new exotic adjustable-rate mortgages provided the answer. With a few alterations, dull home loans magically transformed into flashy new ARMs. The complicated instruments allowed even members of society with the least impressive incomes to own a slice of Americana. Suddenly posh houses formerly reserved for doctors, lawyers, and the upper crust were affordable to practically everyone.

Although consumer advocacy groups argued that lenders failed to warn applicants of the considerable risks associated with adjustable-rate loans, it's highly unlikely that a banker's diatribe would have been of much avail. The housing gold rush was firmly underway and the consumer wasted little time staking a claim. The new exotic ARMs were simply irresistible.

We Can Do This

In addition to new debt instruments, millions were lured into McMansion debt traps by home builder incentives. Fancy new kitchens with granite countertops, cash-back incentives, free plasma screen TVs and even new cars were the lures that concealed the debt hook. But after two years many ARMs reset with a vengeance, leaving home buyer minnows dangling on the fishing line. Sadly, refinancing into a fixed-rate loan was no longer an option to pull desperate borrowers free from mortgage tackle. Thanks to the return of stringent lending practices and offices filled to overcapacity with stacks of paperwork, it became practically impossible to renegotiate mortgages. Borrowers were caught on the cold steel hook of debt.

In retrospect the consumer-driven Goldilocks economy of 2002–2007 was the product of easy credit. No down payment, no document loans, endless credit card applications, rent-to-own, easy car loans, and check cashing services were important components of the "economic miracle."

But the miracle transformed into a nightmare as the tidal wave of subprime defaults washed across the nation from 2007 to 2010. Hundreds of major lenders and thousands of smaller firms entered bankruptcy. The surviving mortgage providers were understandably nervous—it was only a matter of time before the subprime infection spread to the prime mortgage market.

By 2009, the toxic subprime debt sludge did in fact ooze into the prime loan arena. Crashing home prices and unemployment were the culprits threatening the higher quality mortgages. Despite excellent credit scores, prime mortgages entered default at a record pace.

Typhoon Option Only

During the housing market frenzy, millions were lured into dangerous mortgages by the universal mantra, "Home prices always go up." But the housing crash revealed that home prices don't always rise, sometimes they collapse 20 percent in a single year. Indeed, by October 2008, half a trillion dollars' worth of ARMs had reset. Although the tidal forces of the category 5 housing typhoon did eventually subside somewhat in 2009, it proved to be merely the eye of the storm. In fact, most ARM holders are barely making minimum monthly payments. Unfortunately, the second phase of the housing tempest is approaching, spurred forward by the option ARM.

Option ARMs were often sold as second mortgages. Second mortgage liens came into vogue in 2005 and were offered by most major lenders. Since the loans required little to no income or documentation, the risky debt opened Pandora's box to aspiring home debtors who never should have been extended such credit. Large financial institutions such as CITI, Wells Fargo, WAMU, Chase, National City, and Countrywide seized the opportunity to corral a fresh herd of unsuspecting borrowers.

ARMed and Dangerous

During World War II aerial bombardments, London residents took refuge in subterranean shelters and subways. After the air raid passed, unexploded ordinance and raging infernos presented equally dangerous threats. In similar fashion, while the subprime barrage has come and gone, an equally imposing force is threatening the populace—the option ARM.

Unfortunately, not even fortified subterranean bunkers offer adequate protection against the option ARM ordinance. The cunning enemy deployed option ARMs with low teaser rates in order to draw timid buyers into expensive McMansions. The toxic prime rate loan came with several alluring alternatives:

1. Pay principal and interest.
2. Pay interest only.
3. Pay the minimum amount.

In order to purchase luxuriant new houses far beyond their means, many chose the most risky option 3, to: pay the minimum amount. While the terms constrained monthly payments for a few years, the principal amount actually increased, not decreased as borrowers made monthly mortgage payments, that is, became negatively amortized. A shocking 80 percent of all options ARMs are negatively amortized to some degree.

Furthermore, once a negatively amortized loan climbs above the 110–125 percent principal threshold, monthly payments recast, to much higher levels. The ramifications of an $800 monthly payment resetting to $1,600 are profoundly negative. Plus, as easy mortgage payments evaporated, the toxic mortgages deteriorated the borrower's financial condition to such an extent that refinancing into a fixed-rate loan became virtually impossible. The only wise choice for most was to send the house keys back to the lender.

Currently, one in four option ARM borrowers is delinquent on their monthly payment schedule. Not only are monthly payments increasing but the total amount owed is as well, a.k.a., negative amortization. After warning GSR listeners since 2007 regarding the option ARMs threat, experts are finally acknowledging the reality of the dilemma. They were only two years late.

Furthermore, Fitch analysts expected roughly $67 billion in mortgages to recast into higher monthly payments by the end of 2010. Such staggering figures ensure that the downtrend in housing will persist well into 2011–2012 (see Figure 9.1).

Although most lenders are returning to their senses and implementing a moratorium on exotic loans, the cure is only further threatening the housing patient. Tighter lending benchmarks restrict the funds available for purchases, in turn drying up the pool of available buyers. While returning to traditional lending practices is a positive step forward toward healing what ails the sector, in the near term the consequence will be a glut of inventory and lower prices.

With millions of Americans facing default, the mainstream media attempts to put a positive spin on the calamity. Myopic experts perpetuate false hopes that the inventory of nearly 20 million unsold homes will be absorbed by bargain hunters. But with years of supply overhang in many troubled areas, the housing glut is certain to be a conundrum for years to come. As the toxic loans reset into higher monthly payments, most will choose an unlisted mortgage option—to walk away. Clearly, the new option ARM implosion will persist for at least two more years, perhaps rivaling even the

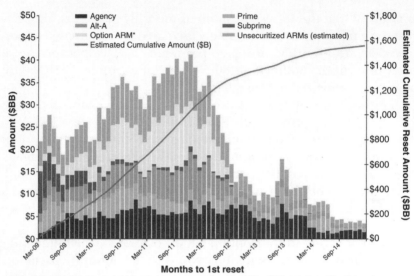

Option ARMs show estimated recast schedule based on current negam rate; Source: Credit Suisse (US Mortgage Strategy), LoanPerformance, FH/FN/GN

Figure 9.1 Option Arm Resets

Source: Credit Suisse.

subprime meltdown. The reprehensible mortgage will continue to send chills down the spines of borrowers for decades to come.

Carnivorous Loans

The 2/20 ARM is another little known but widely dispersed mortgage variant. The 2/20 begins with a two-year fixed rate followed by a 20-year ARM. The financial Venus fly trap lured unwary borrowers with the sweet aroma of fixed rates. Salespeople insisted that higher rates weren't a concern because borrowers could always refinance at a later date. With the typical family moving every three to four years, few gave much thought to signing an ARM. But after a few years of low payment bliss, the housing and credit crisis trap slammed shut, ending with the dark and putrid abyss of ever higher monthly payments for 20 years.

A further variation on the interest-only loan is the hybrid mortgage. Hybrid interest-only loans start life as fixed mortgages. But after the grace period of three, five, seven, or 10 years passes, the loans reset into ARMs. Because hybrids were classified as prime in

2003–2006, low FICO scores, marginal incomes, and minimal down payments were deemed acceptable. The 5/1 hybrids started to recast in 2008 and will continue to do so well into the new decade.

Doomsayer of Omaha

With the housing bust fully underway, the Oracle of Omaha, Warren Buffett, commented on the fiasco at a fund-raising lunch in San Francisco,

> You can't turn a financial toad into a prince by securitizing it. . . .
> Wall Street started believing its own PR on this—they started
> holding this stuff themselves, maybe because they couldn't sell it.
> It worked wonderfully until it didn't work at all. . . . Wall Street
> is reaping what they've sown. . . . It will sort itself out over time
> with a fair amount of pain. We have an economy that can take
> it. . . . It's very profitable selling toxic waste to customers, but it's
> still not a sound business practice.

Furthermore, Buffett, the world's richest investor, is fond of saying that if he can't understand a company business model, he won't purchase the stock. In similar fashion, Buffett admitted that he didn't understand the toxic debt instruments so he never purchased them. If only ignorance were always so profitable.

Buffett went on to say, "We're like a very rich family; we own a farm the size of Texas but want to consume more than the farm generates. . . . Every day, we sell off or mortgage a piece of the farm . . . over time, the rest of the world will own more of our farm." Clearly the Oracle believes that Americans are rapidly becoming indentured servants on their own sovereign land.

Buffett's concerns regarding debt were shared by American founding father Thomas Jefferson. Jefferson feared that debt would lead Americans into serfdom:

> If the American people ever allow private banks to control the
> issue of their currency, first by inflation, then by deflation,
> the banks and corporations will grow up around them and will
> deprive the people of all property until their children wake up
> homeless on the continent their fathers conquered. The

issuing power should be taken from the banks and restored to the people, to whom it properly belongs.

If Buffett and Jefferson are proven to be correct, future generations will be unfairly forced to pay dearly for the housing bubble debt and subsequent bailouts.

Greatest Wealth Transfer (Swindle) in History

Many reporters, politicians, and economists continue to scratch their collective heads when queried as to why trillions of housing bubble dollars evaporated and where it all went. Yet understanding the greatest wealth transfer in history does not require a degree in finance. All that is needed is to use the investigator's maxim, "Follow the money." Ergo, the key to solving the economic quandary is determining who benefited the most financially and who lost most heavily:

Who Lost?

1. Borrowers with down payments now in foreclosure
2. Banks and lenders of foreclosed homes
3. Bank and lender shareholders/bondholders
4. The American taxpayer responsible for at least $10 trillion in bailouts and related promises

Who Benefited?

1. Investment bankers peddling MBS derivatives products
2. Builders
3. Realtors
4. Short sellers

Of the four primary housing bubble suspects, institutions promoting MBS and related derivatives deserve a thorough cross examination. History will not be kind to anyone in the MBS field. Winston Churchill's comment, "Never have so many owed so much to so few," regarding how the Royal Air Force saved London during the Battle of Britain, reveals the significant effect that a small group can have on an entire nation. Conversely, never have so few benefited so much (MBS industry) from the ruin of so many (millions facing foreclosure and the unemployed).

Renters' Paradise

As the housing boom reached its penultimate peak, second and third homes were often purchased under the guise of investment properties and posh vacation palaces. In addition, flippers bought houses for quick resale via the Internet, often without as much as inspecting the premises. But with the median home price off the peak by more than 30 percent across the nation, condominiums and single-family homes are entering the rental market at a record pace. Plus sky-high mortgage costs have convinced many to divest over-priced homes and instead choose the rental option.

Every economics student knows that too much of a good or ser-vice leads to a shift in demand. Likewise, the glut of unsold homes has effectively pushed supply far beyond the equilibrium point, cre-ating a surplus of houses available to buyers and renters alike. Un-der typical conditions, crashing house prices would create a shortage of rental opportunities as crowds of foreclosure victims flooded the rental market. But times are far from typical, thanks in no small part to massive overbuilding. Instead, millions are opting to move in with family and friends—living in basement apartments to reduce monthly expenses.

In general, renting is preferred to owning until the average mortgage payment approaches the typical rental cost. Another use-ful metric is to forgo a purchase until home prices drop to 100 times monthly rental fees. For example, assuming a typical home rent pay-ment of $1,000 per month, the rule of thumb suggests that renting is preferred until a desirable property in the $100,000 price range is identified (this method and several others is covered in detail in the capstone real estate chapter):

$$(\$1,000 \text{ avg.} \times 100 = \$100,000)$$

Yet the typical American house costs over $160,000. The broad discrepancy between home prices and rental costs is a wake-up call for mortgage holders. Difficult times loom ahead, especially when one considers the following:

- Never has a housing market bottomed with the average rent/ average home price ratio so far out of balance.
- Low rates have failed to resuscitate the housing patient.

While stubborn home debtors argue that monthly rent payments make poor financial sense, renters rejoice over lower home prices and vastly reduced costs. Indeed, using a mortgage to build equity in an environment of rapidly deflating prices is tantamount to financial suicide. The true extent of home debtor risk is staggering. Now that the impossible has occurred, that is, home prices are crashing; the wise are simply shunning home ownership in favor of renting, at least until prices fall back in line with historic averages.

Furthermore, the stigma associated with renting a home is disappearing as quickly as lofty home prices. Millions are coming to the obvious conclusion that renting is often far less expensive than a mortgage and related costs. Indeed, property ownership includes the added expenses of a monthly mortgage check, HOA fees, interest payments, property taxes, repairs, and home maintenance fees. Alternatively, renting involves a single monthly check and far fewer headaches.

Rewarding Failure—Punishing Success

With government housing bailout dollars flowing like treats from a battered piñata, millions of frugal and hard-working renters wonder why they are being punished. Indeed, why should the taxpayer fund socialistic banking and housing sector bailouts? Ideally, the system would right itself independently. In so doing, home prices would decline to the natural equilibrium point, reducing the cost of home ownership and encouraging new purchases.

Correspondingly, a $300 billion foreclosure-rescue bill designed to help refinance loans that should never have been issued in the first place became law. Officials promised that the legislation would altogether eliminate the housing problem.

However, before too long the bottomless MBS pit required more bailout funds. The taxpayer was irate. In fact, when the $700 billion Economic Stabilization Plan was proposed, public outrage was intense. According to many members of Congress, their constituents strongly opposed the bailout plan by 20 to 1. Furious voters quickly filled their representatives' e-mail and voicemail boxes with disturbing messages.

Initially, the House of Representatives rejected the plan. Yet despite massive public disapproval, Congress ultimately complied with

Figure 9.2 Stock Market Meltdown
Source: Stockcharts.com.

the moneyed lobbyists' wishes. The Senate and House capitulated and passed the $700 billion Economic Stabilization Plan.

Nonetheless, Wall Street threw a temper tantrum—the NASDAQ crashed nearly 10 percent. But it was the Dow Jones Industrials that stole the spotlight. Blue-chip stocks turned blood red virtually overnight. The index hemorrhaged 777 points in a single session, the worst point decline in its history, at the time. Within two days the benchmark Dow plunged an earth-shattering 1,000+ points. (See Figure 9.2.) The Street understood all too well what Congress had missed. The real estate crash was only in its beginning phase, and battling the crisis with more debt was a losing proposition.

There's No Place Like Home

Although millions of households have found the transition from living beyond their means to living within quite difficult, many more are turning away from debt trap mortgages in favor of the freedom offered by more frugal living arrangements. Seniors will recall the time when extended families lived together for much if not all of their adult lives. Likewise, moving in with parents and friends is once again becoming a popular alternative.

Moreover, experts project that vacant houses and rental inventory will rise above the current 20 million unit figure. Millions of mortgage holders are expected to walk away from underwater mortgages, sending just as many units back onto the market. Plus, second homes will be sold to raise cash and reduce debt.

The New Housing Boom—Tent Cities

In 2008 Goldseek.com Radio was one of the first media outlets to break the tent city story. With more than 300 full-time residents the Ontario, California, tent city was destined to reach overflow capacity. The scenes from ground zero were surreal, resembling video footage from a banana republic refugee camp. The streets surrounding the tent city were lined with makeshift RVs and earth embankments to protect camp dwellers from deranged motorists.

Only weeks earlier, many of the tent city inhabitants were enjoying a typical middle-class lifestyle with everyday conveniences such as running water, electricity, refrigerator, toilet, shower, and privacy. In the blink of an eye, the 300+ inhabitants were reduced to a pitiful existence consisting of shared port-a-potties and two garden hoses for bathing.

With such inadequate/deplorable facilities, GSR leaped into action. Years of volunteer experience with Meals-on-Wheels allows one to better empathize with the plight of the tent city dwellers. Clearly, a fine group of decent people had fallen on hard times—caught off guard by the housing crisis. Thanks to the kind and generous donations of GSR listeners, especially Steven in Florida, GSR was able to toss a humble lifejacket to those living in the Ontario, California, tent city.

While it's pleasing to know that GSR listeners were ready and willing to part with hard-earned profits to help people in distress whom they did not know, the number of tent villages has ballooned since early 2008. For readers interested in contributing, a small donation can make a big difference in the lives of real Americans in need.

Global Housing Contagion—Across The Subprime Pond

The housing crash first appeared on the West Coast before spreading eastward across the nation. Next the U.S. housing distress soon traversed the Atlantic Ocean. The contagion made landfall in the

United Kingdom and Spain. The two nations were hardest hit thanks to overbuilding and the widespread usage of exotic loans. Similar to the United States, the Spanish construction industry employed one in five workers. As a result of the credit contraction, estimates of as high as 75 percent of national real estate companies will close their doors.

In 2008, Great Britain posted its first annual home price decline in 12 years. The typical house lost 1 percent in value from the April 2007 average price of £180,000. However, the UK housing bubble actually eclipsed the U.S. bubble in scope—prices had only just begun to deflate. Fortunately, many British listeners heeded the GSR warning and vastly reduced exposure to mortgage debt.

Anecdotally, unlike Americans, UK residents were actually warned of the impending housing smash. Officials at the Bank of England alerted the public of a potential 25 percent to 40 percent slide in housing prices. By 2009, the prescient forecast came to pass—UK home prices followed the U.S. market into the abyss.

Meantime, a member of the Bank of England's interest rate–setting committee, David Blanchflower, announced his expectations that British homes would decline back to 2003 price levels. Blanchflower's dismal forecast represented a $100,000 loss for the typical UK home. The estimate proved to be quite conservative. Blanchflower further insisted that lower rates would spare the economy from the financial backlash. He was only partially correct. While lower rates did stabilize general economic conditions, nothing could stop the world's biggest housing boom from coming apart at the seams.

From the United Kingdom and Spain, the credit and housing crisis fallout quickly spread around the globe. Toxic MBSs were far from isolated aberrations. Foreign bankers and financial institutions held half of all U.S. mortgage-backed securities. Global banks eagerly devoured the high interest rate, "low-risk" debt instruments also known as structured investment vehicles (SIVs). Swiss banking mogul UBS and German Deutsche Industriebank purchased a disproportionate number of American debt instruments. Additionally, one media source revealed that eight towns in Norway lost at least $125 million on U.S. mortgage securities. Several pension funds in Japan recorded significant losses via Fannie Mae and Freddie Mac bonds.

Interestingly, the European housing bust significantly lagged that of the United States. As a result, eurozone central banker Jean-Claude Trichet was slow to cut rates. Yet in October 2008, UK and European bankers capitulated, quickly following the footsteps of their Federal Reserve counterparts with sharp rate reductions. In response, the euro, sterling, and competing currencies dropped sharply, sending the dollar into the stratosphere.

Since the U.S. overnight lending rate was less than half of its European contemporaries, investors understood all too well that there was plenty of room for further eurozone rate cuts. Ergo, the much anticipated dollar rally of 2008 came to pass with a vengeance. The financial sea change diverted global money flows away from stocks, commodities, and euros into greenbacks.

Chapter Stabilization Plan

The unprecedented multidecade housing advance fomented an atmosphere of hubris throughout the entire industry. Overconfident lenders extended mortgages to risky borrowers with little or no down payments.

However, borrowers are waking up to the fact that a foreclosure rarely haunts a credit score for more than two to three years. Plus with millions already in the foreclosure pipeline and millions more facing default, the stigma associated with foreclosure is far less pronounced than in the past.

Thanks to the toxic effects of exotic ARMs, domestic home prices are expected to drop another 10–15 percent by the end of 2012. Afterwards, prices will likely remain flat, only occasionally punctuated with temporary relief rallies, which inevitably end in further disappointment.

KEY POINT

Due in part to millions of risky ARM defaults the median residential house price will likely decline an additional 10–15 percent by 2012. Renting will remain the preferred alternative to owning a home until the average mortgage payment falls back in line with monthly rental costs.

Q&A

Listener Comment: Duane writes, "Hi, Chris. Please let me start off by saying thank you for your accurate insights on the economy. If only government officials would listen to your GSR program, it would undoubtedly wipe that 'deer in the headlights,' look off their faces when they attempt to resolve our present economic dilemma. It's nice to follow your programs and to be 'in the know' of what is really happening.

"The reason I contacted you is that a few months ago you gave GSR listeners a challenge to get out of debt, pay all bills, and keep you informed of our progress. I am very happy to announce that my 2004 Chevy truck is now paid in full. We made the last payment in the middle of July. It is such a good feeling. We will be putting the money we would have spent on the truck payment toward another loan. When we get that paid off I'll write you again with our progress. Please keep up the good work."

Answer: Hello, Duane. Congratulations—you are clearly on the road to financial independence. Every time you start the engine of your 2004 Chevy truck, remember that the vehicle is paid in full and entirely yours. Try to recall that feeling as you pay off subsequent bills. Thanks, Duane, and please keep us updated with your progress.

CHAPTER 10

Mortgage Epidemic

THE CRISIS CONTINUES

"In a real estate man's eye, the most expensive part of the city is where he has a house to sell."

—Will Rogers (1879–1935)

As house prices began to slip in 2007, media pundits insisted that the event was a mere pothole on the expressway to higher prices. But the rut in the pavement quickly morphed into the deepest recession sinkhole in 50 years. The Case-Shiller 10-city house-price index recorded a 29 percent decline, the worst reading in its 20-year history. By 2008 liar's loan delinquencies leaped 17 percent, even worse than their dodgy subprime counterparts.

Fast forward three years and the same group of mainstream talking heads who missed the crisis now claim that U.S. housing has staged a miraculous recovery. Chapter 10 presents compelling evidence in support of the view that the experts will once again be proven wrong—the bottom has not been reached in real estate. Instead, the hull has been breached and is now filling to capacity thanks to toxic ARM resets and a bleak employment outlook.

Ultimately, the water line will rise an additional 15 percent from the 2006 peak, ending with a total decline of 50 percent in the median house price. Linear regression analysis suggests that the typical house price of $160,000 will drop to approximately $130,000. The unexpected slide will present substantial bargains for patient home shoppers.

The MBS Story

During the housing bubble, home flippers were responsible for nearly half of all sales. No money down, no document mortgages, and related easy credit were primary collaborators. But the housing crisis inverted the world of real estate. Lenders returned to their senses, convinced it was time to readopt more traditional standards. But it was too late. The pool of available buyers evaporated the instant that lenders returned to the conservative and rigid framework of stringent, time-honored lending practices. At that point mortgage lenders/borrowers were destined to earn a place on the endangered species list. Formerly arrogant home sellers faced a market virtually devoid of home buyers.

Adding to woes, a seemingly endless array of exotic lingo worked its way from the real estate and mortgage banking sectors into everyday parlance. Until 2006, only the mortgage bankers issuing the toxic debt were familiar with now common terms like subprime, Alt-A, MBS, CDO, and SIV.

Another important piece of the MBS jigsaw puzzle is the high number of borrowers who acquired multiple home loans and lines of credit. According to reports, lax lending standards and prime credit ratings encouraged the purchase of second and third mortgages. MBSs actually drove demand for toxic loans, which created a virtual sea of available mortgage money. Easy credit convinced millions of people to live far beyond their means precisely when spending habits should have been curtailed. As long as the housing game of musical chairs continued, the unending stream of "free money" flowed. But the demise of the housing bubble was the death knell for easy credit and the beginning of the sharpest real estate plummet in history.

Had the real estate boom been financed through traditional venues, such as local banks, the implications of the downturn would have been far less severe. Instead, thousands of lenders sprung up across the country offering dodgy home loans. The debt was then packaged and sold in large blocks of bonds referred to as mortgage-backed securities (MBSs). Since domestic home prices had experienced an astounding 75-year winning streak, the seemingly risk-free mortgage debt received undeservedly high ratings along with enticing interest rates. While the better than average interest rates should have raised red flags, few institutions anticipated the associated risks. Banks around the globe accepted the bogus MBS story, hook, line, and sinker. By the time that the Moody's and S&P rating agencies downgraded MBS bonds backed by subprime and Alt-A loans, it was too late for most investors. The MBS catastrophe was predicted by Frank Partnoy's seminal work, *Fiasco*.

In merely a few years, millions of toxic mortgages were processed and packaged into tranches. A tranche is merely a component of a MBS, a slice if you like, comprised of bonds with a specific rating, that is to say, AAA, BBB, and so on. Under such a cloak of deception, it became virtually impossible to uncover which lender owned the mortgage and which borrower owned the house. Convoluted packaging methods transformed seemingly innocuous bonds into financial dead falls.

MBSs were bundled by the thousands into CDOs, collateralized debt obligations. The typical CDO contains over 100 MBSs, which are comprised of up to one million home loans. Placing an accurate market value on a single CDO made up of such diverse components is, for all intents and purposes, impossible. In fact, the feat would require an army of analysts with cutting-edge computer models to derive a fair estimate. While many institutions purchased such bonds with the intention of risk diversification, they ignored the cardinal rule of investing: caveat emptor let the buyer beware.

The MBS proved to be the perfect vehicle for passing the risk of default from the seller to the buyer. As a result, thousands of financial firms have invisible, unexploded MBS ordnance hidden within their balance sheets. In 2008–2009, shares of many such institutions literally imploded before the eyes of shareholders. The economic morgue is now filled with MBS-related fatalities: Bear Stearns, Lehman Brothers, Fannie Mae/Freddie Mac, and IndyMac, to name but a few.

Liar's Loans

While most of the subprime fallout passed by the summer of 2008, danger is ever present in the realm of high finance. The next threat on the horizon was the liar's loan. The uninspiring term was reserved for Alt-A mortgages, a step above subprime on the credit ladder and a rung below the more credit-worthy prime mortgage.

By 2008 delinquencies for Alt-As leaped higher by 17 percent, even higher than the14 percent subprime mortgage default rate. As usual, most market watchers were slow to recognize that Alt-A loans were following in the footsteps of their less credit-worthy subprime cousin, down to Dante's default Inferno.

Moreover, the sheer scale of the looming Alt-A and ARM disaster dwarfs any economic calamity in modern history. Subprime and Alt-A mortgages comprise 14 percent of all loans outstanding. More than $800 billion in subprime bonds and $700 billion of Alt-A bonds are expected to default. The total is roughly equivalent to $1.5 trillion dollars of ARM time bombs scattered among the domestic banking system. As a result, Moody's Investors Service joined forces with Standard & Poor's, dropping the boom on Alt-A bond ratings. The downgrades suggest the market for mortgage backed securities will fully capsize, especially nonsecured bonds, perhaps threatening the entire domestic banking system.

Upside Down

By early 2008, the banks and major lenders were clearly crashing along with the housing market. Yet few tears were shed for ailing bank executives with their golden parachutes. Unfortunately for mortgage holders, home loans do not include such extravagant failsafes. Conversely, by the summer months of 2008, nine million home debtors found themselves upside down on their home mortgages, also known as underwater, where the borrower actually owes more than the home is worth. By 2010, the figure rocketed to 12 million unfortunate souls. Before the housing bust passes, estimates reveal that half of American mortgage holders, up to 25 million, will find themselves in the unenviable position. As a result, millions of additional people will turn in their keys and walk away from their debt trap nightmares in search of far more affordable rentals, adding inventory to the already saturated market.

Shiller Knows Best

Yale professor Robert Shiller was one of a handful of economists to accurately predict the housing crisis. A co-creator of the Standard & Poor's/Case-Shiller Home Price Index, his original forecast of a 20–25 percent decline in the national median home price has already come to pass. But Dr. Shiller eventually found his forecast to

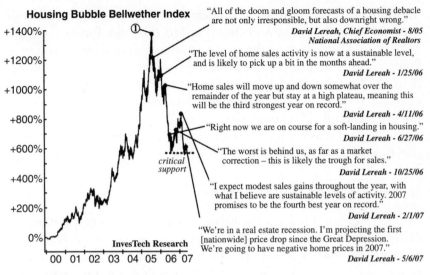

Figure 10.1 is described by the following text within the image:

Housing Bubble Bellwether Index

"All of the doom and gloom forecasts of a housing debacle are not only irresponsible, but also downright wrong."
David Lereah, Chief Economist - 8/05
National Association of Realtors

"The level of home sales activity is now at a sustainable level, and is likely to pick up a bit in the months ahead."
David Lereah - 1/25/06

"Home sales will move up and down somewhat over the remainder of the year but stay at a high plateau, meaning this will be the third strongest year on record."
David Lereah - 4/11/06

"Right now we are on course for a soft-landing in housing."
David Lereah - 6/27/06

"The worst is behind us, as far as a market correction – this is likely the trough for sales."
David Lereah - 10/25/06

critical support

"I expect modest sales gains throughout the year, with what I believe are sustainable levels of activity. 2007 promises to be the fourth best year on record."
David Lereah - 2/1/07

InvesTech Research

"We're in a real estate recession. I'm projecting the first [nationwide] price drop since the Great Depression. We're going to have negative home prices in 2007."
David Lereah - 5/6/07

00 01 02 03 04 05 06 07

+1400% +1200% +1000% +800% +600% +400% +200% 0%

Figure 10.1   Housing Crash

Source: Robert J. Shiller, *Irrational Exuberance*, 2nd ed., 2006. With permission from www.doctor housingbubble.com.

be far too conservative. His latest prediction calls for even more declines before a bottom in home prices is confirmed. The Case-Shiller index is divided into regional markets, with the majority of cities showing much lower prices and sales.

Furthermore, by 2009, the Case-Shiller 10-city index collapsed by 29 percent, the worst reading in its two-decade history. Only a year earlier, mainline media pundits claimed that a meager 2 percent decline was nothing more than an anomaly. Conversely, on GSR, I announced the expectation of at least a 30 percent slide. I now expect the median home price to plunge by 45–55 percent before the storm passes in 2012. A 50 percent decline will push the typical American house price down to approximately $110,000, as seen in Figure 10.1. However, my economic training tells me that a linear regression of the data will provide a better projection, which results in a $130,000 median house price nadir.

The Captain Descends with His Ship

Housing insiders recognized the precarious state of the market long before the headlines reached the nightly news. For example, the CEO of major homebuilder D.R. Horton, Donald J. Tomnitz, announced his dire housing market prediction in 2007. At the JP Morgan Homebuilding and Building Products Conference at Mandalay Bay, Tomnitz said the housing sector would be far worse in 2008, citing concerns over mounting foreclosures and delinquent debtors. Additionally, according to a Federal Reserve report, foreclosures require repair and resale costs of $50,000 on average— benefiting neither borrower nor lender. The vicious cycle of foreclosures only increases unsold inventories, in turn putting downward pressure on already dwindling home prices.

No One Suffers Like the Poor

By far the greatest tragedy of the financial calamity is revealed by the societal effects. Millions of middle- and working-class individuals spent vast sums on student loans, credit cards, and McMansions at the peak of the 2006 housing bubble. Now that the bubble has burst, many will pass through the sequential stages of grief as outlined by Dr. Elisabeth Kübler-Ross. Dr. Ross's work predicts that millions of Americans will experience denial, anger, bargaining, depression, and finally acceptance as a result of the economic meltdown.

Indeed, most are only now acknowledging the degree to which they've been robbed by the Ponzi scheme of the century. Those who are unable to fully pass through the five stages of grief will wait in vain for conditions to improve, frozen like a deer caught in the headlights of an oncoming 18-wheel semi. But the Mac truck brakes have failed. Prices will not recover from cyclic lows for up to one decade.

Most borrowers simply desired a home with potential for a reasonable capital gain. The desire is no more selfish than buying and holding stocks, bonds, or precious metals. Still, the innate human desire for safety and personal improvement is not the issue. As the late George Carlin pointed out in an inspirational comedic performance, the people are not to blame for anything other than their own ignorance.

Nonetheless, as mentioned in the previous chapter, if any group deserves to carry the burden of the housing bubble, it's the mortgage bankers who sold MBSs, CDOs, and SIVs to the legion of unsuspecting institutions. Also responsible are government officials who retracted the protective safeguards that had protected investors since the Great Depression, such as the Glass-Steagall Act and the up-tick rule which limited short selling transactions. Lastly, the

Fed's decision to slash rates down to 1 percent set the financial temperature gauge to the boiling point. The net result was insatiable global demand for toxic MBSs.

The House That Greenspan Bilked

Angry mobs with torches and pitchforks may one day storm Wall Street seeking retribution for the MBS fiasco. But the event would bring justice to merely a fraction of the housing bubble villains. The Federal Reserve shares a hefty portion of the blame, especially Alan Greenspan for lowering rates to 1 percent. Absurdly low rates and the soaring money supply acted as a catalyst for escalating house prices, which allowed the once tame Ponzi scheme to blossom into a modern tulip mania.

However, the tulip mania has produced a hideous batch of new bulbs. Millions are being forced to abandon their homes, often leaving with less than when they arrived. The situation illustrates the risks associated with home ownership in an environment of broadly declining prices. One market pundit described the dire situation, "I've always found it laughable that a home was viewed as the best investment you could ever make, an asset that does not typically generate positive cash-flow, and only appreciates at 1 percent over the rate of inflation, is somehow a great investment?"

Indeed, one wonders how housing and its traditional 1–3 percent annual return can be fairly compared with that of commodities such as gold, which has returned more than 20 percent on average annually for 10 consecutive years.

In like manner, who could blame an observer for believing that the American Dream of home ownership is merely a ruse designed to separate the middle and working classes from their savings? In fact, the fallacious notion helped to spawn an army of mindless drones, eager to oblige the wishes of the lending institutions. Only after their mortgage slips underwater and they fall behind on credit card payments will the naïve wake up to the disaster. For many it may require bankruptcy or the remainder of their lives to repay the mountain of personal debt.

Zero Monthly Payments

In his must-read treatise, *The Total Money Makeover*, Dave Ramsey outlines the story of a young couple who promised their grandfather to never accept any form of debt. Despite the protestations and ridicule of co-workers, friends, and family, the couple scrimped and saved while living in a humble garage apartment for three years. At the end of the ordeal they had amassed an impressive $150,000 nest egg.

Instead of attempting to impress their friends and neighbors by becoming McMansion owners, the couple wisely purchased a reasonably priced starter house for $150,000 in cash. With no monthly rent bill, mortgage payment, or HOA fees, the couple was truly on their way to financial freedom. The biggest recurring bill simply vanished, forever. They owed absolutely nothing to anyone—a foreign concept in today's world.

Living in a garage apartment while saving to purchase a house may have been the American Dream 50 years hence, but thanks to the advent of easy credit the aspiration changed drastically in recent years. Some might argue that living such a frugal lifestyle robbed the couple of life's finer pleasures. But searching for peace and happiness in the form of ever bigger houses with granite countertops is certain to disappoint. A home is merely a depreciating asset in the current market conditions, which requires 1 percent per year simply to maintain.

Furthermore, when one considers that the unemployment rate has registered the most severe reading in decades, their decision to purchase a house outright was brilliant. The current recession is likely to claim at least one of the wage earners' jobs. With soaring health care, gasoline prices, groceries, and insurance costs plus a $1,000 mortgage payment, the family budget would deteriorate rapidly. It doesn't require a PhD in finance to recognize that a job loss would put the couple underwater post-haste. Their dream house would enter foreclosure and the original down payment would be forfeited. At that point, the only refuge would be to rent an apartment or to cohabit with family or friends.

Under almost any scenario, the young couple's original goal of paying for the entire home was an ideal choice. By simply adhering to the wisdom of their grandfather as well as Poor Richard's time-honored adage, "Neither a borrower nor a lender be," no matter how bad conditions become, they'll always have a roof over their heads.

It's unlikely that many family members, friends, or co-workers could make the same bold claim. One might imagine that the couple was regularly teased for their frugal living arrangements. However, the credit crisis certainly silenced the envious group. The same folks likely purchased homes near the peak of the housing boom, with no money down, no documentation loans, Alt-As/option ARMs. Under such a scenario, mortgage payments ballooned by 100 percent or more and equity performed a vanishing act. In fact, many are likely to be so deeply underwater that SCUBA gear is required just to enter their homes.

Furthermore, since the housing sector was responsible for as many as one in five domestic jobs, many of the young couple's original detractors suddenly found themselves in the unemployment line. Making matters even more unbearable, rapidly declining disposable incomes will be funneled away from leisure activities toward far more mundane expenses, such as soaring mortgage payments, gas-guzzling SUVs, and grocery bills. Some will be forced out of extravagant estates while the frugal couple enjoys a far more conservative, yet comfortable home.

Sadly for many, the previous story will seem all too familiar from 2010 to 2012. Yet there is a silver lining. Eventually, the crashing real estate market will discount prices to much more affordable levels. Plus, strict lending standards, which seem like a curse to sellers, will soon be viewed as a blessing to aspiring homeowners who will be far less likely to face home foreclosure in the coming decades.

KEY POINT

Amid the deepest recession in over 50 years, house prices are expected to further erode for at least two more years. Readers are encouraged to embrace frugality and self reliance while avoiding risky exotic mortgages/debt.

Q&A

Listener Question: Bob asks, "Chris, do you feel that Nebraska farm land is a good investment for the long term, if purchased correctly?"

Answer: Hello, Bob. It's interesting that you should ask about Midwest farmland. When I spoke with *Adventure Capitalist* Jim Rogers about relocating in a recent interview, he suggested purchasing farm land in the Midwest. I'm sure he based the opinion on the fact that demand for commodities such as grains has been climbing steadily while farm property has become more attractively priced.

There are many important questions to ask before making such a move. Are you buying the land for speculation or as a home farm? Will you lease the land to farmers? Have you and your family visited the area and become spellbound by the local charm? Thanks for the thought-provoking question and best of luck with the house hunting.

The Ideal House Price

BARGAIN HUNTING, 2012

"Ninety percent of all millionaires become so through owning real estate."

—Andrew Carnegie (1919)

Part 2 covered the real estate bubble/crash, particularly the widespread use of dangerous mortgages. Toxic ARMs encouraged millions to accept loans of up to nine times the annual household income, 300 percent higher than recommended. Such debt levels cannot be sustained indefinitely. Thus, up to half of all mortgage holders are expected to be underwater by 2012. But after the tidal wave of foreclosures washes away the excess inventory/high prices, bargains will abound. Eventually owning a mortgage will again be a prudent decision. But how will you know when it's time to reenter the market? Indeed, what separates a bargain dream home from an overpriced nightmare?

Chapter 11 provides three simple rules of thumb that every home hunter needs while stalking real estate prey. Armed with such easy to use, capital-preserving survival tips, the reader will steer clear of the mine field and instead locate a personal field of dreams. Hunting rule number one: Search for properties priced less than three times household income.

Three Times Method (3×s)

Although a mountain of empirical evidence indicates that the real estate downturn will persist until 2012, eventually inflated prices will reach more reasonable levels and owning a house will once again become an attractive proposition. Since home ownership is generally the biggest investment decision of a lifetime and usually involves purchasing a mortgage, annual household income is a primary determining factor in choosing the right property. For decades, multiplying gross household income by three has remained a reliable method for estimating the ideal mortgage size. For instance, assuming a median gross income of $50,000, the ideal house price for the area is $150,000 ($50,000 × 3 = **$150,000**).

Aspiring house buyers are encouraged to adjust the median family income figure to better fit their personal specifications. If household annual gross income is $70,000, the acceptable mortgage increases to $210,000 ($70,000 × 3 = **$210,000**).

However, during the housing bubble years, the three times gross annual income procedure (3×s) was tossed out the McMansion window. Toxic mortgages of as high as nine times the gross household income were approved. The no income, no documentation loans roped the unsuspecting herd into debt traps while salespeople reaped huge profits packaging and selling the MBSs to Wall Street.

Although simplicity is an obvious advantage of the 3×s method, it is not without its detractions. Homes with exceptional qualities such as: mountain views, finished basements, beach/lake frontage, large acreage, or exclusive community locations will understandably command higher prices. Demand for vacation homes, rentals, and flippable properties often drive prices far beyond local income levels. In such cases, the 3×s multiplier is adjusted by dividing the average price of recent home sales by the gross annual income figure. For example, assuming that the typical household income is $50,000 and the average sale price of three comparable homes is $200,000, the ideal multiplier increases to 4×s ($200,000/$50,000 = 4×s). Please note, however, paying more than 3xs the household income for most buyers is unadvisable.

Since anyone can multiply his or her gross income by three, the 3×s rule of thumb should become an integral part of every real estate investor's toolbox.

Thirty Percent Solution

Another widely accepted rule for identifying the best mortgage size, the 30 percent method, requires a bit more number crunching. The 30 percent rule hinges on the understanding that monthly mortgage payments should never exceed a fixed percentage of income. In general, lenders allow home buyers to borrow up to 30 percent of annual gross income, depending on FICO scores and related considerations. Ergo, a couple earning a combined monthly gross income of $3,333 is advised to only accept a mortgage with monthly payments of $1,000 or less ($3,333 × 30% = **$1,000 payment**).

Clearly the 30 percent technique is closely tied to the borrower's income level. The 30 percent method does, however, have at least one important limitation. When exotic loans are employed, the technique must be adjusted to compensate for the ARM reset.

Numerous mortgage borrowers were lured by low ARM initial monthly payments. The card trick provided oversized fees to lenders, allowed home builders to sell more homes, and let realtors earn additional commissions. But once the initial ARM grace period expired, monthly payments more often than not soared into the stratosphere. The sleight of hand actually distorted monthly payments, essentially encouraging unqualified buyers to move "all in."

Correspondingly, monthly payments for the typical 2/20 option ARM remained safely fixed for two years. However, afterwards the payments reset to alarmingly high levels. See Equations 11.1 and 11.2, where the 30 percent rule is in effect.

Equation 11.1 Before Reset

$ 3,000 monthly income
$ 1,000 monthly payment
$ 1,000/$3,000 = **33%**

Equation 11.2 After Reset

$ 3,000 monthly income
$ **2,000 monthly payment**
$ 2,000/$3,000 = **66%**

Once the option ARM resets, suddenly the total monthly income directed to a mortgage payment increases from a manageable

33 percent to an impossibly high 66 percent. Put simply, two out of every three dollars of income are required just to service the mortgage payment. If left uncorrected, the scenario will almost certainly end in foreclosure.

Enhanced 30 Percent Hybrid

The enhanced 30 percent home buying method protects home buyers from accepting toxic mortgages such as the option ARM by revealing the hidden reset danger. The technique is simply a hybrid of the 30 percent and 3×s methods. First, the buyer multiplies annual household gross income by 3. Next, monthly income is multiplied by 30 percent (see Equations 11.3 and 11.4).

> **Equation 11.3 Acceptable Mortgage**
>
> $\$\,3,000$ mo. Inc. $\times 30\% = \$1,000$ **payment**
>
> $\$\,150,000$ mort./$\$50,000$ gross ann. Inc. $= \mathbf{3{\times}s}$

> **Equation 11.4 Unacceptable ARM Mortgage**
>
> $\$\,3,000$ mo. Inc. $\times 30\% = \$1,000$ **payment**
>
> $\$\,200,000$ mort./$\$50,000$ gross ann. Inc. $= \mathbf{4{\times}s}$

In Equation 11.4, although the 30 percent method failed to identify the danger posed by the impending ARM reset, the 3×s method acted as a fail-safe. Clearly four times the annual gross income is well beyond the established safety level—the borrower is advised to reject the loan.

100 Times Rent Method (100×s)

The next valuation rule evaluates general house prices, not personal loan compatibility. The 100×s method examines the relationship between local home prices and rental costs. Generally speaking, when homes are selling above the typical monthly rent multiplied by 100, renting is preferred to owning. Conversely, when homes are selling at or below the average monthly rent multiplied by 100, home ownership makes financial sense.

Using a sample size of at least three comparable houses and rental properties, a quick assessment is possible. Services such as Realtybid.com and Craigslist.com are excellent free data resources.

To illustrate, assume that a query of rental homes on the Chicago Craigslist.com website reveals that the typical 1,400 sq. ft. house in the desired neighborhood currently rents for **$1,200** per month. Similarly, the average 1,400 sq. ft. home sells for **$150,000**. Using the 100xs method, the monthly rent is multiplied by 100 and then compared with the average house price. (See Equation 11.5.)

> **Equation 11.5 The 100×s Method**
> 1, 400 sq. ft. rental: $1, 200 \times 100 = $**120,000**
> 1, 400 sq. ft. home for sale: **$150,000**
> Defference: $\underline{$30,000}$

Clearly, the typical house for sale is overpriced by approximately $30,000. Until prices fall back in line with more traditional metrics, the home rental option is preferable. Plus, owning a home is expensive, entailing numerous responsibilities and expenses, including annual taxes, repairs, maintenance, and insurance. Contrarily, renters avoid all of the above hassles and are only required to send a single check to the landlord each month.

All things being equal, the 100×s method provides an accurate estimate of intrinsic home value. After searching through online real estate sources and becoming more familiar with the method, readers will find that it makes identifying bargain houses a snap.

Rent or Own? A Real-World Example

With domestic home prices crashing on average 30 percent and 12 months of inventory overhang, it remains a renter's market. In fact, Jennifer and I are listed among their ranks. After months of searching through local newspaper classifieds via websites and Craigslist.com, we found an impressive house for rent in the resort town of Sapphire, North Carolina. Sapphire is a quiet ski and golf resort village nestled in the eastern North Carolina mountains. As one might imagine, the town earned its name from the rare gemstones distributed throughout the geological strata. Equidistant from Asheville and Greenville, the quaint town of Sapphire offers the scenic beauty and privacy of Mayberry with modern conveniences such as high-speed Internet access.

Needless to say, we were pleased to find a reasonably priced rental home in the area. Only two years earlier, near the peak of the housing bubble, a similar rental property could fetch $1,500 per month. But by the fall of 2008, we secured a long-term lease for the reasonable price of $950 per month. The almost new home has a long list of enticing accoutrements: breathtaking mountain views, a cathedral ceiling, three bedrooms and 2 bathrooms, comfortably furnished and much more. In the winter months, a mere five-minute drive is all that's required to enjoy the ski slopes. In the summer, nearly endless national forests beckon for hiking, fishing, and camping.

Nonetheless, in 2008, before making the house rental plunge we made offers on several houses. We became so convinced that house prices would continue their perilous descent, we actually forfeited $3,000 in earnest money on one particular property. So was renting the best decision? To find out, the following methods are considered: 3×s, 100×s, and the 30 percent rule.

3×s Rule

Since the typical income in this area hovers near $40,000 per year, the 3xs rule yields an ideal house price of $120,000. (See Equation 11.6.)

Equation 11.6 3×s Rule

$$3 \times \$40,000 = \underline{\$120{,}000}$$

100×s Method

Considering the fact that Sapphire is a highly sought-after vacation town, house rental fees are surprisingly low, $1,000 on average. Ergo, the 100xs method provides a low home price. (See Equation 11.7.)

Equation 11.7 100×s Method

$$100 \times \$1,000 \text{ rent per month} = \underline{\$100{,}000}$$

Thirty Percent Rule

Finally, if one again assumes that the typical gross income in the area is $40,000 or $3,333 per month, the 30 percent rule results in a reasonable mortgage payment of $1,000. (See Equation 11.8.)

Equation 11.8 30 Percent Rule

$$30\% \times \$3,333 = \underline{\$1,000 \text{ mortgage}}$$

Currently a fixed-rate mortgage with a $1,000 per month payment will purchase a $160,000 home.

Next, the average of all three valuation methods provides a reliable price guideline for aspiring house hunters. (See Equation 11.9.)

Equation 11.9 Price Guideline

$120,000 + $100,000 + 160,000 = $380,000
$380,000/3 = **$130,000**

Therefore, a solid benchmark for purchasing a home in this area is **$130,000**. Given that Sapphire is a resort village, a luxury bonus of $50,000 is added to the $130,000 estimate. Therefore, a typical house is worth approximately $180,000.

Our current rental home was listed with a sale price of **$340,000**. Yet according to the area house price guideline provided by the average of the three home valuation metrics, our rental unit is worth, at most, **$180,000**, almost 50 percent less than the asking price.

Similarly, the $340,000 asking price is wildly overvalued according to the 100×s rule. By simply reversing the process and dividing the market value by 100, the expected monthly rent payment is $3,400. (See Equation 11.10.)

Equation 11.10 Expected Rent Payments

$340,000/100 = **$3,400**

Therefore, under normal market conditions a home worth $340,000 should command a $3,400 monthly rent payment. But our monthly rent payment is only **$950**, including perks such as a fully furnished home and access to recreational facilities. Plus, house

KEY POINT

Eventually owning a house will become a prudent decision. The ideal mortgage size is three times the household annual income. Readers are encouraged to rent a home until average monthly mortgage payments are comparable with monthly rental costs.

prices have plunged since we made the decision to rent instead of own a house. As a result, as much as $100,000 in capital losses was avoided. So was renting a house a wise decision? I leave the question with the reader.

Q&A

Listener Question #1: Paul says, "Chris, I love your show and listen when I can. It seems that this talk of a bailout in the trillions of dollars is not possible. The money doesn't exist, and the printing press doesn't seem likely to work either. I can't imagine China or another foreign nation lending more money to the United States. It seems that the powers that be are stalling for time. These bailout Band-Aids are only temporary. Do you have any thoughts on this?"

Answer: Hello, Paul. You are correct that the money for the bailouts does not exist. However, thanks to the magic of the fractional reserve banking system, the Treasury Department may borrow as much money as is required from the Federal Reserve. For the time being, I expect officials to keep the printing presses running 24/7 if necessary to keep the Ponzi scheme going. Thanks, Paul, for the question.

Listener Question #2: Sharif says, "Chris, a guest explained on GSR how defaulting mortgages are causing the money supply to shrink. Isn't that only occurring in terms of paper money, since the money has already been spent? This seems inflationary to me, since currency that would have otherwise returned to the bank will remain in circulation."

Answer: Hi, Sharif. The answer to your question is contingent upon the time frame observed. For instance, plummeting house prices/MBS values are deflationary, albeit in the short term. Also, homeowners are no longer able to withdraw funds from the home ATM, that is, via lines of credit and second mortgages.

However, in the long term federal bailouts, near 0 percent interest rates and debt monetization will result in soaring inflation. Thanks, Sharif, for the great question.

PART III

BANKING—SUPER PROFITS

CHAPTER 12

American Central Banks

LEARNING FROM PAST MISTAKES

*"Bankers own the earth; take it away from them but leave them with
the power to create credit; and, with a flick of a pen, they will create
enough money to buy it back again. . . . If you want to be slaves of
bankers and pay the cost of your own slavery, then let the bankers
control money and control credit."*

—Sir Josiah Stamp, Director, Bank of England, 1940

Following eight years of war with the reigning global superpower,
in 1782 America won its independence from Britain. Yet only
30 years later amid the War of 1812, the United States once again
found itself embroiled in a death match with its former rival. Although American forces narrowly emerged victorious in both conflicts, the United States actually lost the economic war. How so? In
both instances, the central banks that quickly sprung up wreaked
havoc on the economy.

However, in 1836 President Andrew Jackson removed the last
remaining vestiges of the national banks. Set free from the heavy
burden, the economy thrived for decades. Yet in the aftermath of
the 1907 panic, the sinister banking cartel seized the opportunity to
once again consolidate financial power. In 1913 under a shroud of
secrecy, the Federal Reserve was created. Since that time numerous
calamities have befallen the financial system, including the 1929

crash, the Great Depression, the 1970s stagflation, the 1980s S&L crisis, the 1990s dot.com boom/implosion, and the 2007–2008 housing/credit crashes. Most troubling of all, the dollar lost over 95 percent of its purchasing power.

Part 3 begins the investigation into the American central banking experiment, starting with the recent 2008 financial crisis. Next a thorough examination of the first three central banks reveals the hidden flaws that threaten the very foundation of the current Federal Reserve System. The section concludes with an overview of the heroic figures that strived to unshackle the nation from the usurious banking cabal.

Financial Shock and Awe

Millions of investors, analysts, and economists were caught off guard by the 2008 credit crisis. Even the world's richest man, Warren Buffett, watched helplessly as the price of his Berkshire Hathaway shares plunged by approximately 50 percent from peak to trough. In addition, the former head of the Federal Reserve, Sir Alan Greenspan, claimed ignorance regarding the "once-in-a-century credit tsunami," noting that the crisis

> has turned out to be much broader than anything I could have imagined. . . . It has morphed from one gripped by liquidity restraints to one in which fears of insolvency are now paramount. . . . Those of us who have looked to the self-interest of lending institutions to protect shareholders' equity (myself especially) are in a state of shocked disbelief.

In front of a congressional panel, Greenspan released himself from personal responsibility for the crisis, citing his "underpricing of risk" remarks: "In 2005, I raised concerns of a protracted period of underpricing of risk, if history was any guide, would have dire consequences." However, Greenspan's warning wasn't enough to stop the looming disaster. In 2008 Greenspan acknowledged the severity of the crisis,

> Given the financial damage to date, I cannot see how we can avoid a significant rise in layoffs and unemployment . . . a marked retrenchment of consumer spending as households

try to divert an increasing part of their incomes to replenish depleted assets, not only in their 401k's but in the value of their homes as well. . . . The necessary condition for this crisis to end is a stabilization of home prices in the U.S.

Interestingly, not once did Greenspan admit that the credit crisis and housing bubble were directly related to an overly dovish FOMC rate policy and open market operations.

Nevertheless, hundreds of major lenders closed their doors two years before the economic storm made headline news. In fact, more than 300 mortgage lending companies went out of business by 2006, well in advance of the first bank bailout. Given the fallout in the lending sector, one wonders how the housing crash and related economic deluge that followed could have possibly come as a surprise to the former Fed chairman. Indeed, how did leading economists fail to foresee the financial storm of the century? In the sections ahead, a review of earlier economic crises as well as the central banking system provides the solution to the puzzling question, beginning with the S&L crisis.

The Savings and Loss Crisis

Economic disasters are hardly a new American phenomenon. During the infamous S&L crisis of the 1980s, more than 700 savings and loan institutions closed their doors. The event is widely viewed as the primary precursor to the 1990–1991 recession. In July 1996 the General Accounting Office (GAO) put the final price tag on bailing out the 747 bankrupt savings and loans, that is, lenders, at $480.9 billion, half a trillion dollars. Much of the blame for the financial mayhem was put squarely upon the shoulders of lax S&L regulation, the Tax Reform Act of 1986, and soaring short-term interest rates.

Similar to the hundreds of now defunct lenders in the current housing bust, S&Ls offered loans to practically anyone with a pulse during the 1980s housing boom. Next, the Tax Reform Act of 1986 vastly reduced the value of real estate–related tax shelters and thus by proxy, real estate. The net effect was a glut of homes held by investors who had neither the resources nor the incentives to pay their mortgages. The situation compares remarkably well with the current domestic situation comprised of 7 million delinquent mortgage holders and 12 million underwater home debtors.

A contributing factor in the S&L bust was the domestic inflation of the 1970s. As prices soared, borrowers demanded higher interest rates. While the low fixed rates were a positive for mortgage holders who secured rates at favorable levels, the rate differential created significant stresses within the already troubled S&L industry. Financial institutions garner a significant proportion of their fees by offering long-term loans while borrowing at slightly lower rates. Put simply, most S&Ls were heavily invested in fixed loans near 5 percent just as inflationary forces bid rates up to levels unseen in generations. The loans and mortgages represented not only an opportunity cost but a considerable threat to bank solvency.

At the peak of the S&L crisis, hundreds of thrifts closed their doors. An infusion of cash was required to keep the FDIC, and by proxy, the entire banking system solvent. In similar fashion, after a mere handful of bank closings in 2008, the FDIC was already bracing for a potential bailout request. Evidently, those at the helm of the FDIC expected a tidal wave of trouble to wash over the industry.

The Only Thing to Fear Is Debt Itself

As damaging as the S&L crisis was to the national economy, the Great Depression was by far the greatest domestic banking disaster. The events that transpired during the 1930s remain seared in the minds of thousands of American seniors. Even the Long Depression of 1873 and the panics of 1893 and 1907 were merely economic turbulence when compared with the Great Depression.

Following the Allied Powers' WWI victory, the unprecedented prosperity that followed led to the Roaring Twenties. With only 70 domestic bank failures per year, the national economic underpinnings were deemed to be rock solid. Yet conditions changed abruptly following the Wall Street crash of 1929. Over 700 banks closed their doors annually, culminating in an unthinkably large 3,000 defunct banks before the crisis passed. In fact, President Franklin Delano Roosevelt's famous sound bite from March 3, 1933, "The only thing we have to fear is fear itself," was in reference to the cataclysmic banking disaster. One wonders if our current commander-in-chief will utter a similarly haunting phrase such as, "The only thing we have to fear is debt itself."

While analysts ponder whether economic history is repeating or merely rhyming, headline reports mirror those of the Great Depression. Just as deregulation and greed fomented the reckless loans of the 1920s and the 1980s, the current housing crash has saddled countless millions of consumers with mortgage debt and bailout bills.

Nonetheless, if history proves to be a reliable guide, society will once again demand a sacrificial scapegoat for the economic calamity. Just as Herbert Hoover was singled out as a primary culprit for the Great Depression, a new boogie man will become the target of national scorn. Will Bernie Madoff or Alan Greenspan earn the title? Stay tuned.

(Dollar) Bill and Ted (Rothschild's) Excellent Adventure

On GSR I occasionally use theatrical audio props to better illustrate significant, albeit abstract economic concepts. Following in the footprints of H.G. Wells and his classic science fiction novel, *The Time Machine*, GSR listeners occasionally are treated to the sounds of the Tesla-Einstein-Kaku-Maxwell-Hawking-Reflector (TEKMHR). The proprietary, yet imaginary quantum teleportation device requires the entire electrical resources of a nuclear power plant. The TEKMHR was modeled after Tesla's electromechanical wizardry, Einstein's relativity theory, Maxwell's electromagnetism, Michio Kaku's string theory, plus a dash of Stephen Hawking's work on singularities and wormholes. Conceptually, the TEKMHR harnesses the mass of a mini black hole to create a gateway to parallel universes. Simply put, the machine allows the user to travel back and forth through space-time.

First on the TEKMHR itinerary is a rendezvous with arguably the most successful investor in history, Mayer Rothschild, whose name loosely translates as Red Shield. Rothschild was the founder and head of an international banking dynasty and the most successful European business family. Controversial and unconfirmed estimates of the Rothschild family fortune range from $10 trillion to as high as $300 trillion.

Mayer Rothschild was one of eight children born in 1744 in a Jewish ghetto in Frankfurt, Germany. Often referred to as the founder of international finance, Mayer Rothschild built the banking empire squarely upon the shoulders of his 10 offspring. His eldest son was sent to England, another to Austria, a third to Naples, and still another to Paris, France.

Mayer Rothschild grasped a profound economic concept that still eludes many even today. The most crucial component to controlling any civilized nation is its money supply, as illustrated by his famous statement, "Let me issue and control a nation's money supply, and I care not who makes its laws." In yet another telling quote, his son Nathan Rothschild, head of the London branch, mirrored his father's sentiments: "I care not what puppet is placed on the throne of England to rule the Empire. The man who controls Britain's money supply controls the British Empire and I control the British money supply." The Rothschild's were not concerned whether the money was soaked in blood, as long as the family business controlled it.

Meanwhile, turning the TEKMHR dials forward in time to 2010, Mayer Rothschild would be impressed with and even perhaps envious of the Federal Reserve System's stranglehold on the domestic money supply. Unlike the Central Bank of Canada, a nonprofit institution that is actually "owned" by the government and by proxy the people, the Federal Reserve is an altogether different creature. The U.S. central bank is the "Federal Reserve System," which does not belong to "We the People." Instead, the Fed is owned by the shareholders of the 12 regional Federal Reserve Banks. The shares of the member banks are actually traded in a private forum. However, the board of governors is an independent government agency, whose members are appointed by the president with the consent of the Senate.

The first stage in the domestic money creation process involves the issuance of bonds by the Federal Reserve on behalf of the U.S. Treasury Department. Next, the Treasury Department sells bonds to investors in exchange for funding. At this stage in the process, the fiat money is only backed by the good faith of the American taxpayer and has zero intrinsic value. Not until the Treasury bond interest payment is received do the dollars gain value.

As a result of the fractional banking system sleight of hand, the U.S. dollar is based primarily upon debt. The arrangement is particularly appealing to the government because direct taxation on the unsuspecting populace is not required. After all, when a people are taxed beyond their means, they sometimes throw tea parties and toss imports into the Boston Harbor, or even worse, organize a revolution.

Nevertheless, as Mayer and Nathan Rothschild's earlier statements indicate, those who own the Federal Reserve, including foreign powers with questionable agendas, wield far more power than do the elected officials on Capitol Hill. In my opinion, the corrupt Federal Reserve System will ultimately bring this mighty nation to its knees.

What You Don't Know Can Cost You

Next the TEKMHR time machine propels the reader back in time several decades to the age of the twentieth century's most renowned economist, John Maynard Keynes. Ironically, the very economist whose work forms the basis of the entire central banking system made peculiar comments regarding monetary deception. Keynes said:

> By a continuing process of inflation, governments can confiscate, secretly and unobserved, an important part of the wealth of their citizens. . . . There is no subtler, no surer means of overturning the existing basis of society than to debauch the currency. The process engages all the hidden forces of economic law on the side of destruction, and does it in a manner which not one man in a million is able to diagnose.

Keynes warned that uncontrolled central banking allows governments to pillage the hoi polloi's savings with only one in a million realizing what occurred.

Close Encounter of the Rogers Kind

Billionaire investor Jim Rogers has been a good friend to GSR and a regular guest since 2006. Rogers frequently points out the perpetual struggle against the tyrannical central banking system. In a 2008 interview, Rogers mentioned that the Fed would eventually follow the previous two U.S. central banks into bankruptcy. After hearing his comments I decided to delve more deeply into the enigmatic banking system, which culminated with the following investigation into the three previous domestic central banks.

Unearthing the roots of the national central banking system requires a TEKMHR time machine jump back to 1763, 13 years before the signing of the Declaration of Independence. While on a trip to England, founding father Benjamin Franklin was asked by officials at the Bank of England how the colonies would manage their finances. Franklin proffered:

> That is simple. In the colonies we issue our own money. It is called Colonial Script. We issue it in proper proportion to the demands of trade and industry to make the products pass easily from the producers to the consumers. . . . In this manner, creating for ourselves our own paper money, we control its purchasing power, and we have no interest to pay to no one.

Not surprisingly, British authorities were displeased with Franklin's comments, in particular King George. After all, domestic banking interests were of great interest to the monarchy and the Bank of England. Under the Currency Act of 1764, Americans were asked, ever so politely, to cease and desist printing their own money or face an unpleasant jail sentence.

Although the colonists were far from keen to maintain the royal agreement, the colonial script was eventually exchanged at a rate of two-to-one for British notes. The Currency Act of 1764 led to severe unemployment and depression. Poor Richard, Ben Franklin, described the outcome, "In one year, the conditions were so reversed that the era of prosperity ended, and a depression set in, to such an extent that the streets of the colonies were filled with unemployed."

Accordingly, for many of the colonists the honeymoon period with their former island homeland was over. The British approval rating sank to the lowest level since the foundation of the colony. As every student of history knows, excessive taxation and economic depression eventually lead to war. Rumors of a war for independence were rife.

In like manner, the lust for independence from Old World rule led to eight bloody years of conflict. Despite the harrowing odds, Continental Commander George Washington's iron will led his forces to victory in the bid for independence. Yet freedom always demands substantial sacrifices and the American struggle for independence was no exception to the rule. The war exacted a heavy toll on battle-weary soldiers as well as government coffers.

The new nation was also saddled with costly economic tribute in the form of the first true American central bank, also known as the Bank of North America.

American Central Banks

In the Ship of Theseus paradox, the Greek philosopher Plutarch delves into the illusory nature of identity. During Theseus' harrowing return voyage from Crete, legend has it, Theseus and his Athenian crew was forced to replace most of the vessel's wooden planks. Plutarch ponders whether the original ship still remains intact after nearly every component has been substituted. For example, if the old planks were used to build a new ship, does the original exist or has a clone taken its place?

In similar fashion, since 1781, the nation has endured four central banks. The current Federal Reserve System shares striking similarities with the earlier versions. But do their flaws doom the Fed to failure? To find out, the investigation begins with a review of the three failed American central banks.

American Central Banks

1. The Bank of North America (1781–1785)
2. The First Bank of the United States (1791–1811)
3. The Second Bank of the United States (1816–1836)
4. The Federal Reserve System (1913–Present)

First Central Bank

The first national experiment with central banking began with the Bank of North America. The private commercial institution intimately linked private banking interests with those of the government. On December 31, 1781, the Congress of the Confederation and Robert Morris, the superintendent of finance, signed the bank's charter. The sleight of hand allowed the U.S. Treasury to loan the U.S. government the funds required for basic operations.

Yet monetary expansion proved to be as tempting in 1782 as it is today. Fortunately for posterity, the bank charter expired in 1785 and the doors were closed after only four brief years. Among the reasons cited for its demise: **favoritism toward foreign interests and unfair competition against state banks**. Although the institution was reopened two years later, severe constraints ensured that no central banking powers remained intact. While curtailing central banking power and tenure set an important precedent, unfortunately it is one that was destined to be ignored.

Second American Central Bank

While the danger of fractional reserve banking was well known at the time, the allure of easy money once again became irresistible to men of power. Six years after the first national bank ended unfavorably, officials agreed to a second attempt. Known as the First Bank of the United States, the second central bank received its charter in 1790. The institution was the brainchild of Alexander Hamilton, the secretary of the Treasury. The newly formed First Bank of the United States was inspired, according to legend, by powerful banking interests primarily in Great Britain and Europe.

Meanwhile, at least one wise leader recognized the dangers posed by the central bank. Thomas Jefferson, the secretary of state, fiercely opposed the institution, noting:

> I believe that banking institutions are more dangerous to our liberties than standing armies. . . . If the American people ever allow private banks to control the issue of their currency, first by inflation, then by deflation, the banks and corporations that will grow up around [the banks] will deprive the people of all property until their children wake up homeless on the continent their fathers conquered. The issuing power should be taken from the banks and restored to the people, to whom it properly belongs.

Nevertheless, amid the protests of Jefferson and many others, on April 25, 1791 George Washington signed the document that granted the second central bank a 20-year charter. The national lending institution proved to be a disaster for the American people. In the first five years of operation, the government borrowed $8 million, which led to hyperinflation-like price levels.

The (Bank) War of 1812 Twenty years after the First Bank of the United States opened its doors, in 1811 the U.S. Congress voted down a bid for contract renewal. At last the financial parasite was dislodged. The new nation was entirely free from tyrannical central-ized banking. But instead of ushering in a period of great prosper-ity, the move to reject the second central bank thrust the tiny nation into global conflict.

Moreover, the nefarious global banking cartel understood all too well that where diplomatic deviousness had failed, military conquest might succeed. The vast American resources wouldn't be relinquished without a fight. In fact, Nathan Roths-child, head of the London banking branch, reportedly commented on the failure to renew the First Bank of the United States, "the United States would find itself involved in a most disastrous war if the bank charter [First Bank of the United States] was not renewed." Not surprisingly and far from coincidentally, only a few months after the First Bank of the United States closed its doors, the British declared war on the United States, igniting the War of 1812.

Fortunately for Americans, Britain was also embroiled in an epic struggle against its French neighbors and their beloved emperor, Napoleon Bonaparte. In early 1814 English resources were fully committed to the task of subduing the Napoleonic forces. However, the reprieve was only temporary. By April 14, 1814, Napoleon Bonaparte was captured by the allied forces. The emperor of France abdicated his throne, which allowed the British war machine to redirect its full force toward crushing the American insurrection.

Meanwhile, after two bloody years of conflict, on August 24, 1814, the invading British army made landfall in Chesapeake Bay. The 8,000 residents of Washington, D.C., including President James Madison, found themselves under siege not only by swarms of dis-ease-laden mosquitoes, but by 4,000 British Redcoats. Not to put too sharp a point on it, but during the march through Washington, D.C., the president's house, aka the White House, was captured and burned to the ground.

Yet providence once again smiled upon the grand American experiment. After suffering defeat at the Battle of New Orleans, on December 24, 1814, the British fleet and supporting troops with-drew from the nation. Against seemingly impossible odds, the fledg-ling country secured its second bid for independence against the leading global superpower. Yet the military victory was merely the opening salvo in the struggle for monetary freedom.

Third American Central Bank

Since war is always a costly affair, regaining the coveted title of American independence was by no means inexpensive. The War of 1812 culminated with excessive debt levels, which once again stretched the U.S. banking system beyond the breaking point. Demand for funds was a driving factor behind the creation of the third domestic central bank, aka the Second Bank of the United States. The institution opened its doors in January 1817. Similar to its predecessor, the bank was also located in Philadelphia, limited to a 20-year charter, and maintained branches throughout the nation.

Irrespective of all the trouble that wartime debt had caused in the past, once again officials printed too much money. Like a broken timepiece that correctly tells time twice per day, economic history was repeating. The 20-year reign of the third central bank created considerable strife among politicians and competing banks. At the heart of the conflict were government-granted monopoly powers and revenues. In fact, the Second Bank of the United States created such controversy that President Andrew Jackson opened an executive investigation into the matter. The president concluded that the institution was a detrimental influence on American political elections and a threat to national sovereignty.

Furthermore, the irresistible banking force met with an unmovable object, that is, Andrew Jackson. The president was well known for his dislike of banker hubris and for his staunch belief that gold was the only sound money. Jackson learned much from studying the circumstances surrounding the two former central banks. The president insisted that centralized banking concentrates far too much power into far too few hands. In 1936, President Jackson focused his bid for reelection primarily on a platform of quashing the charter renewal for the Second Bank of the United States.

The Great (Debt) Emancipator   The drive to implement a new central bank was as tenacious as a kudzu vine's stranglehold on red Georgia clay. Although Andrew Jackson had thoroughly severed the stalks of the central bank vine, the nefarious roots remained safely concealed several yards beneath the surface.

And as it always does, war required far more funding than could be found in the Treasury coffers. In an attempt to hold the nation together, President Abraham Lincoln refused to sell posterity into financial bondage with usurious loans of 24–36 percent. Instead, the president issued $450 million in greenbacks that carried zero interest obligations. Due to the green ink used on the reverse side of the bills, the term "greenbacks" is still in use today.

President Lincoln's $450 million greenback investment seems trivial in terms of current government expenditures. Today, the sum would barely cover the executive bonuses of a Wall Street bank. Yet for the period, it was a tidy sum and was instrumental in winning the Civil War. According to a report from the Treasury Department in 1972, statisticians determined that by sidestepping the usurious loans, Lincoln's patriotic foresight saved the nation a king's ransom in interest payments. In fact, at a rate of 24–36 percent, the $450 million compares with $4 billion in modern terms. This fact alone earns honest Abe Lincoln the apt title, "The Great Debt Emancipator."

However, Lincoln's decision to avoid the interest rate trap did not go unnoticed. An editorial in the London *Times* responded to Honest Abe's perceived insolence:

> If this mischievous financial policy, which has its origin in North America, shall become indurated down to a fixture, then that government will furnish its own money without cost. It will pay off debts and be without debt. It will have all the money necessary to carry on its commerce. It will become prosperous without precedent in the history of the world. The brains and wealth of all countries will go to North America. That country must be destroyed or it will destroy every monarchy on the globe.

The article's stunning predictive accuracy is confirmed by the unparalleled prosperity of the twentieth-century American economic miracle.

Likewise, Chancellor Otto von Bismarck echoed Lincoln's sentiments regarding the American Civil War and its roots in powerful banking interests:

> The division of the United States into federations of equal force was decided long before the Civil War by the high financial powers of Europe. These bankers were afraid that the United States, if they remained as one block, would attain economic

and financial independence which would upset their financial domination over the world.

Bismarck remarked at Lincoln's death:

> The death of Lincoln was a disaster for Christendom. There was no man in the United States great enough to wear his boots. I fear that foreign bankers with their craftiness and tortuous tricks will entirely control the exuberant riches of America and use it systematically to corrupt modern civilization. They will not hesitate to plunge the whole of Christendom into wars and chaos in order that the earth should become their inheritance.

Moreover, shortly before his assassination, Lincoln commented on centralized banking, "The Money Power (banks) preys upon the nation in times of peace and conspires against it in times of adversity. It is more despotic than monarchy, more insolent than autocracy, more selfish than bureaucracy." Following his tragic assassination, Congress revoked the Greenback Law and enacted the National Banking Act. The decision was made to retire greenbacks from circulation, as the paper notes returned to the Treasury in the form of tax payments. National banks became privately owned and notes once again bore interest.

The reader will recall how Lincoln vehemently opposed interest-bearing debt or currency. Arguably, the crooked National Banking Act set the stage for the Federal Reserve Act of 1913, which usurped much of the principles and the freedoms that so many valiant soldiers shed blood to protect. However, Lincoln's actions did reunite the nation, set the captives free, and sidestep globalist banking entanglements, albeit temporarily. Thomas Jefferson, Andrew Jackson, and Abraham Lincoln understood the toxic nature of central bank fiat money and endeavored as individuals to forever end the despotic rule of the global banking cartel.

Fourth Central Bank—The Federal Reserve

The Panic of 1907 reduced the value of the New York Stock Exchange by 50 percent. The stock market panic continued unabated from January 1904 to January 1908, punctuated with bank runs and corporate bankruptcies. Some sources blame the ensuing chaos on the limited market liquidity of several New York City banks. In many aspects, the panic closely resembled the 2008 economic malaise, even more so than the Great Depression.

Meantime, the task of saving the stock market, banking sector, and even New York City required Herculean efforts. Similar to the current wave of municipal troubles, in 1907 entire cities entered bankruptcy. In fact, a tidy $30 million bailout was needed in order for New York City to avoid bankruptcy.

Yet without a central bank lender of last resort, the task of shoring up liquidity fell upon the private banking sector, more specifically, JP Morgan. John Pierpont Morgan, a.k.a. JP Morgan, was credited with rescuing the U.S. Treasury in the previous market crisis. Arguably the most famous financial figure in American history, JP Morgan's skillful management of the railroad panic of 1893 secured his position at the helm of the rescue efforts in 1907.

In one of his most decisive and well-known operations, Morgan assembled the presidents of every leading bank and held them, for all practical purposes, hostage until they agreed to provide the necessary funds to shore up the economy. His commanding presence and somber gaze was enough to convince the 14 bank presidents to commit $24 million to the cause. The bold decision halted the stock market crash, including the demise of at least 50 brokerage houses. Yet to millions of Americans, it became patently clear that far too much economic power was wielded by one man. After all, from the perspective of the typical American, a financial monopoly too closely resembles a monarchy.

Still, nothing bends the iron will of the people like a good old-fashioned financial meltdown. The bank crisis of 1907 deserves much of the credit for the decision to open the fourth domestic central bank, the Federal Reserve.

The Central Bank from Jekyll Island According to G. Edward Griffin's classic tome, *The Creature from Jekyll Island*, in November 1910 the leading domestic financiers met in Georgia at the Jekyll Island Club. The attendees assembled under the official guise of "a duck hunt." Yet with memories of the disastrous 1907 market panic fresh in their minds, the true purpose of the collaboration was to lay the foundation of the Federal Reserve System.

To shield their true identities even from club servants, the participants only addressed one another by their first names. The list of attendees included the assistant secretary of the Treasury Department, Paul Warburg, a senior partner of the JP Morgan Company, as well as several other representatives of the moneyed class.

Coup d'état   Despite two solid years of stiff opposition in Congress, early in the morning on Monday, December 22, 1913, the Federal Reserve Act finally cleared Capitol Hill. President Woodrow Wilson signed the bill into law the next day. While the majority of Congress was sleeping at home or away for Christmas holiday celebrations, the covert legislation became a law. It was precisely under such a shroud of secrecy that the economic freedoms won by President Jackson, President Lincoln, and thousands of American heroes were lost.

Clearly, President Woodrow Wilson's failure to veto the Federal Reserve Act sealed the fate of the dollar. The legislation ultimately cost posterity over 95 percent of the purchasing power of each and every note issued. The nefarious act transferred control of the money supply from Congress, as defined in the U.S. Constitution, into the hands of the parasitic banking elite.

In an ironic twist, President Woodrow Wilson allegedly realized that he had been duped by the banking cartel. According to one source, after signing the Federal Reserve Act, President Wilson wrote:

> I am a most unhappy man. I have unwittingly ruined my country. A great industrial nation is controlled by its system of credit. Our system of credit is concentrated. The growth of the nation, therefore, and all our activities are in the hands of a few men. We have come to be one of the worst ruled, one of the most completely controlled and dominated Governments in the civilized world, no longer a Government by free opinion, no longer a Government by conviction and the vote of the majority, but a Government by the opinion and duress of a small group of dominant men.

Although some historians question the authenticity of the above statement, considering the Federal Reserve's track record, such an apology was certainly apropos.

The Fed Emperor Has No Clothes

This abbreviated overview of the American central banking system exposed the grand deception that has been foisted upon the nation. The overwhelming preponderance of evidence indicates that the masses have been duped. Not only is the Federal Reserve emperor without clothing, but the entire nation is disrobed. In order for the United States and the rest of the world to break free from globalist economic tyranny, ultimately the unconstitutional fractional-reserve banking system must be repealed and replaced with a sound gold and silver–based monetary system, as prescribed by the U.S. Constitution.

KEY POINT

In less than 100 years, the Federal Reserve has destroyed more than 95 percent of the dollar's purchasing power. Investors are advised to protect their wealth with tangible assets such as precious metals and energy investments.

Q&A

Listener Question #1: Doug expresses his concerns over the impossibly large national debt: "Chris, I've been enjoying your program for a couple of months now. Can you tell me how the pundits came up with the $53 trillion dollar national debt figure?"

Answer: Hello, Doug. You have every reason to be concerned by the national debt statistic: $53 trillion is comparable in size with each and every dollar created by individuals, business, and government programs in the United States over the course of four years. Simply put, the national debt can be expressed as roughly $175,000 for each man, woman, and child. That equates to approximately $700,000 for the typical family. Eventually, the debt must be paid in full or the dollar will devalue by a similar amount. Since the prospect of paying off the national debt is grim at best, I suggest protecting wealth with an investment in precious metals/energy. Thank you, Doug.

Listener Question #2: Mike from Vancouver says, "Dear Chris, firstly I would like to deeply thank you for an outstanding weekly performance. I have been listening religiously since I stumbled upon your show in mid-2007. I quite depend on you all—you have opened my eyes to certain realities that were opaque to me previously. Many thanks in advance.

"As a Canadian, I feel free to observe that Canada, financially at least, seems to go along with whatever the United States does. I frequently have entertaining chats with my local Keynesian banker, but I just can't seem to bring myself to be reassured by the so-called stability of the Canadian banking system, supposedly the envy of the world to hear him speak of it. The task I set myself every week is to translate your teachings.

"My question to you is twofold. Lately the Canadian dollar has been tanking against the greenback, despite the fact the U.S. dollar itself is streaking toward worthlessness relative to all things real. What does all this mean and when can I expect the recession or inflationary crisis to visibly find its way to Canada? I understand that the Federal Reserve is a nonregulated, privately owned financial entity run by a cabal of U.S. and international bank-sters. Is the Bank of Canada privately or publicly owned?"

Answer: Hello, Mike. Regarding your concerns over the soaring greenback, although the dollar is rising relative to most asset classes, I do not expect the uptrend to become a long-run event. The U.S. recession has temporarily contained inflation fears. Before the slowdown passes, I expect 10+ percent unemployment, continued home price declines, and a subdued stock market. Our Canadian neighbors will likely be visited by similar economic issues.

Regarding the differences between the Canadian central bank and the U.S. Fed, the Bank of Canada is actually owned by Canada, and it is a nonprofit institution. However, the U.S. central bank is the Federal Reserve System, which is not owned by "we the people." Instead it is owned by the 12 regional Federal Reserve Banks. In fact, shares of the member banks are informally traded. A primary difference between the Fed and a public corporation is that the board of governors is an independent government agency, whose members are appointed by the President with the consent of the Senate. In a nutshell, the Canadian central bank is a less insidious beast than the Fed. Few Americans are aware that their money supply is controlled by interests from outside the national borders. Thank you for the excellent questions, Mike.

GSEs and FDIC

LEARNING FROM RECENT MISTAKES

"A bank is a place that will lend you money if you can prove that you don't need it."

—Bob Hope (1903–2003)

To help revive the struggling U.S. economy during the Great Depression, President Franklin D. Roosevelt created the mortgage lender Fannie Mae. The concept was simple: Increased home ownership would benefit the nation as a whole. Owning a piece of Americana would encourage thrift and job/family stability and increase property tax revenues. Fannie Mae's cousin lender, Freddie Mac, received its congressional charter three decades later in the aftermath of the Vietnam War.

By the 2000s, Fannie Mae and Freddie Mac expanded far beyond what was originally intended. The government-sponsored enterprises (GSEs) guaranteed over half of all domestic mortgages, $6 trillion in total. The two behemoth hybrid lenders secured more home loans than all of the 8,500 FDIC-insured commercial banks and thrifts combined. The U.S. government had essentially become the landlord of over 30 million homes, approximately 100 million people. The house of cards was destined to collapse.

Meantime, in 2008, low-quality subprime loans and accounting gimmickry crushed the GSEs' share prices. Subprime debt further devastated several Wall Street investment banking icons. The balance sheets of once mighty Bear Stearns and Merrill Lynch were reduced to ashes practically overnight by toxic MBSs. Even the nation's largest financial institution, Bank of America, was up against the ropes. On the West Coast the financial chaos at the Indy-Mac lender led to bank runs. The mayhem threatened to sink the entire nation in true Icelandic fashion.

While officials were able to stem the initial credit crisis tide via $12 trillion in bailouts, there's now mounting evidence of renewed banking trouble. In April 2010, the Fed announced it would no longer support the financial sector with massive purchases of toxic MBSs. Plus the federal housing tax credit expired in the same month. While government policies are following a similar course as in the 1930s, unlike in the Great Depression, fighting stagflation with trillions of additional debt will merely postpone the reckoning day.

With a mountain of ARMs expected to reset from 2010 to 2012, the next wave of foreclosures is bound to impact the banking sector with at least as much force as the 2007 subprime dilemma. Will a second credit dilemma capsize the FDIC as it did during the S&L crisis? All signs point to a similar outcome. Until the ARM reset trouble passes in 2013, the national banking system will likely remain on shaky ground. Chapter 13 continues the investigation into the banking/credit crises beginning with an analysis of the effects of toxic debt on Wall Street.

Banking Bubble, Toil and Trouble

In October 2008, credit crisis shockwaves rattled the pillars of the entire global financial system. Internal financial turmoil lurked behind impressive Wall Street bank towers, reminiscent of Ayn Rand's *The Fountainhead*. Corrosive debt had reduced the formerly rock-solid banking foundation to sandy soil.

In the same manner that the subprime mortgage crisis bankrupted the major mortgage lenders, the credit crisis exacerbated the Wall Street bank collapse. The first high-profile domino to fall was UK bank Northern Rock. Next was investment bank Bear Stearns, which was soon followed by Lehman Brothers. However, it was the downfall of Fannie Mae and Freddie Mac that captured the spotlight. On Sept 7, 2008, the two largest mortgage lenders imploded. Saving the financial titans required the biggest government bailout in history, a staggering $5.3 trillion.

Grin and Bear It

Before the credit crisis became a full-blown mainstream event, the news was virtually devoid of stories regarding the impending disaster. That all changed as reports of trouble at Bear Stearns, the preeminent investment bank, made the headlines. Behind the scenes, Bear Stearns' management team was desperate to keep its two subprime hedge funds afloat. Unbeknownst to most investors, the High-Grade Structured Credit Strategies Fund and its sister group had acquired over $20 billion in highly toxic mortgage derivatives.

While the moniker "High-Grade Structured Credit Strategies" certainly inspires confidence, investors quickly discovered that a fancy title does not a sound investment make. Despite the reassuring nom de plume the fund was suddenly on the verge of insolvency. During the early innings of the credit crisis few people outside the industry had heard of a subprime mortgage. In fact, the entire sector was built on the faulty notion that house prices always increase in value. Ergo, the two Bear Stearns funds held $6 billion worth of subprime mortgage debt in the form of CDOs, that is, collateralized debt obligations. But soaring delinquencies and defaults on subprime mortgages sent MBS values into a tailspin. The bad bets culminated with a 22 percent quarterly loss for Bear Stearns.

Ironically, the once formidable Wall Street icon Bear Stearns had been a white knight lender during the famous $3.6 billion Long Term Capital Management bailout. But despite the chivalrous action, no such leniency was extended to Bear Stearns. Its troubles reached a crescendo when Merrill Lynch, a primary investor, demanded the return of $1 billion in collateral, post-haste. In response, Bear Stearns management requested additional time to reorganize the two ailing funds. But Merrill Lynch executives viewed the plea as a delay tactic and rejected the request. As a result, Bear Stearns mortgage bonds were auctioned off at pennies on the dollar, effectively delivering a death blow to the bank.

News of Bear Stearns' misfortune culminated with an industry wide tidal wave of mortgage debt redemptions. Officials at Bank of

America announced that anything was possible if a financial institution of such impeccable character as Bear Stearns could fail. The comment illustrates how oblivious top industry insiders were to the looming financial disaster.

The Die Is Cast

When Julius Caesar crossed the Rubicon River in 49 B.C., according to legend he uttered the phrase, "The die is cast!" (Latin: *jacta alea est!*) In essence the great general alerted his commanders that by crossing the boundary between Gaul and Roman territory he had broken the law and war with Rome was inevitable. In similar fashion, when Merrill Lynch executives failed to recognize the repercussions of the Bear Stearns debt fiasco, their fate was sealed. Risky MBS bets soon covered the Merrill Lynch balance sheet with blood-red ink.

Meantime, Bank of America CEO Kenneth Lewis agreed to purchase the troubled financial institution. Lewis's decision to acquire Merrill Lynch would come to be viewed as the worst blunder in a year rife with executive mistakes. The Bank of America balance sheet was already riddled with more holes than a firing range target. In fact, the bank was still reeling from the Countrywide Financial acquisition and its huge debt burden. In Ken Lewis's defense, he did attempt to back out of the Merrill Lynch deal. But ignoring his noblesse oblige, Treasury Secretary Hank Paulson twisted Lewis's arm.

Clearly, Merrill Lynch was deemed by government officials as "too big to fail." But perhaps "too toxic to survive" is a more appropriate sobriquet. The mountain of Merrill Lynch debt struck the hull of the nation's largest bank like a mountain-sized iceberg. Above deck it was business as usual. But in the captain's chambers, the silence was deafening. The Countrywide and Merrill acquisitions virtually guaranteed a Bank of America share crash. As the stock market deluge reached its penultimate nadir in 2008, Bank of America shares plunged 90 percent in value, threatening to capsize the vessel.

Financial Transparency (Truth)

Widely credited with slaying the 1970s inflation beast, Paul Volcker served as Fed chairman from 1979 to 1987. More recently, amid the credit crisis the respected economist announced that the United

States was experiencing an "unprecedented" financial crisis—more complex than any other in U.S. history. His dour view of the state of economic affairs quieted the cheering section for Federal Reserve Chairman Ben Bernanke and former Treasury Secretary Hank Paulson.

At a Columbia University Women's Economic Round Table in New York, Volcker said, "We are really going to have to rebuild this system from the ground up." Volcker's comments confirmed what many had suspected, that complex debt instruments, for example, MBSs, CDSs, and CDOs, actually reduced transparency by concentrating and concealing risks. He expressed his firm belief that bailouts created a moral hazard by increasing the expectation of future intervention. Volcker insisted that a far-reaching fiscal stimulus plan was necessary to shore up the ailing economy.

Dishonorable Discharge

In response to the global banking system meltdown, Federal Reserve Chairman Ben Bernanke had a more upbeat view of the domestic economy: "All banks are being challenged by credit conditions now. . . . The good news is that the banking system did come into this episode extremely well capitalized, extremely profitable." Bernanke commented further on the fragile economy, "Persistent strains in financial markets, rising joblessness and housing problems . . . ongoing strains in financial markets; declining house prices; a softening labor market; and rising prices of oil, food and some other commodities. . . . The possibility of higher energy prices, tighter credit conditions and a still-deeper contraction in housing markets all represent significant downside risks to the outlook for growth." In other words, expect unemployment, inflation as well as foreclosures to plague the economy. If only investors had known just how correct he was.

The Fed chairman's sobering assessment of the state of the economy caused an epidemic of fear and foreboding throughout Washington and on Wall Street. Treasury Secretary Henry Paulson and SEC Chairman Christopher Cox teamed up with Ben Bernanke to testify before the Senate Banking Committee. The gloomy meeting highlights included expectations of sluggish consumer spending and a weakening housing sector. Bernanke endorsed the Treasury secretary's plan, which granted the federal government power to shore up Fannie Mae and Freddie Mac with temporary loans. The maneuver amounted to the largest government bailout in history.

Government-Sponsored Enterprises (GSEs)—
Frankin-Mae and Frankin-Mac

Fannie Mae was originally founded in 1938 amid the Great Depression as part of President Franklin D. Roosevelt's plan to revive the struggling U.S. economy. Three decades later while the nation was grappling with the socioeconomic fallout of the Vietnam War, Freddie Mac received a congressional charter. The two government-sponsored enterprises (GSEs) guarantee over half of all domestic mortgages, $6 trillion in total. In fact, the mortgage burden far exceeds that of the combined banking sector, including all 8,500 FDIC-insured commercial banks and thrifts.

For decades the GSE partnership between the private and public sector created a highly liquid market for MBSs. The game of musical mortgages continued without a hitch until the housing bubble burst in 2007. Suddenly, crashing real estate prices and soaring unemployment threatened the entire process.

Financial Master and Commander

The late financial commentator Louis Rukeyser provided my first introduction to Jim Rogers's interesting climb to financial stardom. While working with George Soros at the Quantum Fund, Rogers rewarded clients with a 4,200 percent return on their initial investment. Jim Rogers's performance is even more staggering when compared with the 47 percent S&P 500 return over the same period. The spectacular record still stands as a monumental achievement.

Nonetheless, the expression "talk is cheap" is particularly apropos within the realm of market forecasts. Yet comments from professor and author Jim Rogers often prove to be the exception to the rule. On several occasions Rogers made startlingly accurate predictions on GSR. For example, when gold was trading hundreds of dollars below the millennial mark, Jim predicted that the yellow metal would soar to $1,000. The projection came to pass at the close of 2007, the same year of the forecast. Next, as gold was still trading near $1,000, Rogers insisted that the precious metal would crash before staging a recovery. In the fall of 2008, just as predicted, the king of currencies declined to $680 before building a solid base and soaring to $1,200. With such an impressive track record, his views are always noteworthy.

Meanwhile, in a GSR interview Rogers commented on the Fannie Mae and Freddie Mac dilemma. Rogers claimed that the Treasury Department plan to save Fannie Mae and Freddie Mac was an "unmitigated disaster." In another interview he further underscored the dangers of government intervention, "So we're going to bail out everybody else in the world. . . . it ruins the Federal Reserve's balance sheet and it makes the dollar more vulnerable and it increases inflation."

Accordingly, Rogers said the U.S. taxpayer would be saddled with tremendous debt if Congress agreed to the Fannie Mae/Freddie Mac bailout plan as proposed by Henry Paulson. As always Jim Rogers wasn't afraid to back up his opinion with his brokerage account. The financial master and commander not only shorted GSE shares but publicly announced his intentions to sell more in the event of a stock price rebound.

Moreover, Rogers's former partner and billionaire investor George Soros expressed his negative viewpoint on government bailouts. Soros said Fannie Mae and Freddie Mac faced a "solvency crisis, not liquidity [crisis]." The well-known hedge fund manager and author expected troubles to escalate. "This is a very serious financial crisis and it is the most serious financial crisis of our lifetime. . . . It is an idle dream to think that you could have this kind of crisis without the real economy being affected."

At the time, many viewed the comments from Rogers and Soros as overly pessimistic. Yet the natural progression of time and events confirmed their claims. Investors watched in horror as Fannie Mae and Freddie Mac shares collapsed. In fact, Fannie Mae's shares plunged from $20 to $0.20 in only six months. (See Figure 13.1.)

Jim Rogers made further comments on the major market event,

> These companies were going to go bankrupt if they hadn't stepped in to do something, and they would've gone bankrupt with all of the mistakes they've made. . . . What's going to happen when you put some Band-Aids on it for another year or two or three? What's going to happen three years from now when the situation's much, much, much worse . . . ? The U.S.

Figure 13.1   Fannie Mae Share Price Crash

Source: StockCharts.com.

economy is in a recession, possibly the worst since World
War II. . . . They're ruining what has been one of the greatest
economies in the world. . . . Bernanke and Paulson are bailing
out their friends on Wall Street but there are 300 million Americans that are going to have to pay for this.'

   Meanwhile, another investing legend, Warren Buffett, proclaimed that the rotund lady had sung for the two biggest mortgage
companies. According to the Oracle of Omaha Fannie Mae and
Freddie Mac "don't have any net worth." In an interview on CNBC
the 77-year-old chairman of Berkshire Hathaway said, "They were
able to borrow without any of the normal restraints. They had a
blank check from the federal government." Investors agreed with
Buffett's comments and promptly sold Fannie Mae and Freddie
Mac shares post-haste. On the heels of record home foreclosure
numbers, the wholesale liquidation crushed share prices by more
than 90 percent.

   Former Federal Reserve Chairman Alan Greenspan and Richmond Bank President Jeffrey Lacker soon joined in the chorus.
Greenspan and Lacker concurred with Buffett that the troubled
lenders of last resort should be nationalized. But former head of
the St. Louis Fed. William Poole wasn't convinced. Poole opined
that Freddie Mac was technically bankrupt and Fannie Mae was financially unsound. With half of all national mortgages outstanding
held by the GSEs, Poole the voice of reason, agreed with Jim

Rogers's viewpoint. Ultimately it would be the taxpayer who was stuck with the unprecedented $5 trillion bailout tab.

However, former Morgan Stanley strategist and head of the Traxis Partners LLC hedge fund Barton Biggs defended the government-sponsored bailout, "Fannie and Freddie are way too big and way too big a part of the mortgage system and really the American way of life to say 'Just let them go bankrupt.' . . . The Treasury is doing the right thing." Regardless of who is ultimately proven to be correct, one fact remains certain. The 95+ percent drop in GSE share price is prima facie evidence that mixing government inefficiencies with public companies is a blueprint for economic disaster.

Fool Me Twice

With the full support and backing of the U.S. Treasury, arguably the world's deepest pockets, for decades Fannie Mae and Freddie Mac supplied an endless stream of subprime mortgages. At the peak of the housing bubble, seemingly anyone who could fog a mirror received a mortgage. In essence the GSEs underwrote much of the MBS fiasco. In addition, artificially low interest rates further encouraged investment bankers to repackage and sell the surfeit Fannie and Freddie MBSs with high-interest markups. The perpetual influx of fresh government money fomented a vast pool of gullible home-debtors.

Meantime, the dream of perpetually higher prices ended in late 2006 with a housing bubble nightmare. The real estate crash revealed how the GSEs had lined the pockets of Wall Street debt peddlers at the expense of mortgage holders/taxpayers. Essentially, a handful of industry insiders dined on a grand banquet of profits while millions of families received foreclosure notices.

What Went Wrong?

Years of low-quality subprime loans and lax lending standards doomed Fannie Mae and Freddie Mac. Yet this fact alone fails to account for the brutal 90 percent share price plunge. The final death blow emanated from a far more selfish source. In order to secure annual bonuses, Fannie Mae and Freddie Mac executives fraudulently overstated earnings by underreporting subprime mortgage losses. This maneuver was the death knell for the GSEs. Thanks to intentionally inflated subprime valuations, the GSEs' books were as cooked as a Thanksgiving turkey. The fraudulent activity bankrupted the largest domestic lenders and cost taxpayers millions in related pension fund and retirement account losses as well as trillions in bailouts.

The United States of China

The $5 trillion bailout of Fannie Mae and Freddie Mac was by far the largest single action of its kind in American history. Virtually overnight the national debt doubled to $10.6 trillion. But the unprecedented government intervention wasn't enough to buoy the GSEs' stock prices. Shareholders stared in wide-eyed disbelief as shares plunged like a lead dirigible. The bailout had backfired. Instead of benefiting Americans, the beneficiaries of the GSE bailout were the bond holders, primarily the central banks of China and Japan.

Furthermore, although both GSEs' prospectuses indicate in no uncertain terms that company bonds are not backed by the U.S. government, hundreds of billions in bailout dollars were shipped offshore to compensate for the losses of our largest trading partners. As a result, the bailout became the greatest wealth transfer in American history. Put simply, 300 million American taxpayers were robbed of trillions of dollars by their own government.

FDIM: The Federal Deposit Insurance Mattress

Amid the 2008 economic fiasco, droves of nervous depositors lined up around IndyMac bank branches. On the second day of the crisis, at the Encino, California, branch irate IndyMac Bank customers demanded the return of their deposits. Eventually the police were summoned to suppress the crowd. Conjuring up memories of the Great Depression and John Steinbeck's *The Grapes of Wrath*, three police squad cars arrived to help subdue angry depositors.

After officially closing the doors on a Friday, IndyMac officials reopened the bank on the following Monday under the control of the Federal Deposit Insurance Corporation. With federal regulators at the helm, each depositor/victim was expected to speak with a customer service representative or branch manager before making a withdrawal. Lines outside branches became impossibly long with customers waiting up to seven hours before speaking with a bank official. Clearly the new requirement amounted to nothing more than stalling/intimidation tactics.

In fact, many depositors were sent away empty handed—told to return the next day. While nervous bank clients queued up at 1:30 A.M. the next morning, unbeknownst to many waiting in line, a few depositors had been given secret priority the day before. Thanks to the oversight, crowd tensions flared.

Although individual investor deposits of up to $100,000 were fully insured under the FDIC umbrella, those with funds beyond the $100,000 limit were justifiably concerned. In fact, of the 10,000 IndyMac patrons, a combined $1 billion was uninsured. Hundreds of IndyMac depositors found themselves in a far less enviable position than if they'd stuffed their dollars under an FDIM, a Federal Deposit Insurance Mattress.

Nevertheless, in 2008 every GSR listener with bank deposits in excess of $100,000 was encouraged to transfer funds to a solid FDIC-backed account. By the fall of 2008 the economic stabilization plan increased the $100,000 FDIC insurance cap for individual accounts to $250,000. The original warning still applies to everyone with funds above the $250,000 level.

While Bernanke Fiddled, the Banks Burned

According to legend, infamous Roman Emperor Nero fiddled as the majestic city was reduced to ashes. Historians view Nero as the culprit behind the fiery destruction of the city of seven hills. Just as the mythical Romulus slew his twin brother Remus for control of the city, some sources claim Nero betrayed Rome by encouraging the blaze in order to build an ostentatious palace atop the ruins. In like fashion, the roots of the 2008 global financial firestorm can be traced directly to the loose monetary policies of the Federal Reserve and the actions of Ben Bernanke and Hank Paulson.

By December 2008, Fed officials slashed the overnight lending rate down to a quarter of one point, the lowest level in its 95-year tenure. The Fed's actions spoke volumes. The stock market responded with a diatribe of its own—a 40 percent bloodletting from the peak.

To say that the 2007–2008 credit crises and housing implosion were unnerving is an understatement. Not surprisingly, restoration of public confidence in the financial system became a top government priority. Yet why did the economy require a confidence boost? Shouldn't the lone superpower have boundless economic confidence to spare? Destructive Fed policies were at least partially to blame.

Government of the People?

When quizzed in a Senate hearing as to who would ultimately pay for the bailout, Hank Paulson replied, "The government." But when a senator pressed further, Paulson admitted that it was the taxpayer and not the government who would pay the massive bailout bill. Perhaps the senator should have suggested that Hank "Robespierre" Paulson dip into his own humble $500 million personal savings account and make a noble contribution.

With bank balance sheets trampled underfoot like a rodeo clown, Treasury Secretary Hank Paulson was given the task of guarding the hen house. Who better to hire for the position than the wolf that accumulated $500 million? Clearly Paulson was the ideal public servant to relate to the plight of 100 million hard-working American families struggling to keep a roof over their heads and food on the table. Of course if the Treasury secretary had truly been concerned with the working and middle classes, the $700 billion dollar bailout, which morphed into $2 trillion, might have been funneled to those who needed help most. (See Figure 13.2.)

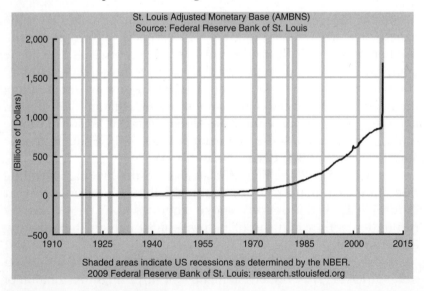

Figure 13.2 Bailout Funds

Furthermore, if one assumes that the $2 trillion bailout was justified and the government was forthright in its intentions to undo the foreclosure nightmare, then why weren't the millions of families facing default its primary beneficiaries? Instead, the first bailout action included the purchase of $250 billion worth of preferred shares in the nation's nine largest banks, a far less noble gesture. Clearly the funds were directed to the banks and bonuses of Paulson's former business colleagues.

Meanwhile, government officials insisted that the bank bailout would resolve credit crisis concerns by putting a floor under the share prices of the ailing sector. In fact, panic in the credit market did subside, somewhat. Bank shares rebounded from their capitulation lows and the Ted Spread gauge of credit market fear dropped nearly 100 basis points. Still, the long-term ramifications of the massive government spending will remain a major concern for several years.

By March 2010, more than 12 million families were upside down on their mortgages and facing the stark reality of foreclosure. Millions will be forced into default in 2010–2012 as options only ARMs and Alt-A mortgages recast to much higher rates. According to one *Wall Street Journal* article, 103 months, or eight and a half years, of unsold inventory is weighing down on the sector. The dire situation illustrates just how poorly the government managed the bailout funds.

Moreover, assuming a typical foreclosure of $200,000, the $2 trillion bailout package was adequate to pay in full all 10 million upside down mortgages. Put differently, the money spent bailing out Wall Street fat cats was sufficient to pay off every reasonably priced mortgage delinquency in the country. In the final analysis, a few hundred bankers and investors were thrown into plush lifeboats while 10 million families, 40+ million Americans, were tossed overboard into the icy ocean water.

However, paying off millions of mortgages is not necessary to save the economy from ruin. Instead of bailing out the banks, a $2 trillion trust fund is a far more practical alternative. At 5 percent annual interest alone, $100,000,000,000 or $100 billion dollars would sufficiently stem the tide of unwanted foreclosures, defaults, and bank closures. Within four years, the option ARM meltdown and related crises would have passed and an economic recovery would have enabled millions to resume paying their monthly mortgage obligations. Just as importantly, the original $2 trillion could be returned to the U.S. Treasury.

Yet the government has chosen a far less savory course of treatment. More than half of U.S. mortgages will eventually be underwater. ARM loan resets will continue to climb, in turn increasing the monthly payment burden of millions of families. Plus thanks to the inflationary effects of massive government bailouts, inflation in the form of higher heating fuel, gasoline, electricity, transportation, food, health insurance, interest charges, and taxes will send even the most prime mortgage holder into default.

Consequently, most mortgage holders will be forced to send in the door keys and simply walk away from their debt nightmare. The typical taxpayer, who benefited least from the housing boom and suffered most from the crash, will ultimately pay the full price of the bank bailout.

Chapter Bailout

For 70 years, strict lending standards diverted toxic mortgage river water away from the banking system tributaries. Yet by the year 2000, lax lending standards and easy credit dissolved a gaping hole in the protective river embankment. Credit subsequently poured through the domestic financial arteries like the mighty Mississippi river. The entire country was inundated with a 100-year credit flood, which gave rise to the greatest global housing bubble in history.

However, the credit crisis of 2008 drained the flood waters, leaving little more than water-logged MBS debris. But instead of allowing the excess credit to evaporate naturally, Fed and Treasury officials opened the liquidity spigots beyond capacity—once again flooding the financial system.

Clearly Fed officials are repeating the same Keynesian policy mistakes as in the 1930s. But, what officials fail to recognize is that conditions are truly different this time. During the 1930s, the nation was an industrial powerhouse. Eighty years later, the economy is shackled with impossibly high debt levels and a decimated industrial base. Against the backdrop of such appalling conditions, a 1930s style course of treatment will only delay the day of reckoning.

Conversely, had a laissez-faire monetary policy been chosen as outlined by Ludwig von Mises and Friedrich von Hayek, the natural economic equilibrium would have already been restored. Although the government is implementing a faulty action plan, there is still time for individual investors to secure their financial future with precious metals investments.

KEY POINT

The national banking system will likely remain under considerable stress until at least 2013. Until the ARM reset trouble passes, bank funds in excess of $250,000 should be transferred to alternate FDIC-backed savings accounts.

Q&A

Listener Question #1: An anonymous caller says, "Hello, Chris. Shouldn't FDIC Chair Sheila Bair's decision to raise the individual savings account insurance cap from $100,000 to $250,000 help alleviate depositors' concerns?"

Answer: Hello, caller. You are correct that the FDIC has agreed to raise the individual account protection threshold to $250,000. However, the big unknown looming over the FDIC is just how many banks will shut their doors in the next few years. If the banking crisis gets out of hand, the FDIC reserves will be stretched to the breaking point. Congress and the Treasury Department will be forced to bail out the FDIC.

This is a new twist on an old Ponzi scheme. As long as investor confidence remains high enough, FDIC protection will suffice. But since most banks loaned out a huge proportion of their funds with practically zero reserves, panicky investors could make a run on the banks and threaten the entire process. Frankly, I'm surprised the system has held up as long as it has.

Furthermore, in 2008, reports of empty ATMs—completely devoid of cash—were commonplace. I refer to this as a run on ATMs. Eventually, the daily withdrawal limit may decline from the typical $500 dollar maximum to $100 or less. In the worst case scenario, bank holidays would freeze all ATM funds.

An alternative to private banks is the home-based savings account. Since most banks offer negligible interest rates, which fail to cover even the lost purchasing power caused by inflation, the opportunity cost of a home safe is insignificant. Once the smoke clears, funds can then be easily returned to savings accounts, money markets, and CDs. Thank you for the interesting question, caller.

Fed Speak

DECIPHERING FED COMMENTS

"As an ex-banker and one who has scuttled quite largely about this country of ours, I give you my solemn word of honor that I have never seen any other class more corrupt, conscienceless, and thieving than bankers."

—Jack Woodford

The Fed FOMC meeting is comparable to an economic Super Bowl. Investors rely on experts to decipher the cryptic phrases and terminology that emerge from the accompanying statements. Known as Fed Speak, the convoluted rhetoric has befuddled even the wisest of interpreters. Why do the FOMC rate-setting events captivate the markets and traders alike? The key overnight lending rate is a determining factor in market liquidity/economic output. Plus, the accompanying statement offers insights into future Fed rate intervention.

Still, for most people deciphering the Fed Speak drivel proves far too mundane a task. Fortunately, a simple alternative method for understanding the latest Fed Speak gibberish can be accessed via the Internet. Will Ben Bernanke and company hold rates steady or raise the overnight lending rate? By simply navigating the Web browser to the Fed website everyone has access to the answer via a free, remarkable tool for determining future FOMC rate decisions.

Armed with the Fed Speak/Fed Funds basics, the reader is prepared for an investigation into the recent unconventional market activities. For example, the Fed slashed rates abruptly during the 2008–2009 market meltdown. Yet the emergency 50–75 basis points cut in the benchmark lending rate was announced well in advance on GSR. In similar fashion, using the simple rules outlined in this section, the reader will never again be surprised by sudden FOMC decisions.

Chapter 14 begins with a simple Fed Speak lesson, including an excerpt from an actual FOMC meeting statement. Next the reader is transformed into an instant Fed rate prognosticator to the amazement of friends, family, and colleagues by means of a few basic guidelines. The section concludes with an anecdotal yet significant glimpse into the $500 trillion credit derivatives threatening the entire economic system.

Fed Speak

Amid the 1,000 known global dialects, Fed Speak distinguishes itself as the most bewildering of all languages. Economists and traders alike spend countless hours mulling over the implications of Fed Speak written within FOMC meeting statements. Of all the Fed chiefs, the most gifted speaker of this cryptic parlance is undoubtedly former Federal Reserve Chairman Sir Alan Greenspan. At this very moment endless hours of the "Maestro's" mind-numbing Fed Speak video footage is racing away from the earth at the speed of light. In fact, the enigmatic messages have now passed beyond the boundaries of our solar system and entered the vast cosmic void of the Milky Way. His words will likely come in contact with an alien species. The human race may be saved from invasion thanks to the difficulty in deciphering the Fed testimonies. On the other hand, the earth may be instantly vaporized by a far advanced race of beings, desperate to shield the galactic federation from a Fed Speak epidemic.

Nevertheless, to mere terrestrially bound beings, Fed Speak is a cipher that must be decoded. Shrouded within the enigmatic phrases are hints to the Fed chief's economic agenda. Like a humorous scene from the movie *Monty Python and the Holy Grail*, the market landscape is littered with the carcasses of unfortunate speculators who incorrectly translated Fed Speak. One cannot help but wonder if the Fed officials themselves truly understand their own gibberish.

Yet to the trained ear, much can be gleaned from Fed Speak. Indeed, any language can be learned given enough time and practice. The GSR Rosetta stone has accelerated the process with the discovery of a few key phrases, basic terms such as *dovish*, that is, the willingness of FOMC members to cut rates, and *hawkish*, a predisposition toward rate hikes. The terms are important components of every investor's repertoire.

It's All Greek to Me

Eight times each year, Fed officials, led by Dr. Ben Bernanke, meet to determine the FOMC overnight lending rate. The event determines the overnight rate for the shortest term government bond that is only available to financial institutions. When the Fed lowers the rate, liquidity is said to increase, which is generally a positive for the stocks and commodities markets. On the contrary, a rate hike tends to absorb liquidity, which in turn puts downward pressure on market prices. Investors monitor the accompanying statements closely for clues to future rate bias. The following quote was derived from an actual Fed statement:

> Strains in financial markets have increased significantly and labor markets have weakened further. Economic growth appears to have slowed recently, partly reflecting a softening of household spending. Tight credit conditions, the ongoing housing contraction, and some slowing in export growth are likely to weigh on economic growth over the next few quarters.
>
> Over time, the substantial easing of monetary policy, combined with ongoing measures to foster market liquidity, should help to moderate economic growth. The downside risks to growth and the upside risks to inflation are both of significant concern to the Committee. The Committee will monitor economic and financial developments carefully and will act as needed to promote sustainable economic growth and price stability.

As far as the typical investor is concerned, the previous Fed statement might as well have been written in Navajo, an American Indian language. Given the fact that the Fed arguably wields more power than the U.S. president, it is essential to make Fed rhetoric comprehensible to every investor. Following each FOMC decision, on GSR I translate the accompanying statement for radio listeners. With a little practice the doublespeak can be transformed into investing nuggets of value. For example:

Fed Speak Excerpt #1: "Strains in financial markets have increased significantly and labor markets have weakened further. Economic growth appears to have slowed recently, partly reflecting a softening of household spending. Tight credit conditions, the ongoing housing contraction . . . "

Translation: Thanks to the housing bubble implosion, MBS meltdown, and record foreclosures, the United States is now facing a financial depression, which threatens to topple the financial markets.

Fed Speak Excerpt #2: "Over time, the substantial easing of monetary policy, combined with ongoing measures to foster market liquidity, should help to moderate economic growth."

Translation: Although the Fed lowered interest rates sharply, officials have lost control of the economy. Wall Street investment banking icons such as Lehman Brothers, Merrill Lynch, and Bear Stearns crashed like lead dirigibles.

In an ironic twist, the last Fed statement was issued before the market crash of 2008. While the Fed should have extended funds to banks in response to the credit crises, instead officials held rates firm amid boos and jeers from the New York Stock Exchange trading floor. By the time that the end was nigh for many top banks, the forthcoming FOMC rate cuts were of little to no avail.

Federal Funds Forecasts

On the days leading up to an FOMC rate announcement, experts appear as guests on business TV shows, offering rate projections. While they often provide compelling arguments in support of their views, on many occasions commentators have supplied inaccurate forecasts and often fall short of the mark.

Conversely, for almost five years, GSR listeners have received startlingly accurate predictions of upcoming FOMC rate announcements. Instead of listening to the endless pontification of talking

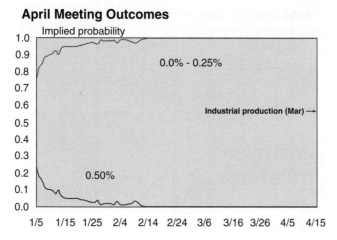

April Meeting Outcomes

Figure 14.1   April 2010 Meeting Outcomes

heads and Fed governors, GSR focuses like a laser on the Fed Funds futures contracts. When investors make bets with hard cash, the markets data is most valuable.

So without the use of Fed Speak or complicated terminology, the three Fed Funds futures contract graphs in this chapter show the likely outcomes of the next three FOMC meetings with a high degree of probability.

Figure 14.1 shows the most likely outcome of the April 2010 FOMC meeting. At the time that the graph was created, the likelihood of rates staying put at the current 0–0.25 percent was 100 percent. The odds of a rate hike to 0.50 percent, was zero. The extremely high probability of the numbers suggest, with near certainty, that the dovish Fed will hold rates steady in April.

In Figure 14.2, the odds of a rate hike at the June FOMC meeting actually increase, albeit fractionally. The chance of rates holding at the current level of 0–0.25 percent dropped from 100 percent to 95 percent. Next, the odds placed on a rate hike to 0.50 percent increase from 0 percent to 5 percent. If we add up the change of both probabilities, investors in the Fed Funds contract are 90 percent confident that the Fed will hold rates steady at the June FOMC meeting.

Figure 14.3 reveals that the odds of a rate hike at the August FOMC meeting increased beyond the June meeting figures. The

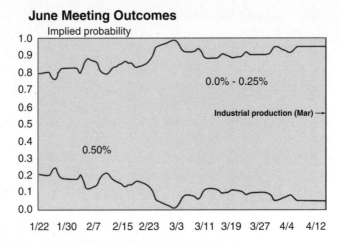

Figure 14.2   June 2010 Meeting Outcomes

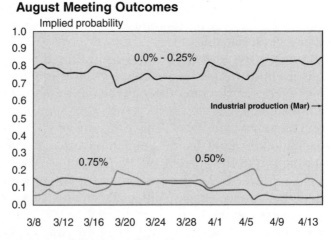

Figure 14.3   August 2010 Meeting Outcomes

likelihood of rates remaining fixed at 0–0.25 percent dropped from 95 percent to 85 percent. Next, the odds of a rate hike to 0.50 percent increase from 0 percent to 10 percent. When the shift in both probabilities is combined, investors are 75 percent confident that the Fed will hold rates steady at the August FOMC meeting.

Plus a new metric is included in the August meeting outcomes, the odds of a rate hike to 0.75 percent. Although the chance of such a big jump in rates is only 5 percent, it does reflect a shift in investor sentiment that higher rates may be forthcoming.

Judging by the probabilities outlined in Figures 14.1–14.3, the next three FOMC meetings will be nonevents. Not until August do the odds of a rate hike climb to 25 percent. But even the 25 percent bias is subject to daily fluctuations. Much can change in a few days, let alone five months. Within a few weeks' time, the August meeting outcomes could drop to 10 percent or less. The key point to glean from the graphs is the big picture: The Fed is likely to hold rates steady over the course of the next several months.

No longer must the reader be confused by Fed Speak. Instead, a quick glance at the Fed Funds futures contracts holds the key to impressing friends, relatives, professors, and co-workers. Simply shift the discussion to the upcoming FOMC rate decision and dazzle your comrades with the most accurate forecast in the room, perhaps even besting the business talk show host of your choice. Readers are encouraged to navigate to and bookmark the source of the charts. The Web page is updated daily in advance of all FOMC meetings: http://www.clevelandfed.org/research/data/fedfunds/index.cfm

Ben "Gutenberg" Bernanke and Hank "Bazooka" Paulson

As the credit crisis unfolded in early 2008, I announced on GSR an impending emergency 50–75 basis points cut in the benchmark lending rate was imminent. Right on cue, the Fed complied with an unconventional half point reduction. "Gutenberg" Bernanke and "Bazooka" Paulson had focused far too long on the inflation specter and were subsequently forced to play catch up via blitz-like rate cuts. Considering the devastating credit collapse, crashing home prices, as well as stricter lending standards for credit cards, mortgages, business loans, and collage loans, the dumbfounded duo simply had no remaining option other than to slash rates.

Correspondingly, when businesses and individuals lose access to easy credit and loans, stagflation shock waves are certain to reverberate throughout the economic landscape. By December 2008, the credit contraction provided more than ample evidence in support of the "stag" in the stagflation hypothesis. Furthermore, the Money Zero Maturity (MZM) and related money supply gauges revealed an astounding 33 percent contraction.

Additionally, in order to bail out the banking system, the government required carte blanche authority to print money via quantitative easing. Although credit was for all intents and purposes extinct, deflation as defined by a major contraction of the money and credit supply was improbable for any meaningful length of time. The sharp price decline in highly leveraged markets was simply distorted due to huge margin calls and related wholesale liquidation. Inflation was still present as revealed by solid prices at the gas pump, as well as grocery bills that never dropped much in price but merely stopped advancing. Every day goods and services remained stubbornly high amid the rubble and ashes of the 2008 crash.

However, a few mainline pundits continued to pound the table over the deflationary effects of lower commodities prices. In reality, the credit contraction vastly reduced the funds available to the consumer, businesses, and financial institutions. The resulting lack of liquidity temporarily stifled the advance. The inflation/deflation debate was ultimately resolved as gold reached a new record high above the four-digit point in 2009. For the small and discouraged band of remaining deflationists who continued to cling to the fallacious belief of crumbling domestic prices, the warning shot across the bow was $1,200+ gold. Amid the greatest financial shakedown since the Great Depression, the yellow metal had finally reclaimed its birthright as the king of all currencies.

In order to offset the damaging effects of the credit crisis, in October 2008 the Congress agreed to a $700 billion economic stabilization plan, which eventually climbed to $2 trillion. Plus the European central bank (ECB) promised $2 trillion to help shore up the ailing banking system. The result was antideflationary, that is, highly inflationary. The Fed's/ECB's careless measures compare with tossing gasoline on the economic barbeque. The resulting inflationary bonfire halted the credit crisis; however, the massive inflation flare-up threatens to consume the global economy.

Saving for a Rainy Decade

Many forward-looking economists insist that the days of global dollar hegemony are numbered. Just as the pound sterling ceased to dominate the global economy early in the last century, the influence of the greenback is beginning to wane. The ongoing decline in dollar purchasing power presents an enticing job opening for a new currency. One possible candidate is the Chinese yuan.

Despite angry protests to the contrary amid an increasingly xenophobic political atmosphere, China's economy does share many similarities with that of the United States during its early ascent to superpower status. An important precursor to the American global reserve currency monopoly was robust domestic savings and investment. However, decades of domestic consumerism dropped the savings rate from near 10 percent per capita to below zero. During the credit crisis, for the first time in national history, Americans spent nearly their entire salaries. Conversely, the typical Chinese saves a remarkable 20 percent or more.

Moreover, the United States and much of the developed nations of the world continue to reel from the effects of the 2008 thermonuclear debt bomb. When credit becomes tight, rather than borrowing more money consumers and businesses must instead pay down debt. Under typical recession conditions, debt repayment is deemed to be the natural progression of events. But following decades of debt accumulation the stock market crash and housing disaster may merely be preludes to much more dire events. It appears that the credit crisis could be the defining moment for the economy, perhaps leading to a doomsday-like scenario.

Furthermore, another sword of Damocles looms over the geo-economy. Due to decades of Keynesian and monetarist policies as well as lax regulation, more than half a quadrillion dollars of illiquid credit derivatives, credit default swaps, and mortgage-backed securities are threatening the entire global economic system with collapse. The worldwide derivatives threat amounts to every dollar created in the United States for nearly 100 years. Clearly, the Fed and most major central banks have embarked upon a destructive course, which can only culminate in the greatest economic collapse in all of recorded history.

Wrap Up

Although Fed Speak is a challenging language, every investor can benefit by adding a few key phrases to his or her repertoire. Another useful tool in the investor's arsenal should be the Fed Funds contract outcomes. With a bit of practice, the reader will be able to anticipate the Fed's next move, to the surprise and delight of many. Lastly, with an interest rate hike looming on the horizon, the ability to anticipate the sea change affecting half of one quadrillion dollars of illiquid/unregulated credit derivatives now threatening the global economic system, may prove to be a useful skill indeed.

KEY POINT

The federal funds futures contracts provide simple to grasp predictions of upcoming FOMC rate decisions. Readers are encouraged to visit/bookmark the Web page: http://www .clevelandfed.org/research/data/fedfunds/index.cfm

---

Q&A

Listener Question #1: George says, "It seemed as though a month ago numerous economists and newsletter writers believed that the domestic economy would remain in a period of inflation. But it appears we are currently in a deflationary environment. How do you think the next couple of years will play out? I recently heard the following potential scenario could unravel: First: a threat of deflation (now); second: inflation; third: real deflation; fourth: hyperinflation."

Answer: Hello, George. The credit crunch caught millions of investors off guard. As a result, several markets, including commodities, experienced severe downturns. The event was a temporary anomaly that offset much of the government money printing. Eventually, due to bailouts, quantitative easing, and low lending rates, inflation pressures will overwhelm credit destruction. The result will be an explosive move higher in commodities and precious metals prices.

Listener Question #2: Jim says, "Thanks for all your time and effort in keeping your listening audience on the cutting edge of wise investing. I do feel sorry for the accepted Keynesian philosophy permeating our culture today. It has already caused many heartaches and I'm afraid it will cause many more. After following your stock 'picks' for a while, I have jumped in with both feet and added most of them to my portfolio. It's a gas (no pun intended) when I find that one of your new recommendations is already in my portfolio.

Speaking of your picks, upon your recommendation I recently added Amerigas. While studying the stock I ran across one of its competitors, Ferrellgas (FGP). It looks promising—especially with an 8.8 percent dividend. Is it on your radar screen at all? I'm wondering what your take is on that stock. It looks pretty sound to me. Keep up the good work. Thanks, Jim."

Answer: Hello, Jim. Since I hand tailor each portfolio in an attempt to keep the individual stock betas as balanced as possible, I would prefer to view FGP in the context of at least two other stocks. The *Spotlight Picks* newsletter portfolio has trounced the indexes with outstanding returns. I credit the success in part to the solid fundamental scores of each stock and strong dividend yields. Please sign up for the free newsletter. Thank you, Jim.

Listener Question #3: Adam from Australia says, "I really enjoy the show. I've been listening via iTunes for a year now. The two-hour program really fits well with my weekly two-hour commute to my remote clients.

I am particularly interested in your real estate discussions and try to correlate your information on the U.S. market conditions with my local property market in Australia. It's a great mind-expanding exercise.

Answer: Hello, Adam. Great to know you found us. I also enjoy listening to business talk radio while driving. Regarding real estate, the English-speaking world is in dire straits. Real estate was our biggest game, as Professor Nial Ferguson is fond of saying. Nearly everyone had a hand in the cookie jar, euphemistically speaking. Wherever there are high debt levels and tricky toxic loans, a housing bubble will be found. Much of what you hear on the broadcast will remain relevant for years to come for our Aussie listeners as well. Thank you, Adam.

CHAPTER 15

Banks and Bailouts

PRESERVING WEALTH

"If you owe the bank $100, that's your problem. If you owe the bank $100 million, that's the bank's problem."

—Jean Paul Getty

At the onset of the credit crisis of 2008–2009, tricky toxic mortgages concealed the looming threat from most banking professionals. However, the multi-trillion-dollar debt firestorm that followed increased the FDIC troubled bank list from 90 to an astounding 702 by February 2010.

Meantime, the investment banks had regularly employed 40–1 leverage. By the end of summer 2008 profits at all 8,500 FDIC-insured banks collapsed by 86 percent. Wall Street legend Bear Stearns was the first to fall to the leverage battle-ax, followed closely by Lehman Brothers, Merrill Lynch, and the nation's largest insurer, AIG. By 2009 the remnants of the shattered banking industry held less than 5 percent in reserves. Much of the remaining 95 percent was tied to nonperforming loans, such as foreclosures/worthless MBSs. Although banks admitted to and wrote off $1 trillion of bad debts, several trillion dollars in losses have yet to be recognized. Wall Street was desperate for cash/emergency loans. Echoes of the old adage, "What's the price of money, Shylock?" were heard throughout the trading floor.

In response, the Fed chairman came to the rescue of the Wall Street elite with three sizable rate cuts. The moves sent the once mighty lending rate to practically zero for the first time in the Fed's 95-year tenure. Congress also implemented emergency damage control measures via the Economic Stabilization Plan, which directed one-third of the $700 billion funds to U.S. bank shares. Bank stocks understandably reacted favorably to the huge sum of government money chasing the fixed number of shares.

Chapter 15 examines the 2008–2009 banking sector collapse in detail, utilizing several revealing graphs to illustrate the degree to which high-flying banks and stocks crashed, including Wells Fargo, which actually survived the ordeal fully intact. The next section outlines the widely varying opinions concerning the $700 million–$2 trillion emergency bailout plan, including comments from the ever skeptical trio, Jim Rogers, George Soros, and Warren Buffett, plus a 2008 proposal from GSR, which urged the use of a bailout trust fund alternative. Interest from the fund alone was sufficient to halt 100 percent of all home foreclosures, in turn saving the families who most needed help instead of the recklass banking sector.

Red Sky at Morning, Banker's Warning

The ancient axiom "Red sky at night, sailor's delight, red sky at morning, sailor's warning" has remained a simple, yet accurate weather forecasting system for thousands of years. Even as far back as the time of the New Testament, the observation was well known. According to Matthew XVI: 2–3, "When in evening, ye say, it will be fair weather: For the sky is red. And in the morning, it will be foul weather today; for the sky is red and lowering."

Interestingly, the basis of the elementary forecasting technique is founded in solid science. The occasional reddish hue in the morning or evening sky is caused by high levels of dust particulates circulating throughout the atmosphere. The dusty air indicates low moisture levels. Since weather patterns generally travel from west to east, a red sunset suggests a dry weather front is approaching, hence "Red sky at night, sailor's delight."

Conversely, a reddish tint in the eastern sunrise indicates that a dry dusty front has passed and more moist air is approaching. High humidity tends to accompany thunderstorms and rough seas. Hence the saying, "Red sky at morning, sailor's warning."

In similar fashion, the financial industry quickly adopted its own twist on the ancient saying: "*Red ink* at morning, *banker's* warning." A multi-trillion-dollar toxic debt storm front led to the highest number of problem banks in years. From April through June of 2008, federally insured banks and savings institutions' earnings collapsed from $36.8 billion a year to a dismal $5 billion. In turn bank profits plunged by 86 percent, according to an FDIC report, and 8,500 FDIC-insured institutions and thrifts set aside a record $50.2 billion to cover losses from defaulted mortgages and various loans in the second quarter of 2008.

To the Emergency Helicopter, Ben

In 2008 amid the credit crisis fallout, numerous banks began a desperate search for Federal Reserve emergency loans. In response, Fed Chairman Ben Bernanke came to Wall Street's rescue with three unexpected rate cuts. The move was viewed as a desperate attempt to stabilize the troubled banking sector and stock market. The first surprise shift in bias involved a huge 75 basis points cut, which was soon followed by a half point reduction. An additional 75 basis point drop brought the once mighty lending rate to practically zero for the first time in the Fed's 95-year history. Additionally, in mid-2008 the Fed dropped its emergency lending rate, offered only to banks, by half a point.

Clearly, Fed officials hoped that by slashing the prime lending rate, banks and lenders would resume the process of extending loans and credit, the very lifeblood of a fiat currency–based economy. By revitalizing the ailing banking sector and ramping up consumer spending, the economic engine could once again fire on all eight cylinders. Yet even with the unprecedented $700 billion economic bailout, banks and financial institutions seemed intent upon stalling the recovery plans. Weary of lending to struggling consumers and ailing corporations, most chose instead to hoard cash, including government funds, refusing to lend to all but the safest borrowers.

Furthermore, FDIC officials were clearly troubled with the dangerous debt exposure in the financial sector. Of particular concern were toxic ARMs, construction loans in overbuilt areas, as well as preferred stock in Fannie Mae and Freddie Mac. Dodgy debt threatened the balance sheets of thousands of domestic banks and thrifts. Currently the number of loans classified as troubled assets, 90 days or more past due is rising briskly. The worrisome figure represents the first time since 1993 that the percentage of total risky loans has climbed above 2 percent. The FDIC oversees the industry-funded reserves used to protect individual accounts of up to $250,000 per deposit.

As the *Titanic* domestic economy rounds the harrowing Cape Horn peninsula, the next major threat is $5 trillion in FDIC-insured deposits and $2.5 trillion in uninsured deposits. Although the FDIC raised its insurance limit, few passengers are aware that the economic vessel has already taken on considerable water below deck and is in jeopardy of capsizing.

By early 2008, the sunrise seen from atop Wall Street's lofty towers was blood red—it was time for bankers to be warned. Toxic MBSs had exposed local and regional banks to enormous risks. Goliath financial institutions carrying huge portfolios filled with debt tipped torpedoes were the biggest threat. For instance, Florida's largest lender, BankUnited, with 85 branches in 13 counties and total assets of $14.2 billion, reported a $200 million loss in the summer of 2008. An astounding 60 percent of its assets were invested in option ARMs. Most option ARMs are now expected to enter default. BankUnited executives watched in horror as its nonperforming loans soared 770 percent in only 12 months and its share price collapsed by 90 percent over the same period.

Moreover, BankUnited was not alone in its troubles. The subprime dilemma quickly morphed into a credit crisis, spreading to every bank with risky debt exposure. Thanks to the acquisition of Countrywide in 2008, the nation's former largest home lender, Bank of America, held $25.4 billion in option ARMs. Only one in four of the borrowers were paying interest due on the loans, while 12 percent were at least 90 days late on payments. By 2010 the numbers were far worse.

Wachovia was yet another major option ARMs casualty. Shareholders and employees suffered thanks to the acquisition of Golden West Financial and its $122 billion in option ARMs, at the peak of the real estate bubble in 2006.

Meanwhile, the fall of major lender IndyMac Bancorp taxed the FDIC far more than anticipated. After IndyMac was seized by the FDIC, a Federal Deposit Insurance Corporation spokesman admitted that the July 11, 2008, failure would cost nearly $9 billion, well above the original $4–$8 billion projection. IndyMac became the second largest U.S. bank default in national history, following the collapse of the Continental Illinois National Bank in 1984.

Safe as Money in the Bank?

The time-honored axiom "safe as money in the bank" has suddenly disappeared from everyday lingo on the Street. Banks and broker-ages alike are reeling from the same toxic sludge that sank hundreds of mortgage lenders in 2007. The banking index is viewed as a primary indicator of overall national economic health. According to the composite, as of 2008, over 75 percent of the banking sector's stock value disappeared in only one year. With thousands of U.S. banks facing disaster due to shaky loans, the 85 components of the S&P financial sector declined $1.3 trillion in value following the 2007 market peak.

In October 2008, a sea change occurred in public opinion regarding the safety of bank accounts. As confidence in banks plunged to new lows, a simultaneous boom in home safe sales was reported by retailers. Fear of further financial sector trouble was behind the huge sales increase. Many Americans had rediscovered a secure and cost-effective banking alternative. Readers are strongly encouraged to direct their Web browsers to Amazon.com. Basic floor safes with digital keypads are highly desirable and may be purchased and delivered for as little as $100. Why not create your own, personalized, anonymous home bank account? The money you save might be your own.

Despite banking woes, reports show that many depositors still refuse to make the switch to safer institutions. What could possibly dissuade an individual from shifting funds at risk to a sound bank? Common answers include lower interest rates, penalties for early withdrawal, paperwork, and related inconveniences involved with transferring savings to a new institution.

However, the cost of inaction is high and collecting interest on lost capital is particularly challenging. Warren Buffett's laws of investing apply: Rule number one, don't lose money. Rule number two, memorize rule number one. Bankrate.com offers free bank ratings to help decide the safest place to park capital.

Wall Street Tremors

Although hundreds of bank dominoes fell in the long row of credit crisis obelisks, as late as 2007 and early 2008, few banking

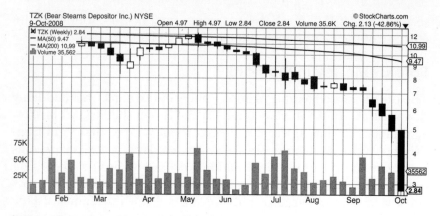

Figure 15.1   Bear Stearns Share Plunge

Source: StockCharts.com.

professionals seemed to recognize the atypical nature of the dilemma. In fact, the debt time bombs were so well masked that the
task of identifying the mountain of debt was impractical at best and
at worst, impossible.

Not perhaps since the 1930s had the general populace been so
fixated on Wall Street's woes. Bear Stearns was the first to implode
along with its stock price (see Figure 15.1).

Next, the nation's fourth-largest investment bank, Lehman
Brothers, filed for bankruptcy protection, sending its shares into
the abyss (see Figure 15.2).

Figure 15.2   Lehman Share Plunge

Source: StockCharts.com.

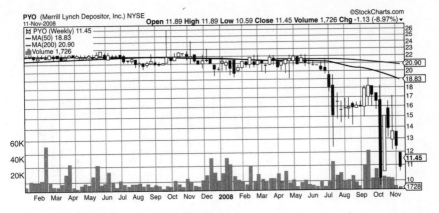

Figure 15.3 Merrill Lynch Share Plunge
Source: StockCharts.com.

Then Merrill Lynch found itself on the chopping block (see Figure 15.3).

Next to fall, the nation's largest insurer, AIG, plunged like an asteroid from its former heavenly orbit (see Figure 15.4).

Then banking behemoth Wachovia saw its share price drop from $23 to $1.23 in merely one week. Shares subsequently rebounded to $5 on news that Wells Fargo had bested a $2 billion Citigroup offer for Wachovia. Anecdotally, Wells Fargo's stock price

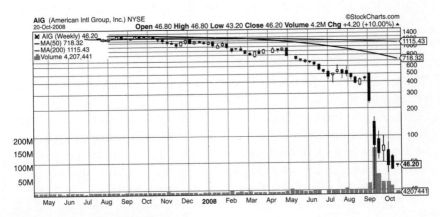

Figure 15.4 AIG Share Plunge
Source: StockCharts.com.

Figure 15.5   Wells Fargo's Shares Strength

Source: StockCharts.com.

held up remarkably well throughout the entire ordeal. Wells Fargo never swallowed the toxic debt poison, as seen in Figure 15.5.

Interestingly, Goldman Sachs and Morgan Stanley made an amphibian-like transformation from aquatic Wall Street investment houses into terrestrial Main Street commercial banks. Yet the evolutionary leap was far from compulsory; it was a necessary step to receive the bailout funds earmarked for the banking sector. Due in part to the online banking/investing revolution, the financial sector had undergone major changes in recent years. Gone were the days of Wall Street's unrivaled monopolistic powers. Instead, much of its wealth was transferred directly into hedge funds and individual brokerage accounts.

Ambac Anonymous

The next steel-tipped boot to drop on the financial sector was the collapse of the bond insurers. From October 2007 to July 2008, the shares of two leading bond market underwriters, Ambac and MBI, crashed by more than 90 percent. But it was the abrupt magnitude of the descent that best illustrates the dilemma. In only a few months' time, shares of MBI plummeted from a 2007 market peak near $70, to a nadir of less than $7 (see Figure 15.6).

The AAA bond rating system failed everyone involved. Many shareholders and bond holders alike would soon require the services of a double A rating system: Alcoholics Anonymous.

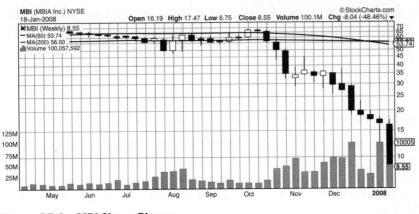

Figure 15.6   MBI Share Plunge

Source: StockCharts.com.

In like manner, financial executives and shareholders alike required many potent potables as the banking calamity roared ever
forward. Besides, if the bellwether bond insurers, MBI and Ambac,
could fail, how safe were FDIC-insured savings accounts? Their
downfall was undoubtedly a significant wake-up call for every individual with an FDIC-backed savings or checking account, not to
mention intangible paper assets in general. A desperate rally cry
echoed throughout the financial community: "Let the saver
beware!"

Super Leverage

From 2008 to 2009, the double-edged battle-ax of financial leverage
continued to slash its way through the financial sector with a ferocious appetite for both profits and losses. The basic 2–1 leverage,
utilized by individual margin accounts, was responsible for devastating losses during the dot.com bust. Ergo, it's easy to fathom the
damaging effects of the 40–1 leverage used by many investment
banks. Decades of reckless leverage eroded the foundations of the
national economy. High debt levels are inherently corrosive and as
a result, most banking and financial institutions are in great peril of
internal collapse.

Currently, domestic banks hold a tiny fraction of the total
$7 trillion of deposits on record. In fact, less than $5 of every $100
in loans is held in reserve. Much of the remaining 95 percent has

found its way into foreclosures, worthless MBSs, and related debt. Although banks have admitted to and written off $1 trillion of bad debts, several trillion dollars in losses have not yet been recognized. This fact alone puts the banking system on a direct collision course with the economy and by default, the FDIC.

CDS—Completely Devastating Securities

In the summer of 2008, Fed officials were bracing for the next systemic financial epidemic to threaten the nation: a mountain of credit default swaps. At the most basic level, CDSs are insurance policies that pass the huge risks associated with toxic loans to third parties. Thanks to lax regulation, such economic time bombs were, for the most part, unregulated. This allowed large institutions to bypass the traditional restraints, such as minimum balances, designed to protect against such a disaster. Just as the MBS fiasco ignited the subprime and lending institution meltdown, CDSs threatened the entire global banking system. In fact, $54 trillion in credit default swaps will continue to unwind for years to come.

With over $54 trillion in CDSs looming over the unregulated global system, there's plenty of unexploded ordnance hidden within the balance sheets of hundreds of financial institutions. Another of Warren Buffett's charming but terse comments is apropos. The credit crisis revealed "who is swimming naked as the economic tide goes out." However, many institutions were found to be not only lacking in undergarments but also caught in the act of flagrante delicto. Indeed, the low tide made transparent what had lain hidden for years. Banks were quietly drowning in trillions of dollars of CDS debt.

Liquidity Crisis? Bank on It

From 2005 to 2007, only three banks entered into bankruptcy. However, by the fall of 2008, a mad dash for cash unfolded, which continued to plague the banking system into 2009. In a page torn directly from the archives of the 2006–2007 lender implosion, hundreds of additional banks would eventually fail.

Furthermore, in October 2008, federal and state regulators closed 15 banks—four of which failed within a tiny, six-week time frame. Yet by 2010, hundreds had failed and more than 700 banks were on the list of troubled institutions. In preparation for the onslaught, FDIC examiners directed all bank executives to raise bank loan reserve requirements. Although the move shielded a fraction of banks from a systemic meltdown, the effects will prove dire for the economy. Limited loan approvals will further curtail business spending and dry up the already dwindling supply of credit to the strapped domestic consumer. As debt-based paranoia sweeps through Wall Street and the banking system, the typical borrower on Main Street stands little chance of securing a loan.

Loan Triage

According to a Federal Reserve survey, three out of four banks have tightened their lending standards for prime mortgages. Strict policies reduced liquidity, which further exacerbated and magnified the recessionary effects. To an economy heavily dependent on consumption, tight lending is the death knell. The already strapped consumer is much more likely to reduce spending as home equity lines of credit, credit cards, and related debt instruments become increasingly unavailable.

However, the banking crisis is not confined to the domestic economy. The Danish central bank announced that its 10th largest lender was on the brink of collapse. Roskilde Bank, a 124-year-old institution, was struggling in the wake of global financial turmoil and mounting losses on mortgage loans. Authorities viewed the situation as "a threat against financial stability in Denmark," which led to a nearly $900 million bailout package from the Nationalbanken. Tumbling house prices across the Scandinavian countryside was cited as the primary domestic cause for the trouble and its inability to secure a takeover suitor.

Bankruptcy She Wrote

As early as September 2007, the FDIC admitted that short-term loans might be required to shore up the wobbly banking industry. FDIC Chair Sheila Bair said the government agency might be forced to borrow money from the Treasury Department to shelter the financial sector from a devastating wave of bank failures. Bair indicated that funds would be used to provide short-term liquidity to help cover depositor demands at the time of new bank closings. The borrowed money would be repaid to the Treasury as bank assets were sold to cover expenses.

By the summer of 2008, the FDIC "problem" bank list grew by 18 percent, to 90 banks with combined assets of $26.3 billion. Next, the number soared from 90 to 117, marking the biggest jump since mid-2003. In a couple of months the number climbed to within earshot of 150. By 2010, the figure reached an unimaginable 702. But few market observers believe that the FDIC troubled institution list offers an accurate assessment of the banking system. For example, conditions deteriorated so rapidly that IndyMac entered bankruptcy before it could earn a spot on the FDIC bank watch list.

Putting the disaster into further perspective, nearly 20 percent of FDIC reserves were devoured by only eight bank failures, including the IndyMac bankruptcy. In fact, IndyMac singlehandedly dissolved more than 15 percent of FDIC funds. Currently, 8,494 banks with $13.4 trillion in assets rely on FDIC.

With the surge in the FDIC "problem" list, Bair said the agency would enact higher premiums to thousands of U.S. banks. Premiums are a primary source of FDIC funding and costs are usually passed on to the consumer. Still, the decision may prove to be a double-edged sword. If the FDIC raises charges too high, it may add to the financial stresses mounting on the sector and actually increase bank failures. Instead, the agency plans to reward lower risk banking behavior while ratcheting up fees on risky lending practices.

Meanwhile, the trend of Friday afternoon bank closings continued into 2010. Apparently, the FDIC prefers working on Friday evenings when the stock market is conspicuously closed. Columbian Bank and Trust of Topeka, Kansas, was the nation's ninth bank to be closed by U.S. regulators amid bad real estate loans. With $752 million in assets and $622 million in total deposits, Columbian Bank and Trust was shut down by the Kansas state bank commissioner's office and the Federal Deposit Insurance Corp.

Indeed, with hundreds of billions of dollars in recently acquired toxic loans sitting on the FDIC's balance sheet, many analysts suspect the banking system is actually putting the insurance agency at risk as well as the economy. In fact, the chief executive of Berkshire Hathaway, Warren Buffett, was so unnerved he put a halt to bank deposit insurance beyond the level guaranteed by the FDIC. Chuck Towle, a senior vice president and employee at the Berkshire subsidiary, Kansas Bankers Surety, said, "We'll work with each individual

bank and work it out with them." Kansas Bankers Surety Co. noti-
fied 1,500 banks in over 30 states in early fall of 2008 that it would
no longer offer "bank deposit guaranty bonds." The perk was
offered as a safety net to wealthy clients. The 18-employee subsidiary
of Berkshire Hathaway, KBS, is one of a small group of insurance
firms to offer such coverage. Furthermore, former IMF chief economist Ken Rogoff announced his expectations that another large
financial institution would close its doors in the next few months.
Rogoff noted, "The worst is to come. . . . We're not just going to
see mid-sized banks go under in the next few months. . . . We're
going to see a whopper; we're going to see a big one, one of the big
investment banks or big banks. We have to see more consolidation
in the financial sector before this is over." Rogoff's dire projections
may come to pass as most banks hold a mere fraction of total deposits on hand.

Moreover, the Harvard economics professor said he expects
Fannie Mae and Freddie Mac to change form substantially in the
coming years, "The world's largest economy is already in a reces-
sion, and the housing market will continue to deteriorate. . . . The
U.S. slowdown will last into the second half of next year." By early
2009, Rogoff's assessment of the GSEs was proven to be correct.
Reports revealed government plans to radically overhaul Fannie
Mae and Freddie Mac.

Lender's Lender of Last Resort

With the financial sector reaching the panic stage, many asked what
would happen if the FDIC also ran low on funds? In such a case, the
lender's lender of last resort, Congress, has the option to protect
depositors with legislation and appropriations. During the savings
and loan crisis in 1989, the Resolution Trust Corp. was created to
manage the closings of 747 failed financial institutions. Although
the government would certainly follow a similar bailout path if the
FDIC became insolvent, the disruption would likely prove to be
highly inflationary.

The 300

According to Gerard Cassidy, an RBC Capital markets analyst, at
least 300 U.S. banks will fail in the next few years due to losses from
real estate–related loans. With analyst expectations ranging from

300 to 1,000 bank closings, the crisis could rival even the Great Depression in real dollar terms. Readers are strongly encouraged to use the time-honored Texas ratio to determine bank solvency when deciding where to park hard-earned cash. Texans suffered particularly during the S&L housing depression. As a result, tough regulations that emerged following the last crisis helped the state to virtually sidestep the entire 2007–2010 real estate crash.

Bank Bailouts

The Road to Socialism—The Paulson Bazooka Bailout

With the economy up against the ropes in 2008, the Federal Reserve offered financial aid directly to companies on an individual basis for the first time since the Great Depression. Similarly, U.S. Treasury Secretary Hank Paulson agreed to assist the Fed to help contain the bankruptcy tide washing across corporate America. Paulson sculpted a plan with top government officials, effectively nationalizing the financial system and transferring losses directly to the taxpayer.

The Economic Stabilization Act passed the Senate on a Wednesday night, with 74 yeas defeating the 25 nays and $100 billion in extra tax breaks. With the approval of Congress and leading bank officials, the government earmarked over one-third of the $700 billion economic stabilization plan funds for the sole purpose of nationalizing U.S. banks. The Treasury Department purchased $250 billion worth of major bank shares, while forgoing voting rights. Among the chosen few were Citigroup Inc., Wells Fargo & Co., JP Morgan Chase & Co., Bank of America Corp., and Morgan Stanley. Bank stocks reacted favorably to the news, undoubtedly due to the huge sum of government money chasing the fixed number of shares.

Superstar investor, author, and economist Jim Rogers voiced his harsh criticism of the $700 billion economic stabilization plan. He called the bill an ill omen for the United States and the global economy. Rogers insisted that the system must be purged, not bailed out, and that the United States will follow the footsteps of 1990s Japan, spawning its own "Lost Decade." Rogers noted that allocating too many resources to the crisis was a mistake. Instead, officials should keep their powder dry in preparation for years of economic turmoil.

Rogers compared the crisis to the 1990s savings and loan dilemma when more than 700 lenders failed. The S&L disaster unfolded over a three-year period with the taxpayer ultimately flipping the bill for the $205 billion bailout, in real terms. Rogers expects many banks to close their doors as the meltdown rolls forward.

Moreover, Rogers said that the U.S. taxpayer would be better served by following the example set by Russia and South Korea. The two nations suffered similar economic crises in the 1990s but overcame the disasters by allowing the ailing companies and banks to fail as well as encouraging new firms to fill the void.

Another vocal billionaire, George Soros, was more reserved regarding the massive government bailout. Soros called the bill "ill-conceived or not conceived at all." The author-investor said the huge economic rescue plan will lead America down a totally wrong path. He added that the current package would unfairly burden taxpayers with a mountain of bad debts. Soros echoed Jim Rogers's thoughts that the taxpayer should not be held financially responsible for the mistakes of bankers and that the companies must be allowed to fail.

However, according to the world's most successful investor, Warren Buffett, the economic air raid sirens were blaring and the skies were filled with enemy dive bombers. With an estimated net worth of $62 billion, Buffett offered his full support to Henry Paulson's Wall Street rescue package. Buffett compared the unfolding credit crisis to Pearl Harbor. In similar fashion, the day the legislation passed will be another day that will live in infamy.

Without the legislation, Buffett insisted, the U.S. economy would come to a screeching halt or worse. The Oracle told reporters on CNBC, "We were at the brink of something that would have made anything that's happened in financial history pale. . . . I'm not saying the Paulson plan will eliminate the problems but it's absolutely necessary, in my view, to avoid going off the precipice." Contrary to Rogers's and Soros's views, Buffett believed the United States can earn a profit from the bailout and urged Congress to act quickly to halt the "economic Pearl Harbor." Buffett noted that if the Treasury Department invests wisely, the American taxpayer would become the beneficiary of such shrewd tactics, "I bet they'll make a profit. . . . They'll pay back the $700 billion and make a considerable amount of money if they approach it like that. . . . I would love to have $700 billion at Treasury rates to buy fixed-income securities—there's a lot of money to be made."

Meantime, in early 2009 Buffet reversed his sell-the-dollar platform from a couple years earlier, noting that the stock market might not have reached the absolute bottom, but it was close. He told reporters he's buying everything American. When Buffett invests, millions of people mimic his every move. He's been heard to say, "Be fearful when others are greedy and be greedy when others are fearful." In like fashion he directed $5 billion into Goldman Sachs' preferred stock, precisely when fear in the banking sector was most pronounced.

$700 Billion/$2 Trillion Trust Fund Solution

Esteemed investors such as Buffett, Rogers, and Soros clearly have widely differing opinions over how to best allocate the $700 billion bailout funds. The logical question is: Will the government plan best serve the nation? After all, a billion dollars is 1,000 stacks of one million dollars. So $700 billion is 700,000 stacks of one million dollars. Assuming that the typical home in foreclosure has a debt burden of $300,000, the bailout funds are more than sufficient to put a halt to every foreclosure in America, as well as alleviate thousands of banks of their toxic loan burdens.

Furthermore, on GSR in 2008, I proposed that the $700 billion emergency bailout money could be far better allocated via a trust fund. As mentioned in a preceding chapter, proceeds would be immediately directed to those facing foreclosure to cover mortgage payments until the economy and housing sector recovered. Interest alone on such a large sum would easily pay for all expenditures. Once the ARM reset threat passed in 2012, the funds would be returned to the Treasury.

Unfortunately, the bailout funds were instead allocated in a wasteful manner. Only bankers received a bailout, essentially delaying the ultimate day of reckoning for the entire economy. The plan included an increase from the $100,000 individual account FDIC insurance to $250,000. This ill-timed move is an impossible burden for the FDIC and virtually guarantees the need for additional government bailout funds.

KEY POINT

Until the credit crises fully passes, readers are encouraged to keep cash reserves in a home-based, fireproof safe as well as think twice before adding financial stocks to their investment portfolio.

Q&A

Listener Question: Ed says, "Hi, Chris. I listen to GSR every week and I love the show. Please explain the nature of a banking holiday. I am trying to get an idea of the mechanics behind dollar revaluation, starting from the actions taken by the government and the subsequent effects. I keep as little money in the bank as possible. I never miss your show. Congratulations on the upcoming release of your book."

Answer: Hi, Ed. Thank you for your kind support. In general a bank holiday involves the closure of most domestic banks and ATMs for an undefined period. In the United States, a bank holiday usually refers to emergency bank closures by executive order or an act of Congress. An example is the Emergency Banking Act of 1933. One can only speculate how far reaching such an announcement would be in today's fast-paced economy. But I think it's safe to say that if a bank holiday persists for longer than one week, the event would trigger a stock market crash, food and energy shortages, and domestic unrest.

For instance, following the tragic events of September 11, 2001, the stock markets were closed for one week. Yet within a couple of months, the equities markets fully recovered and then actually moved above the preattack levels. Hopefully future bank holidays will end with minimal economic disruption. However, it is wise to prepare for a lengthy bank holiday. Thanks, Ed, glad to have you as a regular GSR listener.

CHAPTER

16

Credit Cards

AVOIDING THE DEBT PITFALL

"Modern man drives a mortgaged car over a bond-financed highway on credit-card gas."

—Earl Wilson

For decades obtaining a credit card required a track record of steady employment and financial stability. Strict standards protected the consumer and lender alike. But in the 1990s–2000s easy credit changed the entire paradigm. Suddenly credit cards were as ubiquitous as plastic itself. Today Americans hold 609 million credit cards, 3.5 per person.

The proliferation of credit cards convinced consumers that pocket-sized plastic squares were the key to good credit scores. While it is true that credit cards can help to build a solid credit rating, the temptation to overspend proved to be too much for many. Millions have found, to their dismay, that building credit with plastic cards actually equates to accumulating debt.

Convenience was an important component in the credit card revolution. With the swipe of a card, practically any item was available for purchase. Cash-strapped students were particularly vulnerable to easy credit. By 2008 credit card debt climbed to $1 trillion. Much of it was packaged and sold on Wall Street, similar to MBSs.

While lending standards are once again returning to the historical norm, considerable damage has already transpired. The typical household is swimming in debt, $7,000+ on average (see Figure 16.1). Millions are caught in the downward vortex of minimum payments and usurious interest rates.

Chapter 16 investigates the deception that lured millions of Americans into the credit card trap. Simple, tried and true methods are provided to help set readers free from dangerous credit card bondage. Once all debt is cleared, a family emergency fund takes the place of credit cards as the primary household financial safety net. The next section examines why credit cards may one day be required to include the slogan: "Warning, this plastic device causes bankruptcy, foreclosure, and financial ruin."

Surgeon General's Warning

During the roaring 2000s, life's finer pleasures could be had by practically everyone. New cars, designer suits, exotic vacations, higher education, and jewelry were available at a moment's notice. All that was required was the 16 digits of a credit card and voila, a brand-new Hummer appeared in the McMansion driveway.

Why bother with a boring 9–5 job when a tiny magic card provided one's heart's desires? Once the plastic device lost its uncanny abilities, as they always seemed to do, it could be tossed into the wastebasket. Since everything else was disposable, why not plastic money? Besides, a new card would soon appear in the mailbox to take its place. Of course, the genie who sent the enchanted card sometimes directed his henchmen to make menacing phone calls or send nasty letters. But a peace offering, that is, payment, from a competing card always appeased the anxious specter.

This humorous analogy highlights how millions were desensitized to the malignant cycle of credit card debt. Societies' most vulnerable are particularly susceptible to the financial trap.

Plastic Explosives

While analysts at major media outlets focused their considerable resources on the subprime and MBS debt implosion, an equally disturbing threat flew under their collective radar screens. In the later months of 2008, it was becoming increasingly apparent that the subprime housing dilemma had passed and a new and equally menacing threat was approaching, a tidal wave of $1 trillion in credit card defaults.

For decades, a consumer-based culture made the hollow promise that plastic debt cards were the key to domestic bliss. Simply use a credit card to build your financial credit score. Like so many misguided beliefs, the axiom did contain a modicum of truth. At the time a solid, impeccable credit score allowed one to purchase the best home possible in the nicest suburban neighborhood. After all, wasn't a trendy new McMansion with an elevator, granite countertop, and an upstairs kitchenette essential to achieving the American Dream? Unfortunately, many consumers realized far too late that a system based on instant material gratification and the steady accumulation of debt would transform the American Dream into the American Nightmare.

Building Credit = Building Debt

Exactly how many lives have been ruined by the phrase "Use credit cards to build your credit" remains a mystery. But one fact is certain, easy credit desensitized all but the most prudent to the dangers of indebtedness. In his revealing book, *Maxed Out,* James Scurlock outlines in detail how the temptation of easy credit led the world's most prosperous nation down the slippery slope of credit card dependency.

A key component to the credit card revolution was convenience. Students are particularly vulnerable to easy credit. In fact, student credit card debt has emerged as a major concern. According to Scurlock's research, even college students are bombarded with credit card applications. As many as 50 annual credit card offers per student was commonplace before the credit crisis. Most of the credit card solicitations were sent to those who had never held a steady job. With an average of $4,000 in credit card debt, clearly the cash-strapped college student is in financial peril. In fact, before graduation and entering the workforce, the typical student extends five or more cards to the spending limit.

With millions of young college students falling prey to catchy credit card campaigns, debt co-dependency has inserted its malignant tentacles into a new generation. Students often justify the debt ball and chain with the belief that education is worth the sacrifice. After all, studies claim that college graduates can expect to earn

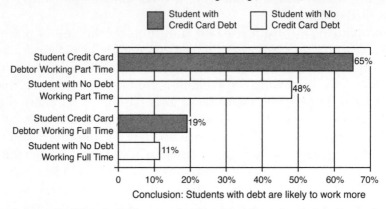

Figure 16.1   **Work Habits of College Students**

twice as much as those with high school degrees. Plus, recruiters and head hunters sometimes lure prospects with the promise of eliminating credit card debts in exchange for signing on the dotted line. However, with soaring tuitions and related fees devouring the monetary benefits of higher education, paying off credit card debt is becoming a daunting task. Plus, one study (see Figure 16.1) showed that students with credit cards were far less likely to hold jobs.

Figure 16.2 shows the differences in credit card debt by age group.

Plastic Savings Accounts

Increased credit card availability helped to fuel the domestic consumer's appetite. In less than 20 years, tens of millions turned to credit cards as a buffer against financial troubles. Put simply, the credit card became a proxy for the family savings account. The consumer lost touch with personal responsibility, instead succumbing to the allure of easy money.

Just as years of lax lending standards aided and abetted a pandemic of subprime mortgages, credit cards were distributed with little concern for the borrower's ability to repay. In fact, credit cards were scarcely more difficult to secure than ketchup packets at a fast-food restaurant drive-through window. Unfortunately, decades of

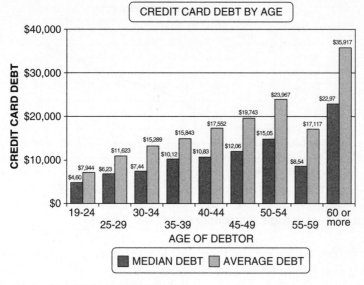

Figure 16.2   Credit Card Debt by Age

loose lending practices encouraged consumers to view toxic credit cards as a reliable means of acquiring everyday needs.

In the 1980s the national savings rate approached 11 percent per capita. However, three decades of steady inflation growth and easy access to credit resulted in a negative savings rate. From the 1980s to the year 2008, an environment of inflation and negligible interest rates discouraged savings while rewarding consumption. In fact, the per capita savings rate declined from 11 percent to –1 percent as millions spent well beyond their total disposable income.

Currently, Americans hold 609 million credit cards—approximately 3.5 tiny ATM machines each. The majority were issued by Visa, MasterCard, and American Express. In only six years, credit card debt has rocketed higher, from $211 billion to $1 trillion, an increase of nearly fivefold. Worse still, $1 trillion of credit card debt was packaged and sold in a similar fashion as the MBS market.

Pocket Loan Machines

An entire generation of consumers turned to plastic loan machines. In fact, the typical domestic family owes credit card lenders $7,000+.

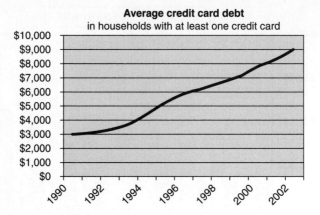

Figure 16.3   Average Household Credit Card Debt

(See Figure 16.3.) Yet the inescapable truth remains, every financial transaction has an equal and opposite reaction.

Hidden behind a veil of barely legible fine print, impossibly high rates prove to be devastating to household budgets. Many credit cards carry usurious rates of 25 percent and higher, which inevitably dooms all but the most prudent cardholder.

Debt End Street

Millions of Americans are bracing for impact as an avalanche of debt hurdles toward credit card–laden family budgets. The event was triggered by the thunderclap of toxic housing–related MBS debt. As a result, the financial industry is returning to the time-honored tradition of far stricter lending practices.

Although tighter lending standards heralded an end to the pushbutton money era and the demise of the home ATM machine, decades of unbridled access to easy money has consumers clinging tenaciously to their former spending habits. While the credit pushers are on vacation, as with most dependencies, the unquenchable desire for money lingers. Like desperate addicts forced to settle for clinic handouts, dwindling credit barely satisfies the money-hungry consumer's appetite.

Plastic Bankruptcy Cards

While banks vastly restrict available funds, new limits make abusing toxic debt cards more difficult. After years of extending oceans of money, lenders are now reducing limits on millions of cardholder accounts, without so much as a warning. The once popular scheme of paying bills via plastic is no longer a viable option.

During a recession-caused debt contraction, the limited profit potential and escalating risks associated with maintaining a high inventory of credit cards equates to financial suicide for lenders. Dominant industry players such as Visa, MasterCard, and American Express are abruptly curtailing the number of credit cards outstanding, while searching through a vast consumer database for any excuse to lower card limits.

While mortgage companies are required to inform customers of credit line adjustments within a few days of the change, the legal system grants credit card companies an extended one-month grace period. As a result, many shoppers are subjected to an unexpected decline in available credit. Millions of cardholders may find that charges as seemingly innocuous as $30 are suddenly rejected by their debt peddlers, despite unblemished payment histories. Unbeknownst to the cardholder, the red flag was often the result of an arbitrary and unrelated debt, such as a delinquent mortgage payment. Public outrage over dwindling credit is inevitable as the once mighty plastic savings account becomes little more than scissors fodder and wastebasket filler.

Furthermore, over the past six years, home equity lines were used to pay off credit card debts. U.S. consumers borrowed $68 billion against credit lines, increasing debt by 7.8 percent, the biggest leap in nearly a decade. The concept was simple and enticing. Pay off credit cards in full with the family equity line in order to reduce interest charges to a far more manageable, single-digit rate. However, the sleight of hand failed now that ARMs are resetting into much higher monthly payments. Credit line debt has essentially increased mortgage payment distress while sending foreclosures to record levels.

Debt: A Four-Letter Word

Among the most prominent credit card lenders, cardholder delinquencies have soared by 50 percent or more. (See Figure 16.4.)

While five out of every 100 credit card-holders fail to pay even a single dollar owed, lending behemoth Capital One wrote off $2 billion in bad debt over a meager three-month period. Now that the

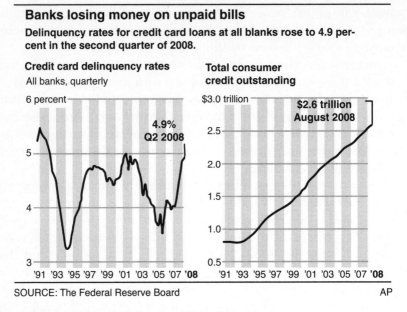

Banks losing money on unpaid bills

Delinquency rates for credit card loans at all blanks rose to 4.9 percent in the second quarter of 2008.

Credit card delinquency rates
All banks, quarterly

Total consumer
credit outstanding

SOURCE: The Federal Reserve Board   AP

Figure 16.4   Costs of Delinquent Credit Cards

credit card bubble has burst, many are taking their cue from the Capital One promotion, asking, "What's in my wallet?" Unfortunately, consumers are answering the question with the four-letter word, "DEBT."

Paper or Plastic?

While credit card lenders receive much of the blame for the debt-burdened domestic consumer, shopkeepers are also complicit in fomenting the cycle of debt. The fact that credit card purchases increase sales figures by 20 percent or more is a well-known industry secret. Nothing encourages impulse shopping as much as the simplicity and convenience of plastic money. As a result, the sector owes much of its existing revenues to the debt-addicted consumer.

Credit card companies actually prefer dependent cardholders. Millions are now caught in the trap of revolving payments and usurious rates. Perpetually maxed out consumers ensure a steady flow of exorbitant interest payments, a primary profit source. Ironically, those who wisely choose to pay their cards in full each month are referred to as "deadbeats." Since 2007, this household is officially a credit card "deadbeat."

In 2006, lenders charged $17 billion for nothing more than late fees. Such penalties compound quickly and only one missed payment can trigger a dreaded credit card adjustment—resetting the credit card interest rate to as high as 29 percent. Yet many will ignore the blatant warning signals and instead fall into the endless karma-like cycle of debt and soaring rates.

Credit Challenge

In his must-read book, *The Total Money Makeover*, radio personality and author Dave Ramsey presents solutions to real-world financial problems for every level of society. Ramsey illustrates the importance of reducing debt, increasing savings, and eliminating credit cards. Following in Ramsey's footsteps, I challenged GSR listeners to pay all their credit cards in full. In order to experience a sense of completion and satisfaction, listeners were encouraged to first pay off the card with the least debt. Next, the highest interest-bearing card is targeted. All that's required is personal discipline and a sharp pair of scissors. In the Q&A section at the end of this chapter, one listener shares his Credit Challenge success story.

He Who Spends Least, Wins

According to Dave Ramsey, every family must embrace a policy of zero credit card debt. First, expenditures should be gradually reduced to make a more economical lifestyle more palatable. Next, fostering an atmosphere of teamwork can be an effective tool to reduce living costs. By organizing a friendly game of cost cutting and saving, family cooperation simultaneously enhances camaraderie and results.

Once household debt is completely eliminated, monthly disposable income is directed toward building an emergency fund. Ideally, the nest egg is ample enough to provide three to six months of living expenses as a buffer against unforeseen difficulties such as job losses, home and auto repairs, and medical expenses. The household emergency fund is the ideal replacement for the malevolent credit cards, the world's most uneconomical savings account. Readers are encouraged to send their debt reduction success stories to gsr@hughes.net.

Conclusion

Although lending standards are once again returning to historical norms, considerable damage has already transpired. The typical American is awash in $7,000 of credit card debt—caught within a vortex of minimum payments and usurious rates.

A time-honored escape plan involves destroying every card in one's possession as well as those that arrive via the postal service. Once all debt is cleared, a family emergency fund replaces the credit card as the primary safety net against unforeseen financial difficulties.

KEY POINT

Credit cards are unnecessary and harmful to financial health. Readers are encouraged to replace credit cards with a cash emergency fund.

Q&A

Listener Question: Duane writes, "Hi, Chris. Thank you for your accurate insights on the economy. If only government officials would listen to your program, it would no doubt wipe that 'deer in the headlights' look off their faces when they attempt to resolve our present economic dilemma. It's nice to follow your program and be 'in the know.'"

"Here's why I contacted you. A few months ago in your GSR Challenge, you asked listeners to eliminate debt and keep you informed of our progress in this area. I am very happy to announce that my 2004 Chevy truck is paid in full. We made the last payment in the middle of July. It is such a good feeling. We will use the former truck payment money to pay off another loan. When the next loan is paid in full, I'll write you again with our progress. Please keep up the good work."

Answer: Hello. Duane. Hat tip to you and your wife for taking steps toward securing your financial freedom. Congratulations on your success and please keep me updated.

Wealth Building Strategies

"There are old investors and there are bold investors, but there are very few old bold investors."

—C.G.W.

The profound financial rewards that accompany exceptional investing results motivate millions of investors to outperform the markets. The seemingly insignificant gap between a 10 percent annual portfolio return and a 20 percent performance differentiates the professional investor from the novice. Yet investing is a dichotomy; the pathway to riches includes potholes as well as dead end streets.

This tome presented the keys to unlocking sizeable profits while avoiding the numerous associated pitfalls. Armed with the weapons of investment success, money management/trend adherence, the reader is prepared to excel in a field that continues to befuddle investors even 400 years after the first financial market opened for trade. A review of the Key Points/introductions from all 16 chapters is included here to better prepare the reader for the challenging investing world.

Although prices typically gyrate in a random manner, eventually all markets enter protracted/profitable trends.

The first step to financial success is a unique understanding of price behavior. Trend investing is arguably the most profound breakthrough in finance since the first exchange opened for trade hundreds of years ago. By examining manias and the people who traded them, the reader will gain priceless insights into market dynamics; including how and why markets enter protracted trends.

Successful investing involves trend and money management skills, which limits losses to no more than 1–2 percent of total portfolio value.

Sir Isaac Newton failed to discover the trend concept and lost his fortune to the South Sea Bubble, whereas Livermore and Dennis embraced market trend investing. However, of the three, only Richard Dennis retained his fortune. The missing ingredient that enabled Dennis to succeed where his two gifted predecessors failed is money management. In addition, we examined three trend trading systems with solid money management parameters to better prepare for financial success.

Precious metals are the ideal insurance plan for every portfolio. Of the two metals, silver represents the greatest opportunity for extraordinary profits.

For several decades stocks and bonds dominated the global financial arena. But in the wake of the devastating 2008 credit crisis, investors are questioning the safety of such intangible assets. A growing number are turning instead to the gold and silver safe haven. Precious metals investments are once again becoming synonymous with financial success. Extensive historical, fundamental, and technical evidence support the case for precious metals as the ideal investment class for years to come.

Due to massive global government bailouts/monetary expansion, an inflation disaster is inevitable. The price of gold will likely reach $2,500 in the coming years. Gold represents the best safety net for every portfolio.

As far back in history as ancient Rome, rising prices have threatened the wherewithal of entire nations. In order to satisfy extravagant desires and to fund expensive wars, currencies are still regularly debased. The result is predictable; inflated prices put basic necessities outside the reach of the masses. Similarly, signs of domestic/global inflation abound. Modern officials are likely to make the same mistakes as their predecessors, culminating in a hyperinflationary disaster.

Due to peak oil/soaring global demand, the age of cheap gasoline has passed. To better prepare for the Energy Crisis Part 2, every portfolio should include energy investments.

The global ebb and flow of petroleum supply/demand has shifted markedly in recent years. Demand for crude oil is accelerating at precisely the same moment when the world oil supply has passed its peak. Against the backdrop of "Peak Oil" and unprecedented global demand, the international chess match is rapidly approaching a checkmate scenario. However, the credit crisis of 2008 sharply reduced demand and the price of energy, providing a much needed time out. The temporary reprieve has presented a rare window of opportunity for the global community and individual investors alike to protect against the corrosive effects of higher energy prices while reaping sizeable profits with minimal risk exposure.

Once an individual investor identifies and conquers personal weaknesses via paper trading, substantial investing profits will follow.

Anyone who spends enough time in the highly volatile financial world eventually comes to the realization that the market is indeed an unforgiving battlefield. One false step in markets and trading capital disappears without a trace. But there is hope for the burgeoning investor. In China more than two thousand years ago, Sun Tzu penned an ancient war tome of enormous strategic significance. Master Tzu's wisdom can vastly enhance trading discipline and performance.

The 75-year housing bubble has burst. A recovery will require several years. Caveat emptor.

In the wake of WWII, the United States emerged virtually unscathed as the lone global superpower. One profound peace dividend was the 75-year domestic housing boom. Relaxed lending standards and artificially low Fed rates further pushed domestic home prices skyward. Generations of mortgage holders became convinced that annual price increases were as certain as death and April 15th. However, the 2007 subprime implosion and the 2008 credit crisis that followed brought an abrupt halt to the housing euphoria. The median U.S. house price tumbled by more than 32 percent. Understanding the similarities between the stock and housing bubbles is crucial to avoiding future crashes as well as benefiting from the next market mania.

Due to the mountain of toxic Alt-A and option ARM mortgages expected to reset in 2010–2012, the number of underwater home-owners is expected to double to 25 million. The resulting flood of inventory will further glut the already crowded market and suppress prices for years to come.

As 2006 came to a close, so did the decade's long real estate boom. In just a few months, years of speculative housing froth were washed away. By April 2010, millions of homes were in some stage of foreclosure. Due in part to the widespread use of toxic mortgages, 12 million stunned homeowners owe more than their property is worth. Before the storm fully passes, the number is expected to surpass 25 million, representing half of all mortgages outstanding. Untold legions will walk away from overpriced properties in pursuit of more affordable housing. The shift away from traditional lending practices and the widespread dissemination of exotic mortgages drove real estate prices beyond all reasonable valuations. Plus, a faulty belief system ultimately convinced millions of borrowers/lenders that house prices "always go up."

Due in part to millions of risky ARM defaults the median residential house price will likely decline an additional 10–15 percent by 2012. Renting will remain the preferred alternative to owning a home until the average mortgage payment falls back in line with monthly rental costs.

The incredible success and stability of the real estate bubble created an atmosphere of exuberance within the lending industry. New and exciting mortgage instruments promised riches beyond the dreams of avarice to banks/lenders willing to accept no down payments from risky borrowers. But now that the residential housing market is in decline, owners without any "skin in the game" have little reason to stay married to toxic mortgages. Plus with millions already in mortgage default amid the worst housing crash since the Great Depression, the stigma associated with foreclosure is now far less pronounced. Thus, 5+ million underwater mortgage holders are expected to walk away by 2012. The resulting inventory flood will be exacerbated by exotic ARMs. The net effect will further push domestic house prices lower by another 10–15 percent by the end of 2012. Afterwards, prices will remain stagnant for years with numerous false rallies along the way. Usurious lending rates and the resulting foreclosures have changed the American Dream of owning a home to renting a home.

Amid the deepest recession in over 50 years, house prices are expected to further erode for at least two more years. Readers are encouraged to embrace frugality and self-reliance while avoiding risky exotic mortgages/debt.

As house prices began to slip in 2007, media pundits insisted that the sea change represented a mere pothole on the expressway to higher prices. But the pavement rut quickly morphed into the deepest recession sinkhole in 50 years. The Case-Shiller 10-city house-price index recorded a 29 percent decline, the worst reading in its 20-year history. By 2008 liar's loan delinquencies leaped 17 percent, even worse than their dodgy subprime cousins.

Fast forward three years and the same group of mainstream talking heads who missed the crisis now claim that U.S. housing has staged a miraculous recovery. Chapter 10 presents compelling evidence suggesting that the experts will once again be proven wrong—the bottom has not been reached in real estate. Instead, the hull has been breached and is now filling to capacity thanks to toxic ARM resets and a bleak employment outlook. Ultimately, the water line will fall an additional 15 percent from the 2006 peak, ending with a total loss of 50 percent in the median house price, of approximately $130,000. The unexpected slide will present substantial bargain opportunities for patient home shoppers.

Eventually owning a house will become a prudent decision. The ideal mortgage size is three times the household annual income. Readers are encouraged to rent a home until average monthly mortgage payments are comparable with monthly rental costs.

Part 2 covered the real estate bubble/crash, particularly the widespread use of dangerous mortgages. Toxic ARMs encouraged millions to accept loans of up to nine times the annual household income, 300 percent higher than recommended. Such debt levels cannot be sustained indefinitely. Thus, up to half of all mortgage holders are expected to be underwater by 2012. But after the tidal wave of foreclosures washes away the excess inventory/high prices, bargains will abound. Eventually owning a mortgage will again be a prudent decision. But how will you know when it's time to reenter the market? Indeed, what separates a bargain dream home from an overpriced nightmare?

Three simple rules of thumb provide what every home hunter needs while stalking their prey. Hunting rule number one: Search for properties priced less than three times household income.

Armed with all three easy to use capital preserving survival tips, the reader will steer clear of the piranha-infested areas and instead locate a personal field of dreams.

In less than 100 years, the Federal Reserve has destroyed more than 95 percent of the dollar's purchasing power. Investors are advised to protect their wealth with tangible assets such as precious metals and energy investments.

Following eight years of war with the reigning global superpower, in 1782 America won its independence from Britain. Yet only 30 years later amid the War of 1812, the United States once again found itself embroiled in a death match with its former rival. Although American forces narrowly emerged victoriously in both conflicts, the United States actually lost the economic war. How so? In both instances, the central banks that quickly followed wreaked havoc on the economy.

However, in 1836 President Andrew Jackson removed the last remaining vestiges of the national banks. Set free from the heavy burden, the economy thrived for nearly 100 years. Yet in the aftermath of the 1907 panic, the sinister banking cartel seized the opportunity to once again consolidate financial power. In 1913, under a shroud of secrecy, the Federal Reserve was created. Since that time numerous calamities have befallen the financial system, including the 1929 crash, the Great Depression, the 1970s stagflation, the 1980s S&L crisis, the 1990s dot.com boom/implosion and the 2007–2008 housing/credit crashes.

The national banking system will likely remain under considerable stress until at least 2013. Until the ARM reset trouble passes, bank funds in excess of $250,000 should be transferred to alternate FDIC-backed savings accounts.

To help revive the struggling U.S. economy during the Great Depression, President Franklin D. Roosevelt created the mortgage lender Fannie Mae as part of the New Deal. The concept was simple: Increased home ownership would benefit the nation as a whole. Owning a piece of Americana would encourage thrift and job/family stability and increase property tax revenues. Fannie Mae's cousin lender, Freddie Mac, received its congressional charter three decades later in the aftermath of the Vietnam War.

By the 2000s, Fannie Mae and Freddie Mac had expanded far beyond what was originally intended. The GSEs guaranteed over half of all domestic mortgages, $6 trillion in total. The two be-hemoth hybrid lenders secured more home loans than all of the 8,500 FDIC-insured commercial banks and thrifts combined. The U.S. government essentially became the landlord of over 30 million homes, approximately 100 million people. The house of cards was destined to collapse.

Meantime, in 2008, low-quality subprime loans and accounting gimmickry crushed the GSEs' share prices. Subprime debt further devastated several Wall Street investment banking icons. The balance sheets of once mighty Bear Stearns and Merrill Lynch were reduced to ashes practically overnight by toxic MBSs. Even the nation's largest financial institution, Bank of America, was up against the ropes. On the West Coast financial chaos at the lender IndyMac led to bank runs. The mayhem threatened to sink the domestic economy.

While officials were able to stem the initial credit crisis tide via $12 trillion in bailouts, there's now mounting evidence of renewed banking trouble. In April 2010, the Fed announced it would no longer support the financial sector with massive purchases of toxic MBSs, plus the federal housing tax credit expired the same month. While government policies are following a similar course as in the 1930s, unlike during the Great Depression, fighting stagflation with trillions of additional debt will merely postpone the reckoning day.

With a mountain of ARMs expected to reset from 2010 to 2012, the next wave of foreclosures is bound to impact the banking sector with at least as much force as the 2007 subprime dilemma. Will a second credit dilemma capsize the FDIC as it did during the S&L crisis? All signs point to a similar outcome. Until the ARM reset trouble passes in 2013, the national banking system is likely to remain on shaky ground.

The federal funds futures contracts provide simple to grasp predictions of upcoming FOMC rate decisions. Readers are encouraged to visit/bookmark the Web page: http://www.clevelandfed .org/research/data/fedfunds/index.cfm.

The Fed FOMC meeting is comparable to an economic Super Bowl. Investors rely on experts to decipher the cryptic phrases and terminology that emerge from the accompanying statements. Known as Fed Speak, the convoluted rhetoric has befuddled even the wisest of interpreters. Why do the FOMC rate-setting events captivate the markets and traders alike? The key overnight lending rate is a determining factor in market liquidity/economic output. Plus, the accompanying statement offers insights into future Fed rate intervention.

Still, for most people, deciphering the Fed Speak drivel proves to be far too mundane a task. Fortunately, a simple alternative method for understanding the latest Fed Speak gibberish can be accessed via the Internet. Will Ben Bernanke and company hold rates steady or raise the overnight lending rate? By simply navigating the Web browser to the Fed website everyone has access to the answer via a remarkable free tool.

Until the credit crises fully passes, readers are encouraged to keep cash reserves in a home-based, fireproof safe as well as think twice before adding financial stocks to their investment portfolio.

At the onset of the credit crisis of 2008–2009, tricky toxic mortgages concealed the looming threat from most banking professionals. However, the multi-trillion-dollar debt firestorm that followed increased the FDIC troubled bank list from 90 to an astounding 702 by February 2010.

Meantime, by the end of summer 2008 profits at all 8,500 FDIC-insured banks collapsed by 86 percent. The investment banks had regularly employed 40–1 leverage. Wall Street legend Bear Stearns was the first to fall to the leverage battle-ax, followed closely by Lehman Brothers, Merrill Lynch, and the nation's largest insurer, AIG. By 2009 the remnants of the shattered banking industry held less than 5 percent in reserves. Much of the remaining 95 percent was tied to nonperforming loans, such as foreclosures/worthless MBSs. Although banks admitted to and wrote off $1 trillion of bad debts, several trillion dollars in losses have yet to be recognized. Wall Street was desperate for cash/emergency loans. Echoes of the old Wall Street saying, "What's the price of money, Shylock?" are still heard on the trading floor.

In response, the Fed chairman came to the rescue of the Wall Street elite with three sizable rate cuts. The moves sent the once mighty lending rate to practically zero for the first time in the Fed's 95-year tenure. Congress also implemented emergency damage control measures via the Economic Stabilization Plan, which directed one-third of the $700 billion funds to U.S. bank shares. Bank stocks understandably reacted well to the huge sum of government money chasing a fixed number of shares.

Credit cards are unnecessary and harmful to financial health. Readers are encouraged to replace credit cards with a cash emergency fund.

For decades obtaining a credit card required a track record of steady employment and financial stability. Strict standards protected the consumer and lender alike. But in the 1990s–2000s easy credit changed the entire paradigm. Suddenly credit cards were as ubiquitous as plastic itself. Today Americans hold 609 million credit cards, 3.5 per person.

The proliferation of credit cards convinced consumers that the devices held the key to solid credit scores. While it is true that credit cards can help to build a good credit rating, the temptation to overspend proved to be too much for many. Millions have found, to their dismay, that building credit with plastic cards actually equates to building debt.

Convenience was an important component in the credit card revolution. With the swipe of a card, practically any item was available for purchase. Cash-strapped students were particularly vulnerable to easy credit. By 2008 credit card debt climbed to $1 trillion. Much of it was packaged and sold on Wall Street, similar to MBSs.

While lending standards are once again returning to the historical norm, considerable damage has already transpired. The typical American is swimming in debt, $7,000+ on average. Millions are caught in the downward vortex of minimum payments and usurious interest rates.

Simple tried and true methods are provided to help set readers free from dangerous credit card bondage. Once all debt is cleared, a family emergency fund takes the place of credit cards as the primary household financial safety net. In the future, regulators may insist that credit cards include the slogan "Warning, this plastic device causes bankruptcy, foreclosure, and financial ruin."

Although this text includes a comprehensive methodology for investment success, the financial marketplace remains a highly dynamic arena. Under such fluid conditions, readers can benefit greatly by participating within a community of like-minded enthusiasts. Please accept my invitation to join the growing ranks of listeners who have made Goldseek.com Radio part of their weekly routine. By directing questions to either the GSR toll-free hotline voicemail, 1-800-507-6531, or the mailbag at gsr@hughes.net, you may not only improve your investing results, but help other listeners in the process. Until we meet again, I leave you with the following words of wisdom:

> "With money in your pocket, you are wise and you are handsome and you sing well, too."
>
> —Proverb

About the Author

Chris Waltzek holds an M.B.A. with a dual major in business economics and information systems. He is currently working toward a doctoral degree in business. Chris hosts a two-hour weekly business talk show, sponsored by Goldseek.com, a leading online precious metals network. The Goldseek.com Radio broadcast was a contender for the prestigious 2009 Peabody Award for Internet radio. The program includes top guests, such as Congressman Dr. Ron Paul, Jim Rogers, and Steve Forbes, and is known industry-wide to be weeks, sometimes months ahead of the competition. In addition to interviews and special segments, Chris and Bob Chapman answer listeners' telephone/e-mail questions. Plus, 400+ hours of free archives are available online at www.radio.goldseek.com.

Chris is editor of *The Market Weatherman Report*. The weekly business newsletter features stock picks with exceptional dividends as well as market forecasts for the coming week. With more than 1,800 subscribers, the flagship periodical is approaching its 180th edition.

Index